The Indictment of a Dictator

The Indictment of a Dictator

The Extradition and Trial of Marcos Pérez Jiménez

By

Judith Ewell

TEXAS A&M UNIVERSITY PRESS
College Station

Library of Congress Cataloging in Publication Data

Ewell, Judith, 1943–
　　Indictment of a dictator.

　　Bibliography: p.
　　1. Pérez Jiménez, Marcos, 1914–　　　2. Trials
—Venezuela.　3. Betancourt, Rómulo, 1908–
4. Venezuela—Politics and government—1958–
I. Title.
LAW　　　　　　　　345.87′0231　　　　　　81–40475
ISBN 0–89096–109–3　　　348.705231　　　　　　AACR2

Manufactured in the United States of America
First edition

Contents

Preface

Most of the scholarly writing on contemporary Venezuela has treated the development of the political party Acción Democrática (AD) and the maturation of political democracy. In a continent which by 1979 was almost entirely dominated by military dictators of various stamps, republican democracy and civilian political parties are indeed remarkable.

The success of Rómulo Betancourt and his party, however, has obscured an equally fascinating phenomenon. The antihero, the antidemocrat, has continued to attract some voters in the thirty-five years that have followed World War II. The recent years of dictatorship from 1948 to 1958 have been depicted by Betancourt and by most social scientists as years of repression, waste, corruption, and incompetent administration. After the fall of Marcos Pérez Jiménez's dictatorship in 1958, the civilian politicians cooperated to try to stamp out all traces of the arbitrary, personalistic governing system which they had known for so long. Yet political polls in the 1960s and 1970s revealed that the former dictator Marcos Pérez Jiménez still had a considerable following in Venezuela.

Betancourt had certainly tried hard enough both to eliminate the characteristics of caudillo government and to ensure that the caudillo himself should not return. Acción Democrática began a long process to extradite and try Pérez Jiménez for his crimes in office. Symbolically, they would purge the nation of dictatorship through the courts. Meanwhile, they tried to distribute the benefits of the oil wealth more widely than had been done before.

Pérez Jiménez, like the good opportunist that he was, could counter the AD moves to some extent and turn the trial to his advantage. The trial patently was not what AD claimed: a regular trial of a common criminal for common crimes. Both Pérez Jiménez and Betancourt turned the trial into a weighing of the two systems of government. Pérez hoped that history, or the electorate, would give him the absolution that the AD courts probably would not. Some of his appeal fell on fertile ground; some Venezuelans had objected to the help which the AD government had been forced to seek from the United States in order to have Pérez extradited. Some Venezuelans could not see that their economic situation was any better under democracy than it had been under the dictatorship. Others may have longed for the predictability and stability of the dictatorship. These people, as well as those who may have been suspicious of the impartiality of AD courts, sympathized with Pérez Jiménez when he claimed that he was being treated arbitrarily by his political enemies. Thus, the trial which was supposed to publicize Pérez's crimes in fact contributed to his brief political rebirth. The antihero represented the disappearance of something familiar from the past.

Acción Democrática leaders and leaders of other civilian parties who had fought the dictatorship in clandestine struggle refused to allow the old caudillo to consolidate his lingering political appeal. Thus, they borrowed a tactic from another caudillo, Juan Vicente Gómez. After detaining Pérez Jiménez for the years of his trial before the Supreme Court, they threatened that he would be detained anew for other crimes if he ever returned to Venezuela. This ploy, which Pérez declined to challenge, successfully removed him personally from the political arena. Fortunately, he was one of the few conservatives who could consistently win a large number of conservative voters; other politicians of the right rose in one election or another but had no stomach for the political organizing that would make their appeal more lasting. Thus, the moderate civilian politicians of the traditional parties finally won. Slowly, the two major parties, COPEI and AD, even began to win the sympathies and the votes of many of the conservative voters.

This study seeks to illuminate the conflict between Rómulo Betancourt and Marcos Pérez Jiménez and the two types of government they represented. In many ways, the trial of Pérez Jiménez was central to that competition; it aired the best and the worst of each administration, and it finally exacted judicial revenge on an arbitrary and personalistic dictator.

Acknowledgments

Many people have contributed directly and indirectly to the completion of this work. Professor Edwin Lieuwen, who suggested the topic and guided my graduate work, deserves special mention. Thanks also go to those who patiently tried to clarify my notions of U.S., Venezuelan, and international law; Howard Westwood, Rafael Naranjo Ostty, Ramón Escovar Salom, Walter Williams, Daniel Guerra Iñiguez, and Marcelino Avila Ferrer were especially helpful. Enrique Sánchez Risso, Secretary of Venezuela's Corte Suprema, was generous with his time and assistance; and Ramón Pacheco, Florencia Fuentes, Maria Elena Bermúdez, Maria Marcano, and other members of the staff of the Venezuelan Biblioteca Nacional offered aid, friendship, and coffee when most needed.

Other friends and associates in Venezuela added immeasurably to my research and understanding of Venezuelan history and politics. I am deeply grateful to Ricardo Montilla, Francisco Alvarez Chacín, José Giacopini Zárraga, Everett Baughman, Martín J. Gutiérrez R., Thomas Allyn Clayton, and Ramón Velásquez.

I would also like to thank those friends and scholars who read and criticized the manuscript: Edward Crapol, Kathy Waldron, and Winthrop R. Wright. A special note of thanks goes to John Lombardi, who offered valuable suggestions for changes in organization and emphasis.

Finally, I am indebted to the American Association of University Women for a dissertation fellowship for the year 1969–1970, to the Organization of American States for a research fellowship for the year 1974–1975, and to the College of William and Mary for a summer research grant in 1978.

The Indictment of a Dictator

1

In the Shadow of Gómez: The Early Careers of Rómulo Betancourt and Marcos Pérez Jiménez

Rómulo Betancourt and Marcos Pérez Jiménez both were born and grew up during the long dictatorship of Juan Vicente Gómez (1908–1935). As infants and toddlers they would hardly have had knowledge of Gómez's seizure of power from his old Táchira colleague and chief, Cipriano Castro. However, by the time of Castro's death in Puerto Rico in 1924, when Betancourt was sixteen and Pérez Jiménez was ten, the two boys had probably heard many times of the events surrounding Gómez's rise. Betancourt devotes some space to Gómez's machinations in his book *Venezuela: Política y petróleo*.[1] Gómez's rise and dictatorship are worthy of note because Pérez Jiménez and Betancourt would as adults reenact the competition between Castro and Gómez. More, the entire lives and careers of the two boys were shaped by their perceptions of and reactions to the type of government that Juan Vicente Gómez represented.

Juan Vicente Gómez was a caudillo of the old school. Born in 1856 in Táchira, he became head of his family at age fourteen when his father died. Native shrewdness, necessity, and the Táchira tradition of hard work enabled Juan Vicente to accumulate a substantial estate in livestock and agriculture. He could, from his relatively isolated mountain home, virtually ignore the political squabbles that surrounded President Antonio Guzmán Blanco and his successors in Caracas. Yet, in the 1890s, Gómez was drawn to the politico-military movement headed by his fellow Tachirense, Cipriano Castro. Gómez became a field general and commissary for Castro and in 1899 accompanied the successful revolutionaries to Caracas, then a city of one hundred thousand. Daniel Joseph Clinton writes: "He was forty-two years old. He still wore the wide hat, ruana and al-

[1] Rómulo Betancourt, *Venezuela: Política y petróleo*, pp. 32–39.

pargatas of his country. After this he would wear different clothes and he would wear the ruana again on occasions, but up to his forty-second year the man who was to become one of the world's richest men had worn the costume of the mountains."[2]

Despite his late start in politics, Gómez's cunning and ability to wait served him well. He was to acquire more talents in management and leadership first as Castro's governor of the Federal District and later as vice-president.

Gómez bided his time and consolidated his power with the revolutionary group. Ramón Velásquez writes:

Juan Vicente Gómez began to represent himself as his stand-in, the anti-Castro. In contrast to Castro, who had become a turncoat, speech-maker, friend of eloquence, dancer, and hardhearted Don Juan, appeared the other man, silent, abstemious, consistent with his old followers. He used his influence in the regime to place his friends in charges of second or third rank, and when the nominee was going to be removed, his protector bound him with the phrase: "Don Cipriano didn't want it, but I got you the position with the Minister." "Go and wait there." "Take care." In the haciendas and ranches that he began to buy, he gave work to dozens of soldiers who had been released by the Army and who could find no protection among the powerful people in the Government, and thus he ensured that they did not return to Táchira at the same time that he was forming the contingents of his select troops, his "boys," his "officers."[3]

In November, 1908, Gómez's moment came. President Cipriano Castro traveled to Europe to seek medical attention and left Gómez in charge of the government. As Betancourt later wrote, Castro had forgotten "the law of the historic *patada*," and Gómez replaced Castro's men with his own and enlisted the help of the U.S. government to see that Castro should not return. Gómez promised the United States and other foreign legations in Caracas that he would settle all outstanding international claims, and he asked the United States to send a warship to La Guaira as a precautionary measure. The U.S. government quickly accepted Gómez's assurances of pay-

---

[2] Daniel Joseph Clinton [Thomas Rourke], *Gómez: Tyrant of the Andes*, p. 82.

[3] Ramón Velásquez, *La caída del liberalismo amarillo*, p. 362. All translations are my own unless otherwise noted.

ment, allegedly at the special pleading of the U.S. asphalt interests, and agreed to extend diplomatic recognition to the new government on February 13, 1909.[4]

Gómez then set out to prevent Castro from returning to Venezuela to challenge him for the presidency. In January and February, 1909, the Corte Federal y de Casación (Federal Court, at that time the supreme court of Venezuela) considered an accusation that Castro had conspired to have Juan Vicente Gómez assassinated in the preceding December. The key document, a telegram in code which Castro had sent to a colleague, existed only as a copy; the original could not be found. The court ignored the loss, found Castro guilty of "treason, abuse of authority against national powers, instigation to crime and homicide" and removed him as president of the republic.[5]

Castro's fate was further sealed when Manuel Paredes accused the former president before the Federal Court of killing his brother, General Antonio Paredes, on February 15, 1907. The charge had been filed earlier by another brother in 1907, but the court had issued no sentence while Castro still remained in power. Again, a telegram in code was a key document to establish Castro's guilt, and again the original version of the telegram had been lost. The court took nine days to decide that Castro was guilty of the crime, and they passed the court record down to a lower court, since the crime was not a political one. One judge abstained, arguing that the record was incomplete without the original version of the telegram. The Federal Court rejected Manuel Paredes's demand for Castro's extradition to stand trial for his crime.[6] Castro's alleged implication in the death of Paredes would be used against him, however, by the U.S. courts and the U.S. Immigration Service.

[4] Betancourt, *Venezuela*, pp. 33–36; J. Fred Rippy and Clyde E. Hewitt, "Cipriano Castro, 'Man Without a Country,'" *American Historical Review* 55 (October, 1949): 39; Ramón Velásquez, "Cipriano Castro y los Estados Unidos," *Resumen* 7 (May 25, 1975): 49.

[5] Velásquez, *Caída del liberalismo amarillo*, p. 364. Velásquez speculates that the code phrase used in the telegram—"La culebra se mata por la cabeza"—sounds more like the language of someone from a rural background like Gómez's than that of the more sophisticated Castro.

[6] Ibid., pp. 365–366.

Immediately following the court decision which established Castro's responsibility in the death of his old enemy, the Gómez government supported a popular movement to make Paredes into a hero. General Román Delgado Chalbaud led the expedition to the Orinoco region where Paredes had been buried; the general's charge was to return the body to Caracas for a hero's burial. On May 27 the body preceded a large following of mourners to the Caracas Cathedral. Juan Vicente Gómez watched from a balcony as men who had been Castro's congressmen, judges, municipal councilmen, military officers, advisers, and friends marched reverently behind the casket which bore the body of Castro's bitter enemy.[7]

The exile himself was apparently undaunted at his loss of friends in Venezuela and, like Napoleon, planned a triumphant return to his homeland. He knew that once he was on Venezuelan soil, enemies could quickly turn to friends. He sailed from France on March 26, but the U.S. press and State Department knew of his plans several weeks in advance. The Venezuelan government consulted with the United States and with other Caribbean nations to prevent Castro from using a Caribbean base to launch a movement to overthrow Gómez. The Venezuelan government, supported by the United States, planned to give Castro two alternatives: either he could return to Europe or he could stand trial in Caracas for the murder of Paredes. The United States pressured other Caribbean territories not to allow Castro to disembark. His ship touched on the island of Guadeloupe, where he was informed by British officials that he would not be permitted to land at Trinidad; when his ship moved on to Martinique, Castro went ashore, only to be expelled five days later. Giving up for the moment, he returned to Europe and arrived back in France on April 24. The U.S. Navy had monitored the movements of his ship in the Caribbean; the U.S. cabinet had discussed the problems which might arise with his return; and President Taft had even taken a personal interest in the affair, terming Cipriano Castro an "international outlaw." The expansive Caribbean policy of the United States could not

[7] Ibid., pp. 369–370.

tolerate the feisty Castro's return to cause havoc in the "American Mediterranean." The *New York Daily Tribune* considered Castro an "international nuisance," and it is clear that in the eyes of the U.S. State Department the former dictator had been guilty of "chronic wrongdoing."[8]

Castro reappeared as a nuisance in December, 1912, when he headed by ship for New York. The State Department turned his case over to the Immigration Service to decide whether he was an undesirable foreigner. When Castro arrived at 9:00 A.M. on New Year's Eve, he was detained at Ellis Island by the immigration authorities. The New York newspapers again publicized his plight, and a legal firm with ties to the Democratic Party petitioned a court for a writ of *habeas corpus* which would release Castro from detention. From his cell, Castro told a French journalist that Juan Vicente Gómez had spent "a fantastic sum of 10 millions" to persecute him, but he also suspected that firms with economic interests in Venezuela were influencing the actions of the United States. Castro apparently hoped that his expressed support for Woodrow Wilson would lead the new Democratic government to assist his ambitions to return to power.[9]

On January 18, while still in detention at Ellis Island, the immigration authorities arranged a secret hearing to decide whether Castro should be allowed to remain in the United States. When queried about his wealth and about the killing of General Antonio Paredes, Castro refused to answer, asserting that he did not recognize the authority of that court to question him. Based on his refusal to answer the questions, Secretary of Commerce and Labor Charles Nagel ordered Castro expelled from the United States. Castro appealed the court's decision and won a conditional liberty on five hundred dollars' bond by the end of January. He was allowed to travel to Albany and was entertained by the New York State governor. The Venezuelan consul in New York protested to the New York attorney general that Castro was fomenting a revolution from New York soil. Just as the U.S. Department of State was

[8] Rippy and Hewitt, "Cipriano Castro."
[9] Ibid.; Velásquez, "Cipriano Castro y los Estados Unidos," p. 50.

considering these new charges, Castro decided to go to Cuba on February 23.[10]

Cipriano Castro continued for the rest of his life to pass between various Caribbean islands and the United States. He remained under the close scrutiny of the U.S. government, especially after he took up permanent residence in Puerto Rico in 1916. It was rumored that he was the object of an assassination attempt in Puerto Rico in July, 1924, but he finally died a natural death in the slums of San Juan on December 4, 1924.[11]

The cooperation between Juan Vicente Gómez and the U.S. government succeeded in making Cipriano Castro an exile for sixteen years. Press opinion in the United States divided on whether the U.S. intervention was well advised and just or not.[12] Venezuelan Pedro María Morantes (Pío Gil), author of the most famous anti-Castro book, El Cabito, expressed some of the ambivalence that many Venezuelans felt about the persecution of Castro. Pío Gil wrote from France in 1913:

Venezuela perhaps has the right and the duty . . . to give Castro four shots in any public plaza; but it is not permitted, without abdicating the privileges of the sovereign Nation, to allow any other foreign government to harass him or to punish him. It is part of the sovereignty of nations not only to protect their citizens, but also to punish them, and the national flag should be extended to protect the despot in exile. . . . Other people will be able to have the right to laugh at the dictator Castro; but the right to hate him belongs to us entirely, to us the Venezuelans. The bad will with which the North American authorities have persecuted him has no other explanation than the millions that they intend to collect from Gómez for police services; or perhaps the Yankees, believing us incapable not only of governing ourselves but also of hating, want to snatch from us not only our independence, but also our grudges.[13]

[10] Velásquez, "Cipriano Castro y los Estados Unidos," pp. 49–51.

[11] Rippy and Hewitt, "Cipriano Castro," p. 51.

[12] Ibid., pp. 52–53.

[13] Quoted by Velásquez in "Cipriano Castro y los Estados Unidos," p. 53. See also "Pío Gil, o la conciencia crítica de Venezuela," Resumen 7 (May 25, 1975): 76–77.

Juan Vicente Gómez, seeing Castro's former allies now placidly serving him, could afford to disregard the judgments of Pío Gil. He had succeeded in neutralizing Castro's popular support by enlisting U.S. assistance to prevent Castro from returning to Venezuela. The U.S. government obviously believed that its economic and military interests were safer with Gómez than with Castro. The pretext for harassing Castro, however, was the accusation before the Venezuelan Federal Court that the old dictator had ordered the assassination of General Paredes. The machination worked, and Gómez continued to maintain good relations with the United States and to allow foreign investors free rein with new oil and trade concessions. Yet his natural suspicions kept him at some distance from the foreigners.

Gómez's staunchest Venezuelan supporters proved to be his own large family, other compatriots from Táchira, the army which he had worked to develop, and many of the Caracas oligarchy and intellectuals. Of particular note among the intellectuals was Laureano Vallenilla Lanz, who in 1919 wrote *Cesarismo Democrático*, a book which became the standard apologia of Latin American dictators who would maintain order and progress "until the country should be ready for democracy." Gómez rewarded each of these groups with government jobs, power, prestige, and opportunities to enrich themselves through their influence with the government. He did much in particular to bind the military officers to him through modernization of the army organization and equipment and access to education. He did not depart, however, from the time-honored tradition of personalist caudillos; he ordered the army to serve him personally, to quell domestic disorder, and to work on his plantations if he so desired. Many of the younger officers were to feel that the disadvantages of such degrading treatment hardly outweighed the advantages of Gómez's favor.[14]

Gómez's regime resembled those of the nineteenth-century caudillos in another way. Just as he considered the army to be his

[14] Winfield J. Burggraaff, *The Venezuelan Armed Forces in Politics, 1935–1959*, pp. 15–20.

personal praetorian guard, he considered the wealth of the nation to be his own personal patrimony. From the sale of oil commissions, from kickbacks, and from land speculation Gómez emulated the old caudillos and quickly became the richest man in Venezuela. The bulk of his property, appraised at Bs126,562,042.60 at his death, was in land acquired since he had reached power. An estimate in 1932 found that Gómez controlled fully one-third of all the cultivated land in Venezuela.[15] The nation had become wealthy and free from debt as a result of the oil bonanza which had begun in the 1920s, but the nation saw few benefits aside from some roads and public works projects.

Gómez's road building projects served several purposes at once. The roads facilitated the movement of troops to put down domestic revolts. They appeared to be a symbol of the new Venezuela which had been ushered in with the oil. Finally, they provided a means for Gómez to harass his political opponents. Political criticism and dissent were not allowed; critics of the regime were badgered into leaving the country or were imprisoned. Many of the political prisoners subsequently became part of work crews who built some of the impressive new highways. There was a congress, of course, and a constitution, and other men even filled the presidential chair in Gómez's place for a few years. Gómez's spy system and allies ensured, however, that there was no real freedom of the press, of discussion, of action, or of criticism.[16]

Gómez, then, was a typical caudillo, notable perhaps only in the length of time that he was able to remain in power. Yet by the latter days of his reign different groups were beginning to rail at the hold of the old dictator. Some lamented the lack of political

[15] Federico Brito Figueroa, *Historia económica y social de Venezuela*, II, 478, 482.

[16] For secondary accounts of the Gómez regime in addition to sources cited, see Pedro Manuel Arcaya, *The Gómez Regime in Venezuela and Its Background*; Edwin Lieuwen, *Venezuela*; Edwin Lieuwen, *Petroleum in Venezuela: A History*; John Lavin, *A Halo for Gómez*; Guillermo Morón, *A History of Venezuela*; Elías Pino Iturrieta, *Positivismo y gomecismo*; Alberto Ramírez, *Esbozo psiquiátrico social del General Juan Vicente Gómez*; and Domingo Alberto Rangel, *Gómez el amo de poder*.

and civil liberties and were especially moved by the examples of the Mexican and Russian revolutions. They attributed the problems of Venezuela to the system of personalistic and arbitrary government which made a mockery of the facade of courts, constitutions, and congresses. They believed that Venezuela should enter the world made safe for democracy and should distribute the national wealth beyond the lucky friends of the dictator of the moment.

Other Venezuelans were embarrassed that Gómez had done so little to modernize the Venezuela of the *alpargatas* and *ruanas* in a material way. They, like Vallenilla Lanz, frequently appreciated the order and stability that the old Táchira general had enforced, but they wished for modern industry, for more construction and roads, for development of a class of well-trained professionals who could direct the fortunes of the country. Especially the young military officers longed for a leader who would allow the army to become truly modern and professional and to assume some responsibility for the progress and development of the nation.

The two groups, as broadly sketched above, were not mutually exclusive. They generally might disagree on whether political institutions or economic infrastructure should receive the top priority for reform, but they could cooperate. They did cooperate in 1928, again from 1945 to 1948, and generally after 1958. Nonetheless, in times of stress, the differences in priorities became apparent.

Rómulo Betancourt and Marcos Pérez Jiménez might be chosen to represent these two schools of thought. Their entire lives were given over to building the kind of Venezuela they envisioned in contrast to *gomecismo*; incidentally, their own careers and ambitions became tied up in the political and economic future of Venezuela. Their visions might logically have been compatible, but their ambitions were not. Their competition for power would last longer than that between Gómez and Castro, but would be no less bitter. Betancourt became the spokesman for the civilian Generation of 1928 which fought for an institutionalized political democracy, while Pérez Jiménez represented the desire for material progress and modernization in a context of absolute order and national unity. Although both Pérez and Betancourt worked for a new and modern Venezuela, they had learned some of their political lessons under the shadow of the old "Catfish" Gómez. Their rivalry would be curiously flavored with some of the traditional methods.

Rómulo Betancourt was born in 1908, the year that Juan Vicente Gómez seized power. The son of a Spanish accountant and amateur poet and a Venezuelan woman, Betancourt grew up in Guatire, Miranda, not far from Caracas. His family had enough financial resources to send him to the Liceo Caracas for his secondary education. There he studied under Rómulo Gallegos, one of the company of Venezuelan liberals who had naively hoped in 1908 that Juan Vicente Gómez would be the democratic leader that Cipriano Castro had not been. The Universidad Central de Venezuela still had not been allowed to reopen when Betancourt finished his secondary education, so he became a bill collector for a wholesale tobacco firm. In *Venezuela: Política y petróleo* he recalled that he and his colleagues had been enthusiastic about news of the Mexican Revolution, the Russian Revolution, the university reforms in Argentina, and the popular struggles in Cuba against dictator Gerardo Machado.[17] Those stirrings of populism must have contrasted sharply with the "election" in 1921 of Gómez for a third term of seven years.

Yet even Gómez had relented a bit by 1927 and allowed the university to reopen. Betancourt fed his awakening interest in politics and ideologies by studying law. His participation in the student protest activities of 1928 has been told many times and need not be repeated here.[18] The leaders of the student revolt were arrested, the university was closed again, and the subsequent revolutionary attempt of the students of the Military Academy in Caracas and the young officers who sympathized with them was quashed.

The events of 1928 were deeply to influence Rómulo Betancourt. He recalls celebrating his twentieth birthday in a jail cell with three colleagues; two of his friends later were to die as a

[17] Morón, *History of Venezuela*, p. 188; Betancourt, *Venezuela*, pp. 87–88.

[18] For example, see Betancourt's own writings; John Martz, *Acción Democrática: Evolution of a Modern Political Party in Venezuela*; and Burggraaff, *Venezuelan Armed Forces*.

result of their continuing fight against Gómez.[19] Betancourt subsequently told a friend and journalist, "A new dimension of human infamy was revealed in the dungeon." When he was released from jail and later went into exile, he determined "to return to Caracas with a triumphant revolutionary group and with the credentials of a man of action earned in the peripeteias of one hundred battles."[20]

If the student revolt of 1928 awakened a lasting bitterness in Betancourt, it also pointed the way to avenge himself. Much to his surprise, a general strike and popular uprising protested the jailing of the students and finally forced Gómez to release them. "That popular pressure opened the gates of the jail for us."[21] More, there were some among the young military officers who shared the hatred of Gómez, and they launched a movement which took the presidential palace on April 7, 1928. That effort failed, but Betancourt was heartened to learn that other Venezuelans longed for the downfall of Gómez. The rebels underestimated the staying power of the old dictator and optimistically supported the 1929 invasion by General Román Delgado Chalbaud. That movement, too, proved as frail as the little boat in which Betancourt and his friends had set forth from Santo Domingo.[22] Betancourt could anticipate the birth of the new, democratic Venezuela which a well-led and well-organized political movement could accomplish. The organization and the leadership were not yet developed enough to overthrow Gómez, so the liberals had to wait for his death in 1935.

The enforced exile from 1929 until 1936 allowed Betancourt time to read, to think, and to work at political organizing in the Caribbean. He read the history of his own country with the same enthusiasm that he read Karl Marx. Like his contemporary Raúl Haya de la Torre of Peru, he sought a peculiarly Latin American and national solution to the problems of his country. He dabbled in marxism with the Communist party in Costa Rica, but broke with the party because of what he considered its rigidity and stereotyped directives. Despite his break with the Communist party, he

---

[19] Betancourt, *Venezuela*, p. 88.
[20] Acción Democrática, *Rómulo Betancourt: Pensamiento y acción*, p. 58.
[21] Betancourt, *Venezuela*, p. 89.
[22] Ibid., pp. 89–90.

retained a lifelong commitment to social and economic justice for the masses. His contact with other Caribbean dictators led him to conclude that it was not the person of Gómez that had to be over-thrown, but the system of personal, arbitrary dictatorship. He also wrote of his experiences and of Venezuelan politics in *Dos meses en las cárceles de Gómez* (1928) and *En las huellas de la pezuña* (1929). He was ambitious for his country and for himself, and he worked to prepare himself to be the leader that Venezuela would require.[23]

The death of Gómez and the temporary political thaw permit-ted by President Eleazar López Contreras gave Betancourt a chance to apply some of the lessons he had learned. In 1936 Betancourt and others of the Generation of 1928 joined with the student gene-rations of 1936 and other liberal sympathizers to found the Movi-miento de Organización Venezolana (ORVE). This rather loose political association gave way in October, 1936, to the Partido De-mocrático Nacional (PDN), a political party that hoped to be able to challenge the López Contreras government in the planned Jan-uary elections. The feverish organization, discussion, and efforts to move the populace were too successful; some of the opposition candidates won in 1937, but López Contreras became nervous about the political activity. He nullified some of the elections and effec-tively outlawed the nascent political organizations. The leaders were termed communists and were expelled from the country. Be-tancourt and some others evaded the police for nearly three years and clandestinely continued their political writing and organizing. Betancourt was finally captured at the end of 1939 and expelled from the country. He traveled and lived in Argentina and Chile be-fore he was allowed to return to Venezuela in 1941.[24]

From 1941 to 1945 President Isaías Medina Angarita provided the political environment which Betancourt needed for his matura-tion as a politician. Medina allowed the political organizers to found and to organize Acción Democrática on September 13, 1941. The four years that followed saw the most extensive political activ-

[23] Acción Democrática, *Rómulo Betancourt*, pp. 46, 58–59.
[24] Martz, *Acción Democrática*, pp. 25–41.

ity that the country had yet experienced as Betancourt and his colleagues tried to ensure that every corner of Venezuela would have a party organization. Betancourt also continued his writing from the newly founded AD newspaper, *El País*. Betancourt further developed his talents to move crowds with his oratory. He was determined to lead his party to victory in this "battle for national opinion," and he hoped for free presidential elections in 1945 when Medina's term was completed.[25]

Betancourt's whole youth then was devoted to politics; he was permitted to know no other occupation. His periods of exile interspersed with periods of frantic political activity produced a man of reflection who was also capable of action. Speaking of his early experiences under the Gómez regime, Betancourt said, "I didn't choose that path . . . , life cast me that way. And that way I will continue until my destiny is fulfilled."[26]

Destiny had provided Betancourt's contemporary, Marcos Pérez Jiménez, with an entirely different experience. Born in 1914 to a farmer and his schoolteacher wife in Táchira, Pérez was isolated from the political activity in the capital city of Caracas. He went to primary school in his home town, but he entered secondary school in the Colegio "Gremios Unidos" in Cúcuta, Colombia, in 1926. His father had recently died, and he lived with an aunt in Cúcuta while his mother resumed teaching. Young Marcos was only fourteen and busily studying in Colombia when the student revolts of 1928 shook the capital city of Caracas. In 1931 he followed his older brother Juan to the Military Academy of Venezuela; following the 1928 revolt, Gómez had moved the academy away from the agitation of Caracas and had relocated it in the more tranquil town of Maracay, where he had his home. Pérez Jiménez would encounter no political activity in Maracay and no interruptions in his academic career. He graduated in December, 1934, having taken top grades in his class for the four years he was there. If he had graduated ten years earlier, he might have found that even his high grades and his Táchira background could not

[25] Acción Democrática, *Rómulo Betancourt*, pp. 33, 43.
[26] Ibid., p. 58.

contribute to his advancement in Gómez's army; the old caudillo had often passed over the better-trained graduates of the Military Academy to promote some of his illiterate cronies.[27] Pérez Jiménez could be patient, however, and he did not have long to wait until 1936, when López Contreras took over the nation and the army.

López Contreras began the badly needed overhauling of the army and of military training in Venezuela. He encouraged young officers to receive advanced training in other countries. The modernization of the armed forces did not proceed nearly quickly enough for young officers like Pérez Jiménez and perhaps frustrated them by raising their expectations too quickly. Nonetheless, Marcos Pérez Jiménez benefited from the new policies. He attended the Artillery School in Lima, Peru, in 1939 and then remained in Lima to study at the Superior War School from 1940 to 1943. When he returned to Venezuela in 1943, he was one of the best trained of the younger Venezuelan army officers. His rise was rapid under the presidency of Medina Angarita. In 1941, he had earned the rank of captain. On January 20, 1944, he became chief of the First Section of the Army Staff. On February 3, 1945, he married Flor Chalbaud Cardona, the daughter of General Antonio Chalbaud Cardona; the general had considerable influence in military and political circles and may have facilitated Pérez Jiménez's promotion to the rank of major on July 5, 1945.[28]

Although biographer Ladislao Tarnói dates Pérez Jiménez's presidential ambitions from the age of twelve, the young officer carefully avoided overt political activity. In fact, he was distressed at the political fervor and uncertainty that followed the death of Juan Vicente Gómez. He approved of General López Contreras's actions in halting the organizational efforts of the ORVE and the PDN and considered them necessary to guarantee national order

[27] Servico Informativo Venezolano, *Venezuela bajo el Nuevo Ideal Nacional*, p. 8; Frederico Landaeta, *Mi General: Breve biografía del General Marcos Pérez Jiménez, presidente de la República de Venezuela*, p. 57; Burggraaff, *Venezuelan Armed Forces*, p. 18.

[28] Burggraaff, *Venezuelan Armed Forces*, pp. 41–46; Servicio Informativo Venezolano, *Venezuela bajo el Nuevo Ideal Nacional*, p. 9; Landaeta, *Mi General*, p. 57.

and unity. His experiences in 1936 and 1937 convinced the young lieutenant that the army was more important than the constitution to ensure stability.[29] He must also have observed that a minister of war has an excellent opportunity to gain the loyalty of the army and thus ensure that he can seize power at the appropriate time; López Contreras had been Gómez's minister of war, and Medina Angarita was López's chief military officer. All of Pérez Jiménez's experience would tell him that his ambition could best be served by rising within the army.

Pérez Jiménez's closest colleagues were some of the other officers who had studied in Peru and had become imbued with the mystique of nationalism and modernization that permeated the Peruvian and Argentinean armed forces. A change had occurred among the young officers who had been commissioned in the late 1930s; they had developed an espirit de corps which encouraged them to see themselves as a unified group. They experienced the common pride in their training and patriotism and the common resentment at the military hierarchy which blocked the modernization of the armed forces. By 1944, a discontented and conspiratorial group of officers in the Caracas garrison had been joined by Pérez Jiménez, Martín Márquez Añez, and Major Julio César Vargas, who had been in Peru together. Julio César's brother, Captain Mario Ricardo Vargas, also joined the group along with many others who ensured that the conspiracy had representatives in most Caracas barracks, the Military Academy, the Maracay garrison, and the aviation branch of the army. Pérez Jiménez's organizational talents guaranteed him a leading role among the group, and he became a member of the executive committee of the secret military lodge, the Patriotic Military Union (UPM), when it was formed in 1945. One of the last to enter the conspiracy was Major Carlos Delgado Chalbaud, the French-trained son of the old anti-*gomecista* General Román Delgado Chalbaud. The UPM wanted to modernize both the military and the political institutions of Venezuela in the name

[29] Ladislao T. Tarnói, *El Nuevo Ideal Nacional de Venezuela: Vida y obra de Marcos Pérez Jiménez*, pp. 38, 47.

of nationalism, patriotism, and progress.[30] Pérez Jiménez was especially concerned about the insulting treatment of the young officers
who "were left to serve as a praetorian guard or as police in the
service of the President of the Republic."[31]

The issue which was to draw these two groups, AD and the
UPM, and these two leaders, Betancourt and Pérez Jiménez, together was the question of Medina Angarita's successor. Medina
had agreed to carefully controlled elections and had proposed the
candidacy of the relatively liberal ambassador to the United States,
Diógenes Escalante. After talking with Escalante, AD's leadership
believed that he, as a transitional president, could guide the country
to a viable democracy. Unfortunately, Escalante became seriously
ill two months before the 1945 election and had to renounce his
candidacy. Medina's second choice of his minister of agriculture,
Angel Biaggini, angered and frustrated the liberals.[32]

The UPM had not accepted the earlier nomination of Escalante
and had decided to carry their conspiracy to its logical conclusion.
The 1928 revolt against Gómez gave them a precedent to try to
cooperate with the dissatisfied civilian politicians, so they arranged
a meeting between the UPM and AD in June, 1945. Pérez Jiménez,
the spokesman for the military group, revealed the conspiracy to the
civilians and invited them to join the officers in overthrowing the
Medina government. On behalf of the officers, Pérez renounced
personal ambition and asked the civilians to help communicate to
the people their desires for an honest, just, and able government.
The officers would accept as leaders any honest and capable men
who had public support. Betancourt later recalled his distrust of
the officers in general and of Pérez Jiménez in particular; the AD
leadership, still hoping in June for the Escalante compromise, rejected the officers' proposal, but the two groups continued to communicate. By September, Biaggini had been proposed, and Betancourt was ready to join the officers' plot. The conspirators had

[30] Burggraaff, *Venezuelan Armed Forces*, pp. 45, 57–59.
[31] Ana Mercedes Pérez, *La verdad inédita, historia de la revolución de octubre revelada por sus dirigentes militares*, pp. 295–296.
[32] Martz, *Acción Democrática*, p. 57; Lieuwen, *Venezuela*, pp. 64–70.

agreed that the first arrest would be the signal to move. Medina discovered the conspiracy in October and arrested Marcos Pérez Jiménez on October 18. The fighting began, but Medina Angarita had little heart for it and surrendered on October 19.[33]

The October 18 rebellion marked the union of the two major groups which had been dissatisfied with the continuation, albeit muted, of the Gómez system. It also forged an alliance of two ambitious leaders who had matured and had been educated under that system. The alliance between Betancourt and Pérez Jiménez was doomed to be brief. Although they both had rejected *gomecismo*, they had done so for different reasons. They found it impossible to trust each other. Each suspected the other's personal ambitions as well as his vision of the new Venezuela. Time would reveal that they both had also learned from Juan Vicente Gómez. Perhaps inadvertently, they had absorbed some practical lessons on gaining and maintaining power and on how to neutralize the strength of a political opponent.

In the long run, Betancourt would have the advantage over Pérez Jiménez because his wider travels, reading, and political organizing had shown him that people could be led to overthrow their tyrants. Nor did Betancourt miss the lesson of the way the U.S. government could be used to bolster one's position at home. Moreover, his interrupted studies and his early experiences with jail, exile, and clandestine activities had made him a tough and determined competitor. He could be the caudillo and the populist politician at the same time.

On the other hand, Pérez Jiménez's more stable youth had sheltered him from the political fervor both within Venezuela and abroad. He, as a well-trained and disciplined military man, could only view the actions of crowds as damaging to the public order. He had faced no real disappointments in his early career and thus felt less hostility to the Gómez system. He would know nothing of political opposition and conspiracy until 1945. Although Pérez might have been impatient with the backwardness of Gómez's army and

[33] Pérez, *Verdad inédita*, pp. 8–9; Betancourt, *Venezuela*, pp. 229–233; *El Nacional*, October 27, 1945, p. 1; April 1, 1958, p. 35.

Gómez's nation, he would be content with modernizing and reforming the existing structure.

From 1945 to 1948, the situation would be one which Pérez could observe and manipulate to his own advantage. He, like many Venezuelans, was more impatient to see signs of material progress than of political reforms. He could wait—as Gómez had—and portray himself as the antipolitician, the one who could produce the desired modernization. If the Acción Democrática politicians alienated people or made them anxious, Pérez would be there. If his chance came, he would also have to emulate Gómez's success in consolidating his power and eliminating his enemies.

2

The Rise and Fall of the
New National Ideal, 1945–1958

The October revolution marked the beginning of the second stage of the careers of Pérez Jiménez and Betancourt. The two men had collaborated to overthrow Medina, and both would hold important positions in the new provisional government. The positions were those that they had independently been preparing for. Betancourt would be the political leader, the provisional president, as the institutions were reformed to construct a representative democracy. Pérez Jiménez, on the other hand, would quietly go about the business of reorganizing and modernizing the armed forces. He became chief of the General Staff of the Armed Forces. The competition and resentment between the civilian politician and the military man would become more intense as the years passed.

The military conspirators made good their promise to take a subordinate role to the civilian politicians when the provisional junta was constituted. On October 19, a meeting of most of the revolutionaries was held to select Rómulo Betancourt as president of the junta and provisional president of the nation; Raúl Leoni, Gonzalo Barrios, and Luis Beltrán Prieto as other AD members of the junta; and Edmundo Fernández as an independent. The army was represented by Major Carlos Delgado Chalbaud and Captain Mario Vargas. The major spokesman for the UPM, Pérez Jiménez, did not receive a seat on the junta. Pérez was absent on October 19 when the rebels met in Miraflores to discuss the makeup of the junta; he subsequently attributed his exclusion to Betancourt's animosity and distrust of him. Others have suggested that he was somewhat embarrassed at having avoided combat by his early arrest or that he sincerely preferred the general staff position to the more political one of minister of war. The most credible account portrays Carlos Delgado Chalbaud as an opportunist who manipulated the situation on that chaotic night to his own benefit. Whatever the cause of Pérez's exclusion, it did appear to deepen the hostility between Pérez and Betancourt.[1]

Outside of the overtly political arena, Pérez Jiménez made good use of his standing with the army after 1945. He is given credit for an improvement of the administration and technical organization of the Venezuelan armed forces. Incidentally, he also fostered a strong personal loyalty to himself and to Luis Felipe Llovera Páez, the second in command of the general staff. Carlos Delgado Chalbaud, the minister of defense, never matched Pérez's influence within the army; his long residence and training in France made him somewhat suspect to the officers trained in America.[2]

Excited by the new phase in Venezuelan political history, the civilian junta from 1945 to 1948 issued a rash of decrees. Acción Democrática oversaw three elections in those years, all of which they won with over 70 percent of the vote. In many ways Betancourt and the AD leaders expressed their commitment to bettering the social and economic conditions of the masses of Venezuelans. The rapid and sometimes confusing changes alienated some Venezuelans and provided political opponents with an opportunity to criticize the politicians for waste, opportunism, corruption, and excessive partisanship. The other civilian parties—the Unión Republicana Democrática (URD), the Comité de Organización Política Electoral Independiente (COPEI), and the Communist party— were poorly organized, but their constant attacks made some impression on the citizenry. Yet most scholars would agree that the greater threat to the AD government would be the military officers

[1] Ana Mercedes Pérez, *Síntesis histórica de un hombre y un pueblo*, pp. 10–11; *El Nacional*, April 1, 1958; Rómulo Betancourt, *Venezuela: Política y petróleo*, p. 238; Winfield J. Burggraaff, *The Venezuelan Armed Forces in Politics, 1935–1959*, p. 74; Glen L. Kolb, *Democracy and Dictatorship in Venezuela, 1945–1958*, p. 19.

[2] *El Nacional*, November 24, 1958; Laureano Vallenilla Lanz, Hijo, *Razones de proscrito*, pp. 32–33; Rodolfo Luzardo, *Notas históricas, 1928–1963*, p. 32; Edwin Lieuwen, *Venezuela*, p. 89.

who were warily watching the progress of the democratic government.[3]

Betancourt introduced two policies to which he was to be loyal for the rest of his political life and which continued to be divisive. In foreign relations, he began to break off diplomatic relations with dictatorial governments in the Americas and elsewhere. His early experiences in the Caribbean had convinced him that democratic governments could best counter *golpista* movements by coordinating their foreign policies.[4] In his observation of caudillos like Juan Vicente Gómez, Betancourt also concluded that they harmed their nations irreparably with their corruption and peculation. In 1946–1947, Betancourt and Acción Democrática initiated a series of trials of former high government officials for graft and illicit enrichment in office. The trials found numerous Venezuelans guilty of peculation and confiscated the property which they presumably had gained from their official positions. Betancourt was determined to wipe out corruption from public office and took great pride in his own poverty when he left office. Many Venezuelans would concede that Betancourt's intentions were laudable, but they often resented the trials as arbitrary and partisan. Critics noted that some friends of Acción Democrática had escaped trial and charged that the trials appeared to be tinged with a spirit of revenge against those who had earlier harassed the AD leaders.[5]

In any case, the period from 1945 to 1948 was an agitated one, with rumors constantly flying and new ambitions rising to challenge the AD monopoly of political power. The pressure finally was too much, and on November 24, 1948, the military-civilian coalition

[3] John Martz, *Acción Democrática: Evolution of a Modern Political Party in Venezuela*, pp. 81–89; Kolb, *Democracy and Dictatorship*, pp. 41–49; Burggraaff, *Venezuelan Armed Forces*, pp. 79–111.

[4] Lieuwen, *Venezuela*, pp. 175–176; Charles D. Ameringer, *The Democratic Left in Exile: The Antidictatorial Struggle in the Caribbean, 1945–1959*, pp. 58–60.

[5] *El Nacional*, March 7, September 14, November 12, November 29, 1947; March 5, June 16, 1948. For a full account of these trials, see República de Venezuela, Junta Revolucionaria de Gobierno, *Recopilación de sentencias . . . por el Jurado de Responsabilidad Civil y Administrativa.*

parted company. Led by Pérez Jiménez, Llovera Páez, and—again belatedly—Delgado Chalbaud, the army repudiated President Rómulo Gallegos's government, his cabinet, and his party.[6] Prior to the *golpe*, the officers had presented a list of demands to Gallegos, and the president refused to accede to all of them. The officers wanted the cabinet to include more officers, wanted Betancourt to leave the country, and wanted a new coalition government to be formed with some participation of the COPEI party. The conspirators claimed that Gallegos could not control his own party or the country. Although Betancourt denied the charge, the officers said that AD planned a general strike and the arming of *campesinos* and workers.[7] In fact, no effective opposition arose to defend the government when the leaders of the revolt arrested the president and members of the cabinet.

In the three-year period, the mutual hostility between Pérez Jiménez and Betancourt had been matched by a growing coolness between the two institutions they represented. Party leaders and army leaders each feared that the other organization aspired to become a state within a state. The military forces, a relatively unified and centralized body, clearly had the initial advantage. AD would need more time to develop the strong populist base which would be able to check the army's natural advantage.[8]

Pérez Jiménez and the conspirators drew considerable support from the Caracas oligarchy who resented the peculation trials and who resented being edged out of positions of power by the largely middle-class AD leaders. They feared the impact of what they perceived as the disorder which emanated from the government headed by the enthusiastic newcomers to politics. The members of the

[6] As a result of the election of December, 1947, Rómulo Gallegos was elected president and took office in February, 1948. Betancourt's provisional presidency lasted until that time.

[7] *El Nacional*, November 24, December 6, 11, 1948; Juan Blanco Peñalver, *Historia de un naufragio*, pp. 179–180; José Agustín Catalá, ed., *Documentos para la historia de la resistencia: Pérez Jiménez y su régimen de terror*, I, 48–51.

[8] *El Nacional*, December 10, 1948; November 24, 1958; Catalá, *Documentos*, I, 31; José Rivas Rivas, ed., *El mundo y la época de Pérez Jiménez: Una historia contada en recortes de periódicos*, pp. 49-10, 49-11.

Venezuelan elite could concur with the *perezjimenistas* that the *golpe* had been the army's defensive move to save the stability of the country and to unify the populace which had been divided by AD partisanship.[9]

After the AD leaders were jailed, Delgado Chalbaud, Pérez Jiménez, and Llovera Páez formed a governing military junta. Delgado became president of the junta and of the nation, even though he had again joined at the last minute a movement which Pérez Jiménez had nurtured. For the second time, Delgado apparently moved quickly at a moment of indecision and claimed the highest position because of his higher military rank. Pérez Jiménez again appeared timid and was either unwilling or unable to challenge Delgado.[10] Betancourt's less than generous first impression of Pérez Jiménez appeared substantiated; he had described the Andean man thus: "In civilian dress, with thick tortoiseshell glasses, an overly careful stutter, not knowing what to do with his hands while he rocked on his short legs, he did not convey much of a martial impression. He seemed like a bookkeeper from the interior provinces. At first glance he appeared a timid and reflective person, more fertile in words than in ideas, lost in a dark forest of vagueness."[11] In 1948 Pérez became minister of defense and continued to reflect, to wait.

Betancourt, too, had to wait. Upon his release from jail, he began another long period of exile and clandestine struggle. He had been betrayed both by his military collaborators and by the people who would not fight to save the AD government. Twenty years of political activity had yielded brief success but had not been enough to prevent errors of judgment. Yet having tasted success and having seen the weakness of the enemy, Betancourt refused to allow Pérez Jiménez the spoils of victory without a fight.[12]

It is difficult to evaluate the military junta headed by Delgado.

[9] Betancourt, *Venezuela*, pp. 161–241, 559–560; Rivas Rivas, *El mundo*, pp. 49-10, 49-11.

[10] Catalá, *Documentos*, I, 35–36; Burggraaff, *Venezuelan Armed Forces*, pp. 112–113.

[11] Betancourt, *Venezuela*, p. 224.

[12] See Ameringer, *Democratic Left in Exile*.

The AD party was immediately outlawed, but other political parties were allowed to operate. Some of the AD initiatives, such as the 1946 constitution and the sentences against the presumed authors of peculation, were rescinded, but the clock was not turned back to 1936 by any means. Political activity and freedom of the press were curtailed, but elections were promised in the near future. Perhaps the ambivalence simply reflected the fact that these military officers had shared some of the objectives of the 1945 revolt. Or perhaps there was a division of opinion among members of the military junta; to some, Delgado Chalbaud appeared to be more moderate and conciliatory than Pérez Jiménez. A new civilian advisor to the military junta appeared shortly after the 1948 *golpe* and would continue to gain in prominence and importance; Laureano Vallenilla Lanz, Hijo, son of the author of *Cesarismo democrático*, became increasingly close to Marcos Pérez Jiménez. Pérez Jiménez himself continued to consolidate his support and influence in the army.[13]

The character of the military junta would become clearer after November 13, 1950. On that date, General Rafael Simón Urbina and a group of comrades kidnapped and killed Delgado Chalbaud. Later investigations never determined under whose orders, if any, Urbina had been acting. Urbina had no opportunity to confess; a trigger-happy policeman shot him shortly after his arrest during an alleged escape attempt. Public opinion and some subsequent testimony suggested that Pérez Jiménez had been implicated in the planning of the crime. At the very least, he was the most obvious beneficiary.[14]

With the death of Delgado, Pérez Jiménez encountered no viable competition for the presidency of the junta. Leaders of the Communist party and AD were in exile or were working clandestinely to overthrow the military government. Jóvito Villaba of URD and Rafael Caldera of COPEI meekly formed the loyal opposition.

---

[13] Kolb, *Democracy and Dictatorship*, pp. 60–75; Burggraaff, *Venezuelan Armed Forces*, pp. 112–121.

[14] Rivas Rivas, *El mundo*, p. 51-59; Luzardo, *Notas históricas*, pp. 168–169; Nicanor López Borges, *El asesinato de Delgado Chalbaud: Análisis de un sumario*.

Llovera Páez displayed no ambition for the presidency, nor did any other military men emerge with sufficient support to seize the top position. The influence and visibility of Pérez Jiménez's one-man brain trust, Laureano Vallenilla Lanz Planchart, increased markedly from this period.[15]

For a third time, however, Marcos Pérez Jiménez turned away from the highest political position in Venezuela. Journalist Arístides Bastidas thought that Pérez refused the presidency in 1950 as a diversionary tactic; fear that public opinion would judge him an accomplice in Delgado's murder led Pérez Jiménez to wait.[16] Whether he had planned Delgado's kidnapping or not, either he was patient enough to bide his time or he did not really feel confident enough to assume the top position.

After an eminent physician, Arnoldo Gabaldón, refused the presidency, a Caracas lawyer, Germán Suárez Flamerich, agreed to fill the position. Pérez Jiménez and Llovera Páez completed the triumvirate. Chosen for his tractability rather than his strength, Suárez Flamerich contributed little of significance.[17]

The election of December 2, 1952, formalized the de facto power that Pérez had acquired after the death of Delgado. Universal suffrage of those over the age of twenty elected a Constituent Assembly to appoint a president and write a new constitution. The main participating parties in the election were the Frente Electoral Independiente (FEI), a government-sponsored "independent" party; COPEI; and URD. Since late in 1948, AD had been outlawed; in 1949 the Communist party was also outlawed, although some small Communist and Socialist factions were allowed to continue their activity.[18] Early election returns indicated victory for Jóvito Villaba's URD party. Then radio and newspaper reporting of election results was halted. When the media announced the final returns, Venezuelans discovered that government (FEI) candidates had handily defeated URD. Then in the interests of national har-

---

[15] Luzardo, *Notas históricas*, pp. 168–169; Catalá, *Documentos*, I, 252; *El Nacional*, August 3, 1958.

[16] Catalá, *Documentos*, I, 4, 252.

[17] Blanco Peñalver, *Historia*, pp. 187–188; *El Nacional*, April 8, 1958.

[18] Robert J. Alexander, *The Communist Party of Venezuela*, pp. 29–31.

mony, Villaba and some of his colleagues were asked to leave the country. Both COPEI and URD, in protest at the apparent fraud, abandoned their pose of loyal opposition to a legitimate regime.[19]

The first action of the Constituent Assembly in 1953 was to name Pérez Jiménez as provisional president. After writing a new constitution, the assembly, mostly FEI members and independents, duly chose Pérez Jiménez as constitutional president for the 1953–1958 term.

With the help of Vallenilla Lanz, Pérez Jiménez began to patch together and express an ideology of economic development. His New National Ideal revealed more by what it denied than by what it affirmed. In effect, Pérez prohibited political activity, personalism, foreign ideology, freedom of expression, and, indeed, any elements of conflict or criticism within Venezuela. Rejecting a pluralistic society, Pérez Jiménez asked Venezuelans to unite unquestioningly behind an administration which promised modernization, economic development, and order. The government assumed that the benefits of prosperity eventually would reach the poor and did not advocate any measures to assure a fairer distribution of Venezuela's oil wealth.

Pérez Jiménez's government was not unique in an age and on a continent which glorified a special military mission, national discipline, and material development usually to the exclusion of social justice. Largely apolitical, Pérez Jiménez did not seek the votes or support of the *descamisados* as had Juan Perón in Argentina. He had no intuitive grasp of politics himself, and he was unfortunate in acquiring an advisor like Vallenilla Lanz. Vallenilla had been educated in France, where he had acquired an enthusiasm for the trappings of modernization and an admiration for the rule of Napoleon III. His elite background and his education prepared him to relive his father's prestige and power under Juan Vicente Gómez but did not equip him to forge a political alliance with the masses he scorned.

[19] Luzardo, *Notas históricas,* p. 171; Catalá, *Documentos,* I, 7; Rivas Rivas, *El mundo,* pp. 52-26, 52-28.

Laureano Vallenilla Lanz Planchart had returned to Venezuela from Europe after the death of Gómez and began to dabble in banking, government, law, and newspaper editing. He married the daughter of Adolfo Bueno, one of Gómez's friends and advisors. In 1946, Dr. Bueno was tried and found guilty of peculation when he had been in the service of Gómez. When the AD government confiscated the larger part of his father-in-law's considerable fortune, Vallenilla could neither forgive nor forget.[20]

Vallenilla's early friendships with his father's friends and associates aided him in securing jobs and a reputation upon his return to Venezuela. He also developed his positivistic philosophy from his father and his associates. Vallenilla advocated a governing oligarchy of talented men, technocrats or mandarins, who would rule Venezuela until Venezuelans proved mature enough for democracy.[21] He encouraged Pérez Jiménez to choose for his cabinet men who had served in the Medina or López Contreras or Gómez governments. As might be expected, this pool of experienced administrators usually came from the upper levels of Caracas society and had attended European or U.S. universities. Also predictably, Vallenilla's colleagues would establish a healthy climate for business and foreign investment at the expense of rural and less affluent groups. Military men, with whom Pérez Jiménez might have felt more affinity, played a role secondary to that of Vallenilla's mandarins. The diffident Andino, like Gómez himself, allowed the more worldly Caracas elite to direct the government and the economy.

In spite of the internationalism of Vallenilla's mandarins and Pérez's advisors and ministers, the New National Ideal did have a strong nationalistic appeal to Venezuelans. The immediate inspiration lay in Venezuelan history and geography. Pérez Jiménez frequently reminded his countrymen of their rich natural resources and of their advantageous geographical position on the northern edge of the South American continent. He also recalled the glorious

[20]Laureano Vallenilla Lanz, Hijo, *Escrito de memoria*, pp. 236–237, 241, 298–299.

[21] Ibid., pp. 109–110, 297, 302–303.

days when Simón Bolívar had freed much of South America and had placed it, at least symbolically, under Venezuelan hegemony.[22] To recover or re-create the national prestige of the past, Venezuelans must unite and hold to common values. A bare four months after the November 24 revolt, Pérez Jiménez had said:

We must admit that we have lacked that fundamental element of the life of people which consists of the clear and precise formulation of a national ideal, capable of binding us into an agreement of wills for its full realization. That ideal, of which so much has been said among us, but for whose concretion we have done so little, has two fundamental forms of objective expression: on one hand the utilization of our historical estate as a fount of moral values, and on the other, the adequate utilization of the material resources of the country to better the luck of living Venezuelans, especially the luck of the least favored, and to bequeath to future generations a more prosperous country.[23]

Other blights in the national character had to be excised before Venezuela again could attain continental leadership, Pérez Jiménez argued. The cult of personalism had thwarted both the team spirit and the technical efficiency necessary for modernization. Also, political leaders had tried to emulate foreign governments and ideologies instead of taking the national realities into account. According to Pérez, Rómulo Betancourt had been guilty of personalism and of dividing the nation by an emphasis on political ideologies instead of work. The AD administration had suffered from all of the characteristics of bad administration: inept political officials, excess of incompetent bureaucrats, overall disorganization, lack of long-term planning, the hegemony of one political party, squandering of public funds, and attempts to weaken the army.[24]

The military man rejected the AD emphasis on human rights, social justice, and political democracy. He argued that order and economic development must precede political development: "Man will defend property more when he has it than when he covets it;

22 Servicio Informativo Venezolano, *Venezuela bajo el Nuevo Ideal Nacional,* p. 35; Marcos Pérez Jiménez, *Pensamiento político del presidente de Venezuela,* pp. 36–37, 59.

23 Pérez Jiménez, *Pensamiento político,* p. 14.

24 Servicio Informativo Venezolano, *Venezuela bajo el Nuevo Ideal Nacional,* pp. 16–17; Pérez Jiménez, *Pensamiento político,* p. 75.

he will preserve his health better when he has felt the full enjoyment of it; he will try to inform himself more when he has felt the benefits of education; and he will use liberty better, protecting it from the ambushes of demagogues or tyrants, when he has lived in its legitimate environment of respect and of order."[25]

Seeking an analogue for the type of government he proposed, Pérez Jiménez depicted the army as a model institution of professional discipline and organization, a repository of national virtues. This army, in which he felt a proprietary pride, was to Pérez Jiménez a microcosm of what he hoped the nation could become. In the army, men learned patriotism, duty, good health practices, a sense of responsibility, reading and writing, and useful trades.[26] Pérez Jiménez might privately have extolled the soldiers' willingness to recognize his managerial skills and to accept his leadership without question.

To effect and implement his new national ideal, Pérez Jiménez relied on the caudillo's proven method of *pan o palo*—"bread or the club." The postwar prosperity made the bread especially rich for some, just as modern police-state techniques made the club heavy and inescapable for others. Increased profits and business opportunities silenced some who might have spoken out in leaner years. Numerous construction projects enriched those who held government contracts and provided work for the immigrants and rural migrants who poured into Caracas. Expansion of power facilities, irrigation projects, and agricultural credit for larger farmers pleased some would-be agribusinessmen. Improvements in transportation and communication developed marketing possibilities for those who lived in the interior of the country. The armed forces were proud of new weapons and the luxurious new Officers' Club.

The new waves of wealth provided opportunities that made the corruption of Gómez's day pale by comparison. Pérez and his collaborators may have had excellent professional and technical backgrounds, but they did not develop a mystique of public service in

[25] Servicio Informativo Venezolano, *Venezuela bajo el Nuevo Ideal Nacional*, p. 47.

[26] Pérez Jiménez, *Pensamiento político*, pp. 15, 20.

the new era of wild prosperity and in the absence of moral leadership from the president. A Venezuelan intellectual who remained in exile during the 1950s, Mario Briceño-Iragorry, described the moral vacuum that the headlong scramble for wealth had left in his country:

To run, run, run toward wherever there is a possibility of profit has been the life plan of many responsible Venezuelans of today. Profit—not just from mining, but from all kinds of concessions: licenses, permits, contracts, commissions—has destroyed the moral fiber of a great number of men who in other times would have been models of rectitude. Also, many, stimulated by the purpose of making or remaking a fortune, have fallen without noticing into grievous obligations with interests that deny genuine nationalism. . . . Traitors and thieves have been protected . . . by the tarnished maxim that *in Venezuela nothing takes away and nothing bestows honor.*[27]

Protests of those who could not be silenced with prosperity or those who did not share in the prosperity met governmental repression. Press censorship encouraged the psychological unity that Pérez Jiménez wanted. Freedom of organization and assembly also was curtailed. The government denied labor unions, formerly led by AD and Communist party members, the freedom to bargain collectively for new contracts; instead, the government dictated new contracts.[28] Restrictions on labor union activity sought to lessen the possibilities of agitation and disorder and to undercut AD's strength in the labor movement.

Venezuelans concentrated their hatred and distrust of the Pérez Jiménez regime on one organization: Seguridad Nacional (SN), a national police force with virtually unlimited powers which operated under the Ministry of the Interior. Its chief from September, 1951, until January, 1958, Pedro Estrada, learned from the FBI in the United States and imported British Scotland Yard agents to conduct classes in the police academy. He also encouraged the police organizations of other Caribbean nations to harass and

[27] Mario Briceño-Iragorry, *Ideario político*, p. 71.
[28] Catalá, *Documentos*, I, 221, 231–232, 236–238; Rivas Rivas, *El mundo*, pp. 50-7, 50-8; Domingo Felipe Maza Zavala, *Paradojas venezolanas: Crónicas de economía y angustia social*, pp. 138–139.

watch over Venezuelan exiles. Mysterious disappearances or deaths of persons who opposed the military regime intensified popular fear of the Seguridad Nacional. Reputedly, agents of SN assassinated Leonardo Ruíz Pineda, Antonio Pinto Salinas, and Luis Hurtado, all of AD, and Germán González, a political independent. The SN and the National Guard also administered the hated prison camp of Guasina in the Orinoco River delta. Infamous for its unhealthful conditions, Guasina later became a symbol of the repressiveness of the government.[29]

Pérez Jiménez's repressiveness brought back memories of the Gómez regime to some Venezuelans. They remarked as well that, like Gómez, Pérez Jiménez enjoyed the support of the U.S. government. President Harry Truman had recognized the military junta shortly after being reelected in 1948, and relations became even more cordial when General Dwight Eisenhower assumed the U.S. presidency in 1953. In October, 1954, General Eisenhower awarded Colonel Pérez Jiménez the Legion of Merit in its highest rank for his outstanding leadership and example in the Caribbean. The letter which accompanied the decoration praised Pérez Jiménez's sound economic policy, his public works program, his initiative in combating communism in Venezuela and in the Americas, and his reform of the Venezuelan armed forces, which made them more valuable to the collective defense of the Western Hemisphere. Eisenhower further commended Pérez Jiménez on the improvements made in education, health, transportation, housing, and general welfare.[30]

---

[29] *El Nacional*, October 29, 1951; June 15, 1958; José Vicente Pepper, *Reconstrucción integral de Venezuela*, pp. 305–309. For accounts of the prison camps and tortures, see José Agustín Catalá, *La denuncia: Crimenes y torturas en el régimen de Pérez Jiménez*, and José Vicente Abreu, *Se llamaba S.N.* The four assassinations became the ones for which Pérez Jiménez was held responsible in the extradition proceedings in the United States. See chapter 4. For a description of Guasina, see José Vicente Abreu, *Guasina, donde el río perdió las siete estrellas: Relatos de un campo de concentración de Pérez Jiménez*.

[30] Rivas Rivas, *El mundo*, p. 54-20; Marcos Pérez Jiménez, Declaración Indagatoria, 1 pieza principal, Archive 59-95, Archives of the Corte Suprema de Justicia, Caracas, Venezuela.

Other foreign relations provided a barometer to Pérez Jiménez's sympathies. The military president reversed the AD recognition of the exiled Spanish Republic and resumed relations with Francisco Franco's regime. Cordial relations were maintained with neighboring Colombia and British Guiana. The Colombian and Venezuelan police forces cooperated with each other. Venezuela did not, however, continue her partnership in the Grand Colombian Fleet, an AD-sponsored association. Venezuela's boundary claim to part of British Guiana provided a source of conflict with the British government but not immediately with Guiana itself; Pérez Jiménez supported the Guiana independence movement.[31]

Other Latin American countries also generally enjoyed good relations with Venezuela during most of the Pérez Jiménez years. Closest allies included the similar military governments of Manuel Odría of Peru, Juan Perón of Argentina, Gustavo Rojas Pinilla of Colombia, Rafael Trujillo of the Dominican Republic, Alfredo Stroessner of Paraguay, Fulgencio Batista of Cuba, and Anastasio Somoza of Nicaragua. The cordiality and personal affinities of these relations led outsiders to refer to the "International of the Sword."[32] Much cooler were relations with leaders who maintained friendship with Rómulo Betancourt, such as José Figueres of Costa Rica.

Pérez Jiménez also kept up good relations with the Vatican and the Catholic Church until 1957. In May, 1957, Monseñor Rafael Arias of Caracas, citing the poverty and social ills of Venezuela, implicitly criticized Pérez Jiménez's indifference to measures of social welfare. Thus began a period of veiled conflict and increasing opposition on the part of Venezuelan church officials to Pérez Jiménez. The conflict became more serious as Pérez Jiménez and Pedro Estrada reacted repressively to the relatively mild clerical criticism.[33]

[31] Rivas Rivas, *El Mundo*, pp. 50-14, 53-14, 53-30, 54-12, 57-3; Rodolfo Luzardo, *Río Grande: Los malos entendimientos en el continente americano*, p. 131.

[32] Marcos Pérez Jiménez, Intervención, December 5, 1967, Archive 59-95.

[33] Luis Colmenares Díaz, *La espada y el incensario: La iglesia bajo Pérez Jiménez*, pp. 71–73; José Rodríguez Iturbe, *Iglesia y estado en Venezuela, 1824–1964*, pp. 208–209; José Umaña Bernal, *Testimonio de la revolución en Venezuela*, pp. 95–96.

Although the reality of repression and administrative graft during the early 1950s contradicted the national ideal of efficient administration and a better life for all Venezuelans, there were some real accomplishments. The international economic situation favored prosperity for Venezuela in the 1950s. The end of World War II released some of the savings accumulated during the war and lessened the scarcity of durable and consumer goods. Venezuelan oil, much in demand during the war, continued to be marketed profitably during the Korean War and the Suez Crisis. Oil taxes, and the new petroleum concessions which Pérez sold in 1956, brought in sufficient wealth to make Venezuela rich among the less developed countries. Venezuelan nationalists considered the sale of new concessions to be a step backwards in the nation's struggle to control its own resources. Moreover, Pérez Jiménez's use of the increased revenues continues to be debated.

Caracas benefited the most from the public works expenditures, always a major part of the annual budget. New projects each year were rushed to completion by December 2 to celebrate Pérez Jiménez's 1952 accession to the presidency; freeways, new avenues, and skyscrapers changed the appearance of Caracas during those ten years. Urdaneta Avenue, Sabana Grande with its exclusive boutiques, Simón Bolívar Center with its governmental offices and underground shopping center, the Armed Forces Club, University City, Hotel Tamanaco, Hotel Humboldt, as well as privately constructed buildings like the Creole Building told the visitor that Caracas was no longer a sleepy one-story town.

A modern national transportation system received high priority, as it had with Acción Democrática. Caracas became a seaport, by virtue of the Caracas–La Guaira expressway, considered to be one of the great engineering feats of the era. Other highways, including the Venezuelan part of the Pan American Highway, which linked Caracas to the Venezuelan Andes and to Colombia, soon crossed the country. In 1953, Pérez Jiménez won the prize for Pan American Highway construction.[34]

The government sought to promote tourism within the country.

[34] Rivas Rivas, *El mundo*, p. 54-14.

The luxurious Tamanaco Hotel was begun: completed, it replaced the older Avila Hotel as the center of Caraqueño social life and provided a lure for tourists. The Hotel Humboldt, perched on top of Mount Avila overlooking Caracas, could be reached by a tramway and boasted an ice skating rink. The Hotel del Lago raised Maracaibo's tourist rating, and other new hotels were built in the interior of Venezuela. The longest tramway in the world was begun in Mérida in an effort to attract visitors to the Venezuelan Andes.

Other building projects sought to entertain the working classes, especially of Caracas and of the armed forces. The fabulous Armed Forces Military Club had several dining rooms, an Olympic swimming pool, a nightclub, and living quarters, and it ranked among the most elegant of military clubs in Latin America. Close to Macuto, the vacation village of Los Caracas was built to allow government workers to vacation within reach of mountains and sea for a minimal price. Claiming to be the first resort of its type in America, it offered many attractions: restaurants, movies, soda fountains, beaches, tennis courts, hotel rooms, clubs, apartments, and child care centers. A luxurious Casa Sindical in Caracas offered a meeting place and recreation facilities for the city workers.[35]

Several major projects contributed to national and regional development. The most spectacular innovations resulted from cooperation between the government and the subsidiary of United States Steel, the Orinoco Mining Company. Commercial iron-ore mining, the beginnings of a steel industry and hydroelectric complex, and channelization of the Orinoco River brought new life to the Guayana region. New jobs and opportunities attracted migration to Ciudad Bolívar, San Félix, and the newer Puerto Ordaz, just as Brasília would draw population to the interior of Brazil. The state of Zulia also benefited from the dragging of the sand bar at the entrance to Lake Maracaibo which permitted the entry of large tankers and simplified the transportation of Venezuelan oil. Finally, the massive national electrification plan and extensive road building did improve life in the interior and lessened somewhat the

[35] Ibid., p. 55-18.

massive gap between the quality of life in the capital and that in the rest of the country.[36]

Less conspicuous were works specifically designed to alter the social structure of the country or to aid the less fortunate. Some hospitals were built, but they often suffered from deficient supplies and personnel. Efforts were made to build lower-income housing, but the unpopular *superbloques* did not meet the demands of the rapidly increasing urban population; private construction companies found it more profitable to build middle-class and luxury housing, which became a glut on the market. Schools were built, but again, they were inadequately staffed. Frequent student and teacher strikes, both a cause and an effect of police repression and censorship, often closed the schools and universities. The government placed little value on the human resources of Venezuela.[37]

Beginning in 1957, the international economic and political situation ceased to favor Pérez Jiménez to the same extent it had earlier. With the end of the Korean War and the Suez Crisis, Venezuelan oil revenues dropped. A worldwide economic recession began. The Joseph McCarthy period drew to a close in the United States; the harshness of the U.S. anticommunist crusade began to relax and permitted a more flexible attitude toward other American governments and toward more liberal political groups. The U.S. State Department tried to modify its uncritical support of military dictatorships. Among the Latin American dictators, Odría, Rojas Pinilla, Perón, and Somoza had all passed from the scene; Batista had to contend with what appeared to be a minor guerrilla activity. Within Venezuela, Pérez Jiménez increasingly ignored, alien-

[36] Based on figures taken from the 1950 and 1961 Venezuelan censuses, Antonio A. López Guinazú asserted that the narrowing gap between the Federal District and the rest of the country derived from improved conditions in the rest of the country, since the Federal District was relatively heavily urbanized and industrialized in the beginning of the decade. Antonio A. López Guinazú, "Modernization in Venezuela (1950–1961)" (Ph.D. diss., Colorado State University, 1970), pp. 59, 63, 86.

[37] *El Nacional*, March 10, 1958; Rivas Rivas, *El mundo*, p. 50-10; Catalá, *Documentos*, I, 143–144; Umaña Bernal, *Testimonio*, pp. 87–88; Talton Ray, *The Politics of the Barrios of Venezuela*, p. 163.

ated, or insulted various segments of the Venezuelan populace. By the end of 1957, these groups were coalescing into a new movement against the dictatorship. The new coalition revitalized the earlier underground activity led by AD and largely destroyed by 1952. Through actions and attitudes, Pérez Jiménez alienated the intellectuals, the political parties, the church, labor organizations, and even the oligarchy. Repressive measures and censorship offended many intellectuals; newsmen were especially bitter against Vallenilla Lanz and his official newspaper *El Heraldo*. Strikes and school closings left students and teachers idle, embittered, and often persecuted. The political parties resented their illegal status or their closely circumscribed "opposition" role.[38] Arrests of priests in January, 1958, sharpened the disaffection of the Church. Workers, previously won over by the low unemployment rate in Caracas, began to worry about the slowing rate of construction and the rising cost of living. The unskilled workers who benefited from Caracas construction projects often found themselves out of work after the push to meet the December 2 deadlines. Venezuelan workers also bitterly resented the presence of immigrants, who often received preference in hiring. The wealthy business and commercial interests also had a wary eye on the deteriorating economic situation and intended to protect their own interests; Pérez Jiménez had been good to them, but if he could not remain in control of the situation, they might be unable to collect debts owed them by the government.[39]

For the actual revolution the people merely neglected by Pérez Jiménez became as important as those he had alienated. The thousands who had clustered in cardboard houses on the Caracas hillsides wanted more than Pérez Jiménez and his government had

[38] Catalá, *Documentos*, I, 124–125, 140, 143–186, 372; *El Nacional*, August 3, 1958; Umaña Bernal, *Testimonio*, p. 103; José Rodolfo Cárdenas, *El combate político: Solo para líderes nuevos*, pp. 25–26.

[39] Rodríguez Iturbe, *Iglesia y estado*, 207–208; Colmenares Díaz, *La espada y el incensario*, pp. 71–72; Umaña Bernal, *Testimonio*, pp. 95–96; *Venezuela Independiente, 1810–1960*, pp. 333–334; Catalá *Documentos*, I, 221, 231–232, 236–238; Rivas Rivas, *El mundo*, pp. 50-7, 50-8, 56-8; Maza Zavala, *Paradojas venezolanas*, pp. 138–139; Blanco Peñalver, *Historia*, pp. 200–201; Alexander, *Communist Party of Venezuela*, pp. 42–43.

been able or willing to allow them.[40] Most damaging, Pérez Jiménez had neglected the military men and had come to depend increasingly on the SN and on his civilian advisors. Some high military officers were insulted by the difficulty of access to their president and general. Civilians dominated all of Pérez Jiménez's cabinets until the last one formed on January 11, 1958; that cabinet had eight military men and six civilians. Moreover, Colonel José Teofilo Velázco stepped into the position of director of Seguridad Nacional. Vallenilla Lanz, Pedro Estrada, and Fortunato Herrera left the country. Unfortunately for Pérez Jiménez, the military conspiracy could not be halted by the last-minute concessions. He had allowed himself too much distance from the officers. Many resented the prominence of a small clique from Táchira. When the SN took from the army the task of assuring law and order in Venezuela, the uneasiness and jealousy of the army grew. The navy and air force had never held the favored position that the army had and were even more ready to rebel. Assigning an admiral, Wolfgang Larrazábal, to the position of hotel keeper for the Armed Forces Club symbolized the carelessness with which Pérez Jiménez treated the naval sense of honor.[41]

The general finally reached the point of insulting the entire Venezuelan nation. Administrative graft appeared more obvious as the list of *perezjimenista* houses, lands, yachts, jewels, Rolls Royces, and other luxuries accumulated. Although Pérez Jiménez had lived fairly simply up until 1950, he adopted the living style of the more cosmopolitan Laureano Vallenilla Lanz as the decade wore on. Tales of orgies on La Orchila island continued to spread; such peccadillos normally would cause little outrage, but in uneasy times people could whisper of the sanctity of the family and the honor of the nation. The final insult was the plebiscite of December, 1957. Pérez Jiménez allowed Venezuelans and resident foreigners to vote on whether or not he should continue as president.

[40] Ray, *Politics of the Barrios,* p. 163.
[41] *New York Times,* January 11,·24, 1958; *Miami Herald,* January 15, 1958; Rivas Rivas, *El mundo,* pp. 58-6, 58-7, 58-8; Lieuwen, *Venezuela,* p. 100.

Of those who went to the polls, 2,374,790 voted yes and 364,182 voted no. Any semblance of hope for an immediate legal change of regime vanished. Segments of civilian political opposition formed the Patriotic Junta to plot a revolt; clandestine leaflets began to circulate. Street fighting increased among students, residents of the *barrios*, and those protesting the arrest of the priests.

But the key to success and to marshaling wide support for a revolution to overthrow Pérez Jiménez came from the armed forces. On January 1, 1958, planes from the air base at Maracay dropped bombs on Caracas; because of poor coordination, conspirators from the army and navy failed to play their complementary parts. Arrest of some of the conspirators, however, could not turn back the clock for Pérez. Weak-kneed civilians, formerly unaware of the military dissatisfaction, took heart, and many supported the general strike ordered by the Patriotic Junta on January 21. The president tried to placate the navy by appointing Rear Admiral Wolfgang Larrazábal as its head, but the gesture proved futile. Larrazábal led the naval revolt against the government on January 22, and Pérez Jiménez rapidly lost what support he had enjoyed among the army officers.[42]

Forced to resign, Marcos Pérez Jiménez fled in the morning hours of January 23, 1958. His coalition had fallen apart. Indignation at the blatant discrepancy between the New National Ideal and the old national reality of peculation, immorality, and repression could openly be expressed when the armed forces showed that they, too, were tired of the regime. The end came so quickly that Pérez Jiménez had little time to prepare for his departure. In the haste to reach the friendly territory of the Dominican Republic, a suitcase full of money, bonds, and documents was left behind. The contents of that suitcase were to plague Pérez Jiménez long after his hasty flight.[43]

[42] Lieuwen, *Venezuela*, pp. 101–102; Umaña Bernal, *Testimonio*.

[43] For a fuller account of the Pérez Jiménez period through secondary works, in addition to the works cited, see David E. Blank, *Politics in Venezuela*; Joseph Doyle, "Venezuela 1958: Transition from Dictatorship to Democracy" (Ph.D. diss., George Washington University, 1967); Philip B. Taylor, Jr., *The Venezuelan Golpe de Estado of 1958: The Fall of Marcos Pérez*

After Pérez's departure, a governing junta of civilians and military officers was set up to rule until elections could be held. Admiral Wolfgang Larrazábal, president of the junta and the nation, promised that the transitional period would be short and that elections would be held by the end of 1958. The civilian politicians prepared for the elections and agreed to cooperate in order to forestall any potential *golpes* from the armed forces. Betancourt and the other AD exiles returned home to campaign. They would quickly discover that their opposition to the dictatorship had reinstated them with the electorate.

The AD leaders could rejoice that Pérez Jiménez had been ill equipped to turn his waiting and opportunities into permanent political capital. He went into exile, like Cipriano Castro, with a considerable fortune. Like Castro, he probably recognized the popular rejection of him as something that could pass if he were again in a position to give out jobs and favors. He may have accepted his political demise and anticipated spending a comfortable life in exile enjoying the wealth he had acquired as president of Venezuela. If he planned either to attempt to return to power or just quietly to spend his money, he reckoned without the determination of his old enemy, Rómulo Betancourt. Pérez would find that Betancourt, too, remembered some of the tactics employed by Juan Vicente Gómez to ensure that his enemies would not return to unseat him.

Jiménez; Daniel H. Levine, *Conflict and Political Change in Venezuela*; and Sheldon B. Liss, *Diplomacy and Dependency: Venezuela, the United States, and the Americas*.

3

From the Streets to the Courts: The First Punitive Actions against Perez Jiménez

From Santo Domingo and later Miami, Pérez Jiménez might have been chagrined, but hardly surprised, at the immediate outburst of feeling against him. The popular reaction and the measures taken by the governing junta to sequester his property were well within the Venezuelan tradition of reprisals against a former caudillo. Pérez himself had witnessed popular riots and legal claims against the estate of Juan Vicente Gómez in 1936. After Pérez's old enemy, Rómulo Betancourt, won the presidential election in December, 1958, however, the official effort to bring Pérez to trial represented a departure from tradition.

The first few months following Pérez Jiménez's departure from Venezuela were chaotic. Venezuelans sacked and vandalized the private and public property of their former leaders. Buildings of the Seguridad Nacional and *El Heraldo* also were looted or burned. Wolfgang Larrazábal, president of the governing junta, implicitly condoned the popular actions by failing to halt them.[1] The attorney general announced that the government was not responsible for damages caused during the plundering.[2] Newspapers fed the public

[1] Rear Admiral Wolfgang Larrazábal headed the junta for the entire year despite his connection with Pérez Jiménez. Two other military figures who were part of the first junta were forced out almost immediately because of a similar connection; they were Colonel Abel Romero Villate and Colonel Roberto Casanova. On May 19, Dr. Blas Lamberti and Eugenio Mendoza left the junta to be replaced by Dr. Arturo Sosa, Jr., and Edgar Sanabria; all of them were civilians. Some observers remarked that Lamberti and Mendoza remained on the junta long enough to ensure that the junta paid off the short-term debts owed to big business by the Pérez Jiménez government. See Juan Blanco Peñalver, *Historia de un naufragio*, and Robert Alexander, *The Communist Party of Venezuela*, for example.

[2] República de Venezuela, Procuraduría de la Nación, *Informe al Congreso Nacional, 1959*, p. 952.

fury by publishing accounts of the crimes and corruption of the *perezjimenistas*; Venezuelans could read of the torturing of political prisoners, orgies on the island of La Orchila, and fantastic riches accumulated by the former dictator and his friends.

Those who had been associated with Pérez Jiménez hastened to proclaim their innocence. Physicians, military officers, and radio broadcasters, among others, condemned their associates who had cooperated with Pérez Jiménez and asked the public to distinguish between the collaborators and the majority of honest and proper professionals.[3] Even Miguel Silvio Sanz Añez, former head of the political section of the SN, testified that he had not had the authority to mistreat prisoners. "Pedro Estrada and the President of the Republic decided everything," he declared.[4]

The Venezuelans who sued the government for psychological, material, or physical damages suffered under the dictatorship hoped to repeat the success of those who had received shares of Juan Vicente Gómez's property after his death.[5] In 1958 Mariano Arcaya sued Laureano Vallenilla Lanz, Pedro Estrada, and Marcos Pérez Jiménez for Bs8,020,000 as compensation for his illegal arrest and subsequent exile in 1952. Arcaya's suit failed, however, for after the government sequestered the *perezjimenista* property on behalf of the nation, private suits were suspended. Failing satisfaction via judicial channels, Arcaya assaulted Vallenilla Lanz at a fashionable resort restaurant in Monaco.[6] Other Venezuelans accused Pérez and his ministers of attempted murder, of stealing property, or of placing them in unhealthful prisons; one plaintiff, for example, re-

[3] *El Nacional*, February 2, 3, March 14, 1958.

[4] Testimony of Sanz Añez, Vol. I, annex 5, p. 10, William Mathes Papers, Zimmerman Library, University of New Mexico, Albuquerque.

[5] Pedro Manuel Arcaya, *La pena de la confiscación general de bienes en Venezuela: Estudio de historia y derecho*, p. 197. See also the Venezuelan Constitution of 1936.

[6] *El Universal*, January 29, 1958; *El Nacional*, February 4, 1958; Laureano Vallenilla Lanz, *Razones de proscrito*, pp. 260–261. The sequestered properties ultimately went to some social use or to various social institutions such as schools, hospitals, and so on. Much of the land went to initiate Rómulo Betancourt's agrarian reform program.

quested compensation for a severe nasal illness contracted in jail.[7] The transcripts of many of these cases were subsequently used to construct the nation's case against Pérez Jiménez, although they contained little firsthand evidence of Pérez's common crimes.

The governing junta initiated official actions against the *perez-jimenistas* when they decreed on January 25 that the SN be abolished and that judicial proceedings begin against those members of the SN who had committed crimes against human dignity. The attorney general called on the public to come forward to testify against former SN members. The junta also ordered that La Orchila, site of a decade of alleged orgies, be converted into a naval air base. Larrazábal created a special commission to study the best way to compensate labor syndicates whose property had been attached in 1949 and 1950.[8]

On February 6, 1958, Larrazábal issued his most far-reaching decree. Decree number twenty-eight authorized the preventative sequestration of all of Pérez Jiménez's property in Venezuela and the property of all persons declared intermediaries. The list of intermediaries originally contained only Pérez Jiménez's father, mother, children, and wife, but subsequently it was lengthened to include many of his associates and some corporations. The junta announced that the decree was justified by the "public and notorious fact" of Pérez Jiménez's illegal actions and responded to the popular demand for sanctions "without unnecessarily affecting the harmonious atmosphere in which the country has begun to live."[9] Acknowledging that the decree held one person responsible for virtually all official actions, Larrazábal defended the unitary assignment of responsibility by characterizing Pérez Jiménez's dictatorship as personal and arbitrary.[10]

One might reason that Estrada, Vallenilla Lanz, and others had had sufficient autonomy to be held accountable for their own ac-

[7] *El Nacional,* March 30, 1958.

[8] República de Venezuela, Procuraduría de la Nación, *Informe al Congreso Nacional, 1957–1958,* p. 699; *El Universal,* February 15, 1958; *El Nacional,* May 2, 1958.

[9] *El Nacional,* February 7, 1958.

[10] Gilberto Morillo, *El enriquecimiento ilícito en Venezuela,* p. 88.

tions, but decree twenty-eight simplified the initial judicial proceedings undertaken by the state. The attorney general's staff did not have to determine the exact ownership of many properties. Nor was it likely that the Venezuelan government would be able to secure the extradition of all the exiles who had scattered to many different countries. Finally, Larrazábal's reference to national harmony was more than political jargon. The peculation trials of 1946–1947 had made enemies for AD and had eroded some of the government's support. If Larrazábal could limit the number of people liable for prosecution, he perhaps could avoid offending the friends and families of many who had done business with the Pérez Jiménez government. The constant theme of the year 1958 was unity, and the governing junta chose to encourage that unity by holding Pérez Jiménez personally responsible for all of the alleged crimes of his administration. Assignment of total responsibility to Pérez Jiménez in decree twenty-eight did not preclude separate charges from being brought against other key *perezjimenistas* and SN officials.

The junta, representing the executive branch of the Venezuelan government, followed the precedent established by the 1936 confiscation of Juan Vicente Gómez's property. Decree twenty-eight expressed in official terms the popular antipathy toward the fallen dictator and a disassociation from him and his allies. The AD government in 1946–1947 had initiated peculation trials which went beyond the arbitrary and vengeful tradition of dividing up the spoils, but, as noted, the trials proved divisive. Indeed, they were misunderstood by many Venezuelans, who saw them as closer to the old spoils tradition than to a modern effort to hold politicians legally responsible for their administrative actions. Critics charged that the laws necessarily were retroactive, that investigations and judgments were not conducted in the regular courts, and that some friends of the AD leaders escaped judgment. In an effort to respond to the criticism, the AD government probably confirmed it by allowing a review commission to return some property which had been confiscated by the trials.[11]

[11] *El Nacional*, March 19, May 8, 29, 1946; March 7, November 12, 29, 1947.

The trials of the 1940s indicated some of the problems which attended the transition from arbitrary, personal government to an institutionalized and impartial system of rule. In passing the Law against Illicit Enrichment, however, AD provided a legal framework that could facilitate similar proceedings in the future. The law required all government officials to make a declaration of property owned upon assuming office and again upon leaving office. They were not to leave the country until the latter declaration had been made and the Investigating Commission against Illicit Enrichment (CIEI) had examined the declarations. The commission, sitting in continuous session, could hear any accusations made against public officials at any time. The Congress elected members of the commission from nominees submitted by the Congress, the president, and the Supreme Court.[12]

Even though the Pérez Jiménez government did not rescind the Law against Illicit Enrichment, there had been no commission or property declarations for ten years. The commission installed on February 13, 1958, began working from estimates of wealth in their effort to determine illicit enrichment of the *perezjimenistas*. The backlog of presumed cases coupled with the public's reluctance to testify and a lack of cooperation from other government functionaries limited the commission's immediate effectiveness. The public generally was more willing to provide testimony on violations of persons than on the subject of administrative graft and corruption. Moreover, people retained a lingering suspicion of the courts and preferred to denounce the previous government's crimes to the newspapers rather than to the judicial authorities. Despite these handicaps, however, the CIEI did begin to compile evidence against *perezjimenista* officials. As they slowly completed files on individuals, they passed the results of their investigations to various governmental offices. If the suspect had committed crimes specified

---

12 See Morillo, *Enriquecimiento ilícito*, p. 58; see also the text of the Ley Contra el Enriquecimiento Ilícito de Funcionarios o Empleados Públicos. The highest court in Venezuela was known as the Corte Federal y de Casación (Federal Court) from 1904 to 1947 and from 1953 to 1961; under the Constitution of 1947 (1947–1953) and the Constitution of 1961 (1961–) it has been known as the Corte Suprema de Justicia (Supreme Court).

in the Penal Code (for example, bribery or embezzlement), the proceedings went to the Public Ministry for legal action. Other cases went to the General Comptroller's Office. If the evidence suggested illegal enrichment of high officials, the attorney general initiated the legal action.[13]

Most of the attorney general's energy became directed toward the case against Pérez Jiménez. Since Pérez was to be held responsible for the bulk of the misdeeds, it was essential to compile substantial evidence against him and to document his financial dealings with his intermediaries. Attorney General Pablo Ruggeri Parra, assisted by Minister of Justice Andrés Aguilar Mawdsley, found that few people who had direct knowledge of Pérez's financial dealings were willing to testify. Ruggeri Parra then had no choice but to try to patch together a case largely from the public record and from papers seized from some of the exiles' homes and offices.

The most incriminating material against Pérez Jiménez was found in a suitcase which he and his wife left behind in their haste to flee the country on the morning of January 23. Containing real estate deeds, bank deposit slips and other documents, negotiable securities, handwritten notes of financial arrangements, and Pérez Jiménez's military uniform, the suitcase was a real treasure. Larrazábal's junta may not have immediately recognized the evidentiary value of the documents, but it did refuse to honor Pérez Jiménez's demand that the suitcase be forwarded to him in Miami.[14]

The suitcase documents, of course, would only prove valuable if Pérez Jiménez and his associates could be brought to trial. Unfortunately, a trial depended on obtaining the extradition of the accused from the country where he had sought refuge. In the Americas, a request for the extradition of a political figure often

[13] República de Venezuela, Comisión Investigadora Contra el Enriquecimiento Ilícito de Functionarios o Empleados Públicos, *Informe presentado al Congreso Nacional correspondiente al período 1959–1964,* p. 20; *El Nacional,* March 6, 1958; Morillo, *Enriquecimiento ilícito,* p. 58.

[14] David Morales Bello et al., "The Extradition of Pérez Jiménez" (mimeographed report on preparation of the extradition case by a group of Venezuelan lawyers who had worked on the case), p. 2; *El Nacional,* March 18, 1959.

was frustrated by a conflicting respect for the principle of political asylum. A political figure might be surrendered for common crimes, but in practice the line between political and common crimes had been difficult to draw for high political officials. Never had a former head of state been extradited to stand trial for common crimes in the Americas.

Thus, we return to the dilemma of the CIEI and the attorney general. Most of the people under investigation were government officials who had fled to foreign countries, so extradition had to be requested in order to complete the judicial proceedings in Venezuela. Success of the extradition requests depended on the existence of an extradition treaty with the country in question and the willingness of that country to recognize the alleged crimes as common and not political. Some Venezuelans were more optimistic than others at the prospect for success in obtaining Pérez's extradition. *El Nacional* estimated that there must be such a quantity of proof against Pedro Estrada and Pérez Jiménez that no country in the world could refuse to surrender them. On the other hand, Dr. José Rafael Mendoza, an authority on penal law, did not hold out much hope for the extradition of the former president but encouraged the Venezuelan junta to continue the proceedings against lesser officials.[15]

Prodded by the press and public opinion, the governing junta did request the extradition of Pedro Estrada and several minor officials in 1958. The Foreign Ministry could not request Pérez Jiménez's surrender, however, because the attorney general did not pass the case against the former president to the Supreme Court for an indictment. Possibly Attorney General Ruggeri Parra could not complete the case against Pérez any more rapidly. Or perhaps Larrazábal and the junta thought that the confiscation of Pérez's property and the prosecution of SN officials sufficed as reprisals against the previous regime. Prying too closely into the former president's business associations might have needlessly angered some Venezuelans if it was unlikely that Pérez Jiménez would ever be tried.

[15] *El Nacional*, July 5, 1958.

There was very little effort to seek the extradition even of minor officials while Oscar García Velutini was foreign minister. He was replaced by René De Sola in May after U.S. Vice-president Richard Nixon's ill-fated trip to Venezuela. Thereafter, the Foreign Ministry moved more deliberately to develop arguments in support of extradition of political officials who were accused of common crimes. Noting that extradition of Pérez Jiménez, Estrada, and Vallenilla Lanz would be nearly impossible because they carried diplomatic or special passports, De Sola pressed to find out how they had obtained these passports which required the admitting country to allow them to enter. Velutini confessed in June that he had issued the special passports, and De Sola moved immediately to recall them and to replace them with regular passports.[16]

Foreign Minister De Sola also tried to narrow the definition of political crime and thus the occasions when asylum would normally be granted. Most of De Sola's arguments applied to diplomatic asylum instead of territorial asylum.[17] Although the types of asylum differ, the judgment of whether the crime is political or common still must be made. De Sola's contention that there was a relationship between political asylum and the survival of democracy in Venezuela subsequently was used in the request for Pérez Jiménez's extradition.

In September, 1958, an abortive revolt against the governing junta sent Venezuelans scattering to Caracas embassies to seek refuge. To each of the embassies which requested safe conduct passes out of the country for the Venezuelans, De Sola replied with the following argument. The Convention of Diplomatic Asylum of Caracas (1954) was signed later than the Charter of the Organization of American States; therefore, diplomatic asylum as defined in the later document should not be granted when it conflicted with the charter and its ideal of democratic, institutional order. Diplomatic asylum should not be accorded for a crime committed against a democratic government. Moreover, asylum pro-

---

[16] Ibid., May 29, 30, June 1, 3, 1958; Milton S. Eisenhower, *The Wine Is Bitter: The United States and Latin America*, p. 211.

[17] Diplomatic asylum refers to temporary refuge in a foreign embassy, while territorial asylum refers to refuge or residence in a foreign country.

vided for the protection of refugees from extralegal and inhumane treatment; it was not intended to protect them from legal and regular trial and punishment, as proposed by the Venezuelan government.[18]

The governments of Mexico, Cuba, and El Salvador rejected Venezuela's argument. The Convention on Diplomatic Asylum, they countered, said nothing about the form of government that a rebellion sought to overthrow. If the government granting asylum judged the democratic nature of each government which requested the surrender of a criminal, it would be intervening in the internal affairs of that country. Nor did the Convention on Diplomatic Asylum distinguish between arbitrary and regular, legal punishment of a refugee.[19] De Sola gave in and issued the safe conducts, although he continued to question the use of asylum to shelter *golpistas*. The Venezuelan government aggressively pressed the De Sola thesis on asylum for several years, pitting democratic ideals of the OAS charter against the traditions of political asylum.

De Sola also encountered frustration in attempting to seek the extradition of Pedro Estrada, principally for the crime of assassination of Leonardo Ruíz Pineda, an AD underground agent killed in an exchange of gunfire with the SN in 1954. In October, 1958, the Federal Court ruled that there was enough evidence to request the extradition of Estrada and Ulises Ortega, another SN agent implicated in the Ruíz Pineda assassination.[20]

Estrada moved several times in 1958 in an effort to find a hospitable country of asylum. He had settled briefly in the United States until informed by a friend that the United States would honor a Venezuelan extradition request for him. Before leaving the United States, Estrada warned Pérez Jiménez that he might also be wise to move elsewhere. Pérez Jiménez remained in Florida, however, confident that Eisenhower's government would not surrender him. After Estrada left for Spain, the U.S. Immigration Service re-

---

[18] República de Venezuela, Ministerio de Relaciones Exteriores, *Libro Amarillo de la República de Venezuela, 1959*, pp. 63–93.

[19] Ibid.

[20] Ibid., p. 107; *El Nacional*, September 26, October 11, 1958.

voked his right to return, an action that was made easier by the June recall of Estrada's diplomatic passport. At the request of the Venezuelan ambassador, Estrada was also expelled from Great Britain while on a visit to London in October.[21] Expulsion or deportation of foreigners can circumvent pragmatically the whole dilemma of whether to judge a crime political or common. Deportation does not remain an option, however, after a formal request for extradition is made.[22] Estrada finally established residence in Switzerland in November after fleeing Spain just ahead of another Venezuelan request for his extradition.

Although the junta did not succeed in having Estrada extradited, the efforts to do so must have pleased Rómulo Betancourt, who was elected to the Venezuelan presidency in December, 1958. Larrazábal's junta had shown some ambivalence in its pursuit of the *perezjimenistas,* but Betancourt did not waver in his determination to force Pérez Jiménez to stand trial for the misdeeds of his administration. In fact, Pérez Jiménez's trial became central to Betancourt's entire political philosophy at the same time it expressed Betancourt's personal animosity toward Pérez.

Betancourt frequently denied any motives of personal revenge in the legal actions taken against Pérez Jiménez. A skeptic, however, would doubt that Betancourt could forgive Pérez's part in casting him and his party from power in 1948. Nor, after ten years of penurious exile, could Betancourt fail to resent his old enemy's luxurious life in Miami. Simply seizing the former president's Venezuelan property without a public trial to establish his guilt did not constitute adequate punishment. Moreover, the Venezuelan government's efforts to extradite Pérez Jiménez forced the latter to spend large sums of the ill-gotten gains that he shipped out of Venezuela ahead of him. Although Betancourt could hardly have foreseen this development, the extradition proceedings indirectly whittled away some of Pérez's apparently safe liquid wealth.

On a less personal level, the prosecution of Pérez Jiménez reflected three major principles that Betancourt promised would

---

[21] *El Nacional,* October 30, 1958.
[22] Marjorie M. Whiteman, ed., *Digest of International Law,* VI, 748–750.

guide his policy in office. First, his administration would encourage a popular insistence on honest government and would insure that stealing from the public treasury would be difficult; second, strict adherence to the rules of due process would develop the independence of the judicial and congressional branches of the Venezuelan government; and finally, Betancourt's government would urge democratic nations to combine to condemn and isolate the dictatorships in the western hemisphere.[23]

Betancourt particularly stressed administrative honesty and fiscal responsibility in his inaugural address:

The Constitutional Government will call for a policy of austerity in order to balance the budget and to set a new keynote for the country. The wastefulness of the newly rich will disappear from official customs. Ornamental and lavish public works will be radically eliminated. And at the same time, firmly, without hesitation or wavering in the moralizing intention, punishment will fall upon the crimes of embezzlement, of traffic of influence, of corrupting commissions, and of favoritism in the distribution of official purchases or in the granting of contracts to private businesses. Immediately the Law against the Illicit Enrichment of Public Functionaries will be put into full force. . . . Any citizen can come before this tribunal to denounce anyone who is dishonestly managing public funds. And the civil servants will, in turn, be able to denounce individuals who propose deals counter to the interests of the Nation, because the person who offers a bribe should be punished as well as the one who accepts one. All public officials who handle public funds will be instructed to make a sworn declaration of their property before a judge, and that declaration will have the character of a public document, accessible to any citizen who wants to know its contents. "It is necessary to make honesty fashionable," Martí claimed, and the Liberator, speaking to the Peruvian Congress, said that it should decree "terrible penalties against the agents of the Treasury who fraudulently mishandle public funds."[24]

Despite the rhetoric on administrative honesty, Betancourt's administration did little immediately to facilitate the work of the Investigating Commission against Illicit Enrichment. The CIEI complained of numerous procedural requirements that slowed

---

[23] Rómulo Betancourt, *La revolución democrática en Venezuela, 1959–1964: Documentos del gobierno presidido por Rómulo Betancourt,* I, 12–17.
[24] Ibid., p. 12.

down, and ultimately thwarted, its goal of investigating abuses, bringing the guilty to trial, and confiscating the illicit wealth. Some members of Congress, including the Communist deputies, proposed reforms in the Law against Illicit Enrichment which would speed up the process of investigation, punishment, and confiscation. Acción Democrática continued to block reforms which would promote rapid action at the expense of deliberate and institutional measures, although the governing party did support some minor, interim reforms.[25] Opting for the slower judicial processes simultaneously expressed Betancourt's political philosophy and insured that a number of persons would escape investigation. Having learned from the 1947 peculation trials, AD preferred to move cautiously and to concentrate their campaign on Pérez Jiménez and his closest colleagues.

Betancourt's government did follow the example of Larrazábal's junta in disposing of any sequestered *perezjimenista* property which was in danger of spoilage or depreciation. Farms and houses were presented to universities and schools, and the presidential yacht was converted into a hydrographic research ship.[26] Institutions deemed "socially useful" might apply to receive some of the impounded property. The most easily seized wealth had been land, and its distribution further illustrated Betancourt's principle of strict adherence to the rules of due process.

Betancourt directed the attorney general to turn over the *perezjimenista* farmland to small farmers to begin an agrarian reform program. On May 7, 1959, the Hacienda San Juan de Dios was transferred with great ceremony; representatives of the National Agrarian Institute (IAN) and the Agricultural and Livestock Bank (BAP) attended the formal presentation to the *campesinos*. The grants were only provisional, since the government had not legally confiscated the land, but the grants served the triple purpose of aiding the landless, seeing that the land was worked, and winning political support for Acción Democrática.[27] Nearly every day in

---

[25] *El Nacional,* January 11, March 3, 6, April 23, May 2, 4, 1959.
[26] Ibid., June 2, 11, 1959.
[27] Betancourt, *La Revolución,* I, 58; *El Nacional,* May 7, 1959.

May, Caracas newspapers reported similar ceremonial allocations of land. Then came the sour note.

On May 26, a group of peasants occupied some *perezjimenista* land without the authorization of the IAN and the BAP. After taking the land, the squatters requested credit, seeds, fertilizer, and agricultural tools from the appropriate organizations. President Betancourt responded immediately and strongly in letters to the minister of agriculture and the minister of the interior: "There is not the slightest doubt that those peasants who behaved in this way are responding to the instigation of groups who want to create a climate of violence in the countryside, because the normal peaceful progress of the constitutional regime stands in the way of their secret objectives."[28] He ordered an investigation by the Ministry of the Interior to discover the instigators of the invasion, and he ordered that the peasants be removed from the land. Leaders of the takeover, if discovered, were to be tried and punished.

Economist and journalist D. F. Maza Zavala criticized Betancourt for his handling of the incident. Seizing land by force was indeed reprehensible, but this particular occupation of the land was not alarming, Maza Zavala argued. The peasants took over a ranch owned by a former government official and afterward solicited help from the appropriate government offices. According to formalities, the request should have come first, but the men were impatient because of the slowness of the legal preparations for agrarian reform. Little had been done, Maza Zavala continued, to improve the lives of the rural masses even sixteen months after Pérez Jiménez's departure. If Betancourt truly wanted to avoid both police repression and illegal occupation of the land, he should give first priority to rapid land reform.[29]

Betancourt ignored Maza Zavala's advice and continued to insist on due process, regardless of delays and accusations that he was insincere in his proclaimed intention to punish the *perezjimenistas*. Even on apparently minor matters, the AD leadership repaired to the regular courts for rulings and abided by the judicial

[28] Betancourt, *La Revolución*, I, 70.
[29] *El Nacional*, May 29, 1959.

decisions. For example, as the attorney general worked on the case against Pérez Jiménez in June, AD leader and lawyer David Morales Bello argued before the Federal Court that the Pérez Jiménez case should be tried in the lower courts; a former president no longer held a status any more privileged than that of an ordinary citizen and should receive the same judicial treatment that an ordinary citizen would. Moreover, Morales Bello and his colleagues argued, trying the case before the lower courts would speed up the judicial actions. Morales Bello's petition failed, and the Supreme Court became the tribunal which would hear the evidence against Pérez Jiménez.[30] The seemingly insignificant decision probably did contribute to the length of the extradition and trial proceedings. The Venezuelan government might better have been able to argue that Pérez Jiménez's crimes were only common ones if he had been tried by the lower courts instead of the highest court in the nation.

On July 23, Attorney General Ruggeri Parra finally set in motion the trial which symbolized President Betancourt's commitment to administrative honesty and judicial regularity. The attorney general presented the charges and the evidence against former president Pérez Jiménez before the Federal Court for an indictment. The eight bundles of documents and ten boxes of microfilm which Ruggeri Parra deposited with the secretary of the court represented eighteen months of work. The initiation of the hearings prompted considerable speculation on the importance of the precedent that was being set. *El Nacional* commented, "It is doubtless one of the most documented accusations that has ever been presented against a Head of State in any country of the civilized world." The paper expressed a national pride at the new democratic government's contribution to the development of international law. Attorney General Ruggeri Parra agreed that the case was important but held a less simplistic view of a trial which assigned the sole responsibility for all crimes to the former president: "These originators of the dictatorship forged its false philosophy and effectively sustained and profited from such a system. *Perhaps their*

[30] Ibid., June 9, 1959.

responsibility will never be totally proved, but it is good to consign their responsibility to History at the precise moment we indict one who exercised the leadership of the regime that has been an almost traditional form of government in the course of the evolution of the Venezuelan state" (italics mine).[31]

Other Venezuelans were even more explicitly worried about the symbolic effort to hold Pérez Jiménez solely responsible for the crimes of the dictatorship. Journalist José Ramón Medina wrote in *El Nacional:*

Nothing has been said among us about the historical responsibility of the groups that helped create and support the dictatorship of the ex-general in defense of their own particular interests. It is ingenuous to continue believing that the only one guilty of the political trauma suffered by the Republic in the ten years of dictatorship was Pérez Jiménez alone. Men as individuals are not makers of history, and a regime of the magnitude of the one from which we suffered is neither invented nor sustained by one man alone. Someone must exist behind him to sustain and defend the dictatorship, not for the regime itself but for the advantages that he generally receives.[32]

Medina further warned of the danger of believing that the possibility of dictatorship could be eliminated simply by punishment of the dictator and his closest associates.

The case against Pérez Jiménez then, despite some protests, became an integral part of AD's campaign for administrative reform. It equally became central to Betancourt's foreign policy of condemning dictatorship in the Americas. The Venezuelan government pressed other American governments, as well as reform-minded groups, to interpret the OAS charter as a political document which required a boycott of nondemocratic governments. In February, 1959, a group of international political and labor groups met in Venezuela and signed a Declaration of Caracas for Continental Unity against dictatorships. The document condemned the dictators of the Dominican Republic, Nicaragua, and Paraguay and asked that those governments be excluded from the Organization of American States. Recalling their own successful revolt

[31] Ibid., July 24, 1959.
[32] Ibid., July 28, 1959.

against Pérez Jiménez, the AD leaders welcomed the defeat of Fulgencio Batista in Cuba but ominously warned that they could not condone any type of dictatorship in the Americas.[33] In June, Venezuela broke diplomatic relations with the Dominican Republic. The Dominican foreign minister responded by warning the Venezuelan government of the possible consequences of their international crusade: "There is no doubt that the present Venezuelan regime is putting into international practice an extremely dangerous concept for the judicial order of inter-American relations in fomenting in the continent an ideological battle without quarter, foreign to the spirit of the American nations. The ideological battle can only serve the international subversive interests of certain powers which are deadly enemies of inter-American solidarity."[34] Despite the *trujillista* concern, dictators of the left had the most to fear from the Venezuelan campaign for ideological unity. The sharpest rupture in inter-American solidarity would come in 1964 when Cuba was expelled from the OAS.

The AD link between administrative peculation and dictatorship became clearer as Venezuela called for the wealth taken out of the country by dictators to be returned to the people of the nation. Gonzalo Barrios, an AD stalwart from the Generation of 1928, traveled to several international parliaments to press the Venezuelan argument. The Interparliamentary Union, the Organization of American States, and the United Nations all considered the issue. Barrios contended that the money taken out of Venezuela by the *perezjimenistas* threatened the democratic government since it could be used from exile to finance attacks on the AD government. Barrios proposed that the Nuremberg trials might provide a precedent for the "extradition" of stolen wealth. The Nuremberg judges had punished or jailed military and political leaders of the conquered power and had restored some part of their booty to the legitimate owners. Barrios claimed that Venezuela would gain prestige and would set an international precedent by requesting the return of the *perezjimenista* wealth.[35]

[33] Ibid., February 16, January 2, 1959.
[34] Ministerio de Relaciones Exteriores, *Libro Amarillo, 1960*, p. 7.
[35] *El Nacional*, May 13, 1958.

In the general condemnation of dictatorships and in the effort to publicize the wealth enjoyed by the Venezuelan exiles, the new AD government aggressively identified itself as "democratic" and responsible. The international image might be helpful if Venezuela's projected social and economic reform programs aroused Cold War fears of radicalism.

As Venezuela expanded its antidictatorial campaign in the Caribbean and in the world, confrontation with the United States was almost inevitable. Marcos Pérez Jiménez's presence in Miami, Florida, called attention to U.S. cordiality toward dictators in the 1950s and U.S. willingness to harbor old friends under the aegis of political asylum. U.S. spokesmen tried to counter the unfavorable impressions. Milton Eisenhower explained that Pérez Jiménez resided in the United States only because that government had extended a courtesy to a holder of a Venezuelan diplomatic passport. Roy Rubottom, U.S. assistant secretary of state for Latin America, told the Senate Foreign Relations Committee that Pérez Jiménez had not received the Legion of Merit as an individual but as a representative of a nation friendly to the United States. Attorney General William Rogers announced that Cuban former dictator Fulgencio Batista would not receive political asylum in the United States but might be allowed to enter as an ordinary visitor. When Fidel Castro demanded the surrender of some of Batista's collaborators from the United States, however, Senator Wayne Morse expressed a popular view when he advised that the request be denied; although he did not approve of Batista, Morse said that the United States should maintain the traditional policy of providing asylum to political refugees.[36]

To further seek favor with the new Venezuelan government, the U.S. Immigration Service, with the approval of the State Department, began deportation proceedings against Pérez Jiménez in March, 1959. Pérez Jiménez, ignoring Pedro Estrada's warnings of the preceding fall, directed his lawyer, David Walters of Miami,

[36] Eisenhower, *The Wine Is Bitter*, pp. 77–78; *New York Times*, January 9, 1959; *El Nacional*, March 6, 1958; January 22, 1959; *Miami Herald*, January 7, February 19, 1959.

to appeal and delay the deportation orders. The Immigration Service also asked Luis Felipe Llovera Páez to leave the country and obtained a court order which would prevent Pedro Estrada from reentering the United States.[37]

The efforts to deport the *perezjimenistas* were a pragmatic attempt to avoid having to deal with a request for extradition and a sign that the Cold War was thawing enough that the United States could distance itself somewhat from the dictators who had preserved "democracy" in the hemisphere in the 1950s. The *New York Times* commended the Eisenhower government for its attempt to deport Pérez Jiménez and hoped that the world would forget that that same government had given Pérez a medal in 1954. Other newspapers, such as the *Miami Herald*, defended political asylum for Pérez Jiménez as consonant with the basic principles of American foreign policy.[38]

The Venezuelan government and press watched the deportation process and Pérez Jiménez's movements carefully. Each time that a new deportation deadline was announced, *El Nacional* noted it on the editorial page. When Caracas newspapers carried the story that Pérez Jiménez was paying off-duty Miami policemen to guard his expensive home on Pinetree Drive, Miami officials hastened to correct the situation. In mid-June, Miami Police Chief Mike Fox announced that his police officers would no longer accept employment from political exiles. The Venezuelan government also refused to accept Miami as a sister city to Caracas in Eisenhower's People to People program as long as Pérez Jiménez lived there.[39]

The Venezuelan government apparently also tried to influence some U.S. press coverage of the former dictator. On June 14, the *Miami Herald* ran an extensive article about Pérez Jiménez's wealth and investments, with photographs of bank deposit slips to illustrate the story. The *Herald* explained vaguely that the documents had "come into their possession."[40] The documents displayed were some of those used by the Venezuelan attorney gen-

[37] *Miami Herald*, March 28, June 20, August 9, 1959.
[38] *New York Times*, March 28, 1959; *Miami Herald*, March 28, 1959.
[39] *Miami Herald*, June 7, 9, 18, 1959.
[40] Ibid., June 14, 1959.

eral in preparing his case against Pérez. In June, when the story appeared in Miami, the case had not yet gone to the Venezuelan Federal Court, and the evidence should have remained secret. Venezuelan newspapers had complained that they could not obtain or reprint any of the documents.[41] The *Herald's* possession of the documents suggested that the Venezuelan government was not overlooking the part that U.S. public opinion could play in proceedings against the former dictator.

The effectiveness of Venezuela's early efforts to influence U.S. opinion on the Pérez Jiménez case was probably minimal. The United States, however, had made no attempts to deport Pérez Jiménez before Rómulo Betancourt became president of Venezuela. Even so, in 1959 there was no indication that these modest efforts to appease the new democratic government of Venezuela would develop into four years of court battles which would accompany a new direction in U.S. policy toward Latin America.

The democratic caesar himself, nestled in the shelter of the community of Latin American exiles, continued to see the Venezuelan actions against him as Betancourt's personal drive for revenge and could not imagine that the United States would intervene in this private quarrel. His ignorance of politics blinded him both to the changes taking place in Venezuela and to the potential impact of a U.S. presidential campaign in which foreign policy would be an important issue.

[41] *El Nacional*, August 14, 1959.

4

The Extradition Hearings, July, 1959–December, 1960: The Venezuelan Case against Pérez Jiménez

Venezuelan interest in Pérez Jiménez's movements in Miami heightened after the Federal Court received the attorney general's charges against the former president in July. The suspense mounted as people waited to see whether Pérez would flee to a more secure asylum or whether the U.S. government would go beyond a token harassment of the former dictator. When Betancourt actually pressed the case into the courts, it became apparent that he considered the prosecution of Pérez Jiménez as central to his domestic strategy and image. Pressing charges against Pérez also served Betancourt's international strategy of attacking dictators and of representing his own administration as one of democracy and stability; he hoped that other democratic nations would prove to be firm allies if he needed them. The key democratic nation was, of course, the United States, and Betancourt's strategy could not succeed without unprecedented cooperation from the neighbor to the north.

In 1959, Betancourt fortuitously encountered some softening in U.S. policy toward Latin America. The Eisenhower government was beginning to consider the thesis that populist governments provided a better bulwark against communism than did dictatorial ones. Any radical change in U.S. policy toward Latin America, however, would probably have to await the inauguration of the new U.S. president in 1961.

Doubtless, as the election loomed nearer, the Eisenhower government would have preferred quietly to deport Pérez Jiménez or to make him uneasy enough to leave. Ironically, Pérez Jiménez played into the hands of his old enemy by appealing the deportation orders and refusing to move to another country. In the summer of 1959, Betancourt's government forced the issue by a rapid and rather surreptitious delivery of the formal request for Pérez's extradition.

Having received the attorney general's documentation on July 23, the Venezuelan Federal Court issued a warrant of arrest for Marcos Pérez Jiménez on August 15 for the crimes of murder and embezzlement. On the same day, the Ministry of Foreign Affairs was directed to solicit the surrender of the accused in accord with the existing extradition treaty (1924) between Venezuela and the United States. Additionally, the Venezuelan government demanded that all property in Pérez's possession be returned to Venezuela.[1] Only six days later, on Friday, August 21, the request for Pérez Jiménez's extradition arrived in Washington, D.C.

The speed with which the Federal Court's warrant moved through the domestic and international bureaucracy was especially remarkable for August, when many government officials take their annual vacations. Moreover, several senior officials in the foreign policy network were attending the Conference of Foreign Ministers of the Western Hemisphere in Santiago, Chile. Marcos Falcón Briceño, Venezuela's ambassador to the United States; Ignacio Luis Arcaya, Venezuela's foreign minister; and Christian Herter, U.S. secretary of state, were all in Chile.[2] Venezuelan Acting Foreign Minister Dr. Miguel A. Burelli Rivas was the one who ordered the chargé d'affaires in the Washington embassy immediately to seek the legal assistance of the international law firm of Covington and Burling.

The Venezuelan government chose not to ask the U.S. Justice Department to represent them, as was common in extradition requests. The selection of Covington and Burling revealed that Acción Democrática intended to make a serious effort to secure the surrender of Pérez Jiménez at any cost. The law firm had a prestigious and well-known international practice, and former U.S. Secretary of State Dean Acheson was a senior partner. Acheson's con-

[1] República de Venezuela, Ministerio de Justicia, *Memoria y cuenta presentada al Congreso de la República de Venezuela en sus reuniones ordinarias de 1959*, p. 379; *El Nacional*, August 15, 1959.
[2] *El Nacional*, August 22, 27, 1959.

tinuing connections in Washington were not to be scorned, and he had known and aided a number of Venezuelan exiles, including Rómulo Betancourt, during the years that Pérez Jiménez was in power.[3] Representation by an independent law firm instead of the Justice Department should have made it more difficult for the U.S. government to employ any last-minute tactics to avoid the initiation of formal extradition hearings.

In fact, the Immigration Service did make one last effort to deport Pérez Jiménez on Friday, August 21, the very day that the extradition request arrived in Washington.[4] Pérez still refused to leave, and his sudden arrest on August 25 effectively ended the deportation efforts until the extradition hearings had concluded. His arrest on Tuesday testified to the frenzied week-end work of the Venezuelan embassy officials, Howard Westwood of Covington and Burling, and representatives of the U.S. Attorney General's Office, the U.S. State Department, and the U.S. Justice Department. Westwood flew to Miami on Monday, August 24, to enlist the assistance of the U.S. attorney for the Southern District of Florida in submitting the arrest order before the federal district judge.[5]

Pérez's arrest only ten days after the Venezuelan high court had issued the warrant and while major foreign policy officials of both countries were in Chile was a tactical coup for the Venezuelan government. Once the proceedings were actually in the U.S. courts, Pérez Jiménez could not leave the country without seriously embarrassing the United States. The former president was freed on twenty-five thousand dollars' bond, certain still that his country of asylum would not surrender him to his political enemy.

The speed with which the Venezuelan government initiated the request for extradition contrasted sharply with the progress of the case for the next fourteen months. Some of the delays were normal and procedural ones, as ground rules for the hearings were established and documents were translated. The judge assigned to the

---

[3] Interview with Howard Westwood of Covington and Burling, November 18, 1969; interview with Ramón Velásquez, June 4, 1970.

[4] *Miami Herald*, August 22, 1959; *New York Times*, August 22, 1959.

[5] José Cayuela and David Pachano, "El juicio del siglo," *Elite* 2219 (April 6, 1968): 45–46.

case, William Mathes, was a visiting California judge who took on some Florida cases to help lighten the heavy judicial load in the Southern District of Florida until new federal judges were appointed. Thus, hearing schedules sometimes had to bow to the pressures of Mathes's California commitments.

Most of the delays, however, were occasioned by the Venezuelan government and its chief counsel, Howard Westwood. The extradition treaty allowed Venezuela sixty days to file documents in support of the warrant of arrest. Miami Consul Manuel Aristeguieta, on behalf of Venezuela, filed several amended complaints which allowed the plaintiff more time. Judge Mathes ruled that the grace period of sixty days began over again each time a new complaint was filed. The Venezuelan government did not rest its case until June, 1960. Pérez Jiménez's attorney argued that he could not prepare his defense until he had seen the final form of the Venezuelan government's charges.

After two years of preparing the evidence against Pérez Jiménez, why did the Venezuelan government need ten more months to submit their documentation? Although international law does not require that a country requesting extradition actually try the accused according to U.S. rules of evidence, the Venezuelan government wanted to increase the chance of a favorable decision. Thus, counsel for the Venezuelan government used the extra ten months to gather better evidence, to take new depositions (or to retake statements under different procedures), to stress common over political crimes, and to ensure that the charges against Pérez Jiménez corresponded to crimes listed in the extradition treaty.

Howard Westwood and other attorneys working on the case went to Venezuela to collect depositions from Venezuelan witnesses on the nature of Pérez Jiménez's government and crimes. Much of the evidence used in the U.S. hearings appeared to have been gathered *after* the request for extradition was submitted. For example, of forty-six sworn statements that most directly related to the case, thirty-three were taken in 1959 after the filing of the second complaint for extradition, ten were taken in 1958, and three were taken in 1960.

The Venezuelan government also used the extradition hearings as an opportunity to secure more exact information on Pérez Jiménez's financial dealings. The U.S. federal court in Miami first subpoenaed the records and then required depositions from the First National City Bank of New York, the French American Banking Corporation, the Royal Bank of Canada, the Hibernia National Bank of New Orleans, and the Chemical Bank New York Trust Company. The banks were ordered to provide information on Pérez Jiménez's deposits, withdrawals, and financial statements for the preceding decade.[6]

Covington and Burling argued the U.S. interest in obtaining the bank documents. The ability and will of the United States to fulfill a treaty obligation were at stake. If the United States did not facilitate the surrender of foreign criminals, other nations would retaliate by refusing to cooperate with similar U.S. requests. Moreover, the United States did not want to become a haven for those who tried to hide their illicit wealth.[7] The U.S. interest was put forward even more forcefully in an *amicus curiae* brief which the U.S. Justice Department filed. The brief asked the court to assist the Venezuelan officials "by every legal means" within its power: "Finally, it is firmly established that an extradition proceeding is an instrument for carrying out a solemn treaty obligation, and that the salutary and civilized purpose of extradition—to prevent national borders from being a shield for criminals—should be fully accomplished by a liberal view of the obligation itself and of questions arising under the Treaty."[8] The support which the U.S. Justice Department offered for an extremely liberal intrepretation of treaty obligations reflected some of the sympathy for Venezuelan President Betancourt.

The banks successfully fought the court orders, claiming that an individual's banking records were private. Moreover, interna-

[6] Order of November 13, 1959 and Order of November 23, 1959, Petition for Writ of Prohibition of Mandamus, Mathes Papers, Zimmerman Library, University of New Mexico, Albuquerque.

[7] Plaintiff's opposition to application for oral argument, Mathes Papers.

[8] Brief for United States as *Amicus Curiae*, Mathes Papers.

tional legal precedent had denied the petitioning country in an extradition case the right to use the courts and police of the country of asylum to seek more evidence. Counsel for the banks argued that a request for surrender of a person, of evidence to convict that person, and of the property allegedly stolen exceeded the limits of normal extradition practice.[9]

Only one bank, the Hibernia National Bank of New Orleans, slipped and surrendered some of the records relating to Pérez Jiménez. Subsequently, that bank demanded the return of the documents that they had turned over to the courts, since they had surrendered them through a misunderstanding of a court order. By June 1, 1960, the Venezuelan government admitted that there was no possibility of wresting the evidence from the banks and gave up the effort.[10]

The Venezuelan government obviously used the time from August, 1959, to June, 1960, to bring their case into line with U.S. judicial practice. Less obviously, the delays may have been a gamble that whoever won the 1960 presidential election would be more likely to surrender Pérez Jiménez than Eisenhower would. Even if the courts ruled that there was a *prima facie* case against Pérez, the final decision to extradite him would be left to the U.S. secretary of state. Doubtless that decision would be made within the context of general U.S. policy toward Latin America.

As the charges against Pérez Jiménez came more nearly to coincide with the definitions of common crimes in the Florida code, the nature of the Venezuelan case against Pérez was altered. In the most general and significant sense, the Venezuelan government held the former president legally and personally accountable for his corrupt, repressive, and arbitrary regime. Specifically, it charged him with graft, murder, and electoral fraud. The effort to hold him individually responsible for all the excesses of his colleagues and the SN agents reflected a new political value system which had first emerged in Venezuela in the 1920s. Traditionally, many Vene-

[9] Affidavit, Mathes Papers.
[10] Motion of the Hibernia National Bank, Mathes Papers; *Pérez Jiménez v. Aristeguieta and Maguire*, 19,507 (5th Cir., 1962), 9:2471–2472.

zuelans had fatalistically accepted a caudillo's corruption and abuse of power as inevitable; his punishment, they believed, would be equally inevitable. His successor would surely denigrate him, isolate him politically, and enact reprisals against him. Betancourt's extensive use of the regular Venezuelan and U.S. courts to weigh the former dictator's crimes and to decree his punishment was novel to many Venezuelans. Pérez Jiménez's defense, on the other hand, rested on the older belief that a president's actions were beyond the jurisdiction of the courts, if not beyond the animus of a political enemy.

Bringing the case against the former president to the U.S. courts, however, shifted and to some extent trivialized the charges against Pérez Jiménez. For the U.S. hearings, the charges had to be characterized as common crimes instead of political ones, they had to be specified in the existing extradition treaty between Venezuela and the United States,[11] and they had to be based on solid, not circumstantial, evidence. Thus, mismanagement of the 1952 and 1957 elections, clearly a political crime, quickly was sloughed off the charges. Additionally, the U.S. counsel for Venezuela increasingly stressed the financial crimes, although the crimes against persons remained in the warrants and arguments. Most Venezuelans probably would have considered the terrorism and repression more serious, but those crimes were more likely to be termed political by the courts. Finally, even the financial charges assumed a different character because of the kinds of hard evidence which were readily available and because of the treaty limitations. The treaty listed embezzlement or criminal malversation as an extraditable offense but did not specify abuse of influence as a crime. The Venezuelan government, then, had to characterize Pérez's financial chicanery as embezzlement, although his actions did not clearly fit the legal definition of embezzlement.[12] What had begun as a

[11] Although a person *may* be extradited for crimes not specified in the treaty, there is no obligation to do so.

[12] Florida statutes provided that to prove embezzlement, counsel must show that the amount converted was within the protection of the statute; that the amount belonged to someone or some entity other than the accused; that the amount was in the possession or protection of the accused at the time of

public international trial of a political value system increasingly became a series of hearings to determine whether a *prima facie* case existed against a white-collar criminal.

The evolution of the charges against Pérez can be seen in the successive complaints for extradition which the Venezuelan government prepared and in the accompanying warrants of arrest. Four complaints for extradition with amendments were filed on August 25, September 14, November 23, 1959, and March 8, 1960. The first complaint charged Pérez with murder, attempt to commit murder, embezzlement or criminal malversation, and acting as an accessory in the crimes cited. In each amended complaint, more details were added and the legal language coincided more closely with definitions of the crimes in the Florida code. The greatest changes came between the September and the November complaints, when the murder charges were watered down somewhat and the part of the complaint relating to the financial crimes was expanded from three pages to six pages.

The later complaints reflected the difficulty in establishing that Pérez had directly ordered the murders or had directly taken money from the treasury. For example, the September complaint on the murders charged: "The defendant, while in Venezuela, in violation of law *ordered the unlawful murders* of Dr. Leonard Ruíz Pineda, of Dr. Germán Gonzalez, of Dr. Antonio Pinto Salinas, and of Mr. Luis Hurtado, by persons purporting to act as officials of an agency known as the Seguridad Nacional whose conduct in fact was fully controlled and determined by the defendant" (italics mine). The November amendment prefaced the above paragraph with: "The defendant, while in Venezuela, in violation of law *confederated, schemed, connived and agreed with persons* connected with an organization known as the Seguridad Nacional to effect the murders of certain persons in Venezuela. In the course of and in

---

the conversion; that the accused's dealings with the property constituted a conversion; and that there was a fraudulent intent to deprive the owner of his property. See Annex No. 6 to Memorandum in Support of Defendant's Motion to Dismiss, Mathes Papers.

pursuance of such scheme, Dr. Leonardo Ruíz Pineda, Dr. Germán Gonzalez, Dr. Antonio Pinto Salinas and Mr. Luis Hurtado Higuera were murdered by persons purporting to act as agents of the aforesaid Seguridad Nacional" (italics mine).[13]

The financial crimes were described even more carefully, indicating that the counsel for the Venezuelan government hoped that they at least might be considered common crimes. The September complaint stated that the defendant "in violation of law misappropriated to his personal use and benefit many millions of bolivares." The November amendment added: "During such period [that he was in power] defendant by himself and in concert with others engaged in a series of acts which had as an objective his and their illicit enrichment at the expense of the public." Moreover, Pérez Jiménez had "while in Venezuela, abstracted and misappropriated funds with the *administration and custody of which he had been entrusted,* in the amount of many millions of bolivares (equivalent to many millions of United States dollars), and *converted them to his personal use and benefit* and the use and benefit of others" (italics mine).[14]

Use of the term *conversion* facilitated the effort to characterize Pérez's crime as embezzlement, as defined by the Florida code. The final amended complaint of March 8, 1960, differed from the November one only in legal wording, emphasis, technicality, and some detail. Names, dates, and amounts of money were specified.

The several warrants of arrest also illustrated the difficulty in forcing a correspondence between Pérez's deeds and the treaty definitions of extraditable crimes. The first warrant stated that Pérez was accused of "murder, attempt to commit murder, embezzlement or criminal malversation, and as an accessory in such crimes, which crimes *are specified by* the Treaty of Extradition" (italics mine).[15] The definitive warrant omitted any mention of attempted murder and charged Pérez Jiménez with "crimes committed by him in

[13] *Pérez Jiménez* v. *Aristeguieta and Maguire,* 2:528–529, 592.
[14] Ibid., p. 595.
[15] Ibid., p. 462.

Venezuela, constituting violations of Articles 195, 196, 199, 205, 407 and 84 of the Penal Code of Venezuela, and charging that such crimes are within the scope of Article II of the Treaty of Extradition between the United States of America and the Republic of Venezuela, *amounting to, among other things,* embezzlement, criminal malversation, fraud, breach of trust, receipt of property knowing the same to have been unlawfully obtained, and murder and accessory before the fact to murder" (italics mine).[16]

Counsel for the Venezuelan government, faced with inadequate evidence for the crimes he wished to establish, had to plead for a liberal definition of the extradition treaty when he characterized Pérez's deeds as *amounting to* the crimes listed in the treaty. Similarly, he had to show that Pérez Jiménez was personally responsible for the actions of his subordinates. Thus, he charged that the "defendant by himself and in concert with others" had committed crimes. Without evidence to link Pérez Jiménez to the specified crimes, the plaintiff resorted to logically weak assumptions that "he must have" known of or benefited from the actions of his cronies and subordinates. Again, it was obvious that the extradition treaty and the Florida code did not easily accommodate themselves to weighing the administrative responsibility of a former caudillo.

As the amended complaints were being refined and filed, Howard Westwood developed the two major charges against Pérez Jiménez: illicit enrichment and murder. He made a stronger case for the financial crimes. Evidence primarily came from the famous "suitcase documents," which gave a glimpse of the extent of the dictator's wealth when he left office. The Venezuelan government had compiled stock certificates, land deeds, and bank statements to indicate that Pérez had invested and deposited at least $13,513,-576.39 during his years in power (see Appendix B). The sum was approximate and included some property that was registered in the names of family or colleagues. Pérez's government salaries from 1949 until 1958 amounted to only $336,810.28, and his net assets in 1949 had been $23,000 (see Appendix A). According to the Venezuelan Law against Illicit Enrichment, the burden of proof fell

16 Ibid., 3:388.

upon the accused to explain the sources of any unusual increase in wealth.[17]

The Venezuelan attorney general estimated that Pérez Jiménez and his intermediaries sent about $12,041,968.57 out of the country during the 1950s. In 1957, the former president had sent a sum of Bs1,500,000 to be deposited to his account in the Hibernia National Bank of New Orleans. Wallace M. Davis, president of the bank, wrote to Pérez Jiménez about the deposit:

Because of the difficulty of converting this sum into dollars without influencing the exchange rate on bolivares which would, in our opinion, be bad for Venezuela as well as decreasing the amount of dollars available from this sum of bolivares for you, and after full discussion with Dr. Gutiérrez, we have advised that this sum will be converted into dollars and deposited to your account over a period of several weeks. In this manner, the exchange rate will not be adversely influenced and you will be able to derive the greatest benefit from the sum which you have so graciously entrusted to us.[18]

This letter was one of the ones turned up by the subpoena process in the United States, and the Venezuelan government would obviously have had a much stronger case if they had been able to elicit more such records from U.S. banks which had dealt with Pérez Jiménez.

It was possible to establish that Pérez had rapidly become wealthy, but it was more difficult to prove how he had done so. Gossip, court testimony, and some documents suggested that Pérez Jiménez and his cabinet ministers frequently had received commissions, or bribes, from firms which obtained government defense or construction contracts. Agents of foreign firms would sometimes testify that commissions were given, but they seldom implicated their own companies. For example, Raymond Smith, a representa-

[17] Plaintiff's Memorandum of the Facts, Mathes Papers; certified copy of the record of sworn declaration of assets, Vol. I, Annex 8, Plaintiff's Evidence, Mathes Papers; Article 28 of the Ley Contra el Enriquecimiento Ilícito de Funcionarios o Empleados Publicos.

[18] Wallace M. Davis to Marcos Pérez Jiménez, November 27, 1957, Vol. I, Annex 10, Plaintiff's Evidence, Mathes Papers. See also Appendix C for estimates of other amounts earned on commissions and sent abroad.

tive for several British aviation companies,[19] testified that his company, Rolls Royce, did not give commissions to increase business but that he knew that many companies customarily paid 5 percent commissions on large contracts and 10 percent on small ones. When his company refused to pay such fees, Smith continued, the SN had threatened him.[20]

Robert Shama, another British citizen, stated that Napoleón Dupouy, Pérez Jiménez's intermediary, had served as a director of the Campenon Bernard of Venezuela company from 1950 to 1957. Dupouy's chief usefulness was in providing introductions to influential Venezuelans who could see that the company received government contracts. If the company obtained a bid through Dupouy's intercession, he was paid a fixed sum; his fee was not usually contingent on profits. For example, Dupouy collected Bs300,000 in 1956 on the Bs23,000,000 contract for construction of a breakwater on the Maracaibo sandbar. Agents for the companies which executed government contracts testified that Dupouy had shared his commissions with his friend, President Pérez Jiménez.[21] Reports of threats from the SN to recalcitrant companies also at least indirectly implicated Minister of the Interior Laureano Vallenilla Lanz and SN Chief Pedro Estrada.

Pérez and his ministers then apparently directly collected a percentage of the value of government contracts issued to foreign companies. Occasionally they also set up dummy corporations to subcontract government business. The shareholders of the front company divided the difference between the original, inflated government price and the lower subcontract fee. Empresa Venezolana de Ingeniería y Construcción S.A. (EVICSA) was one such corporation whose business consisted wholly of six government contracts signed between May, 1955, and June, 1957. The company earned the following net sums for the designated periods: Bs308,-645.25 in fiscal year 1954–1955, Bs2,923,482 in 1955–1956, and

[19] The companies were Rolls Royce, Rotol, Smith, Hawker, and Plessey as well as Vickers Armstrong.

[20] Plaintiff's Evidence, 4:59–61, Mathes Papers.

[21] Ibid., 5:119–121; 9:82, 127, 128; Plaintiff's Memorandum on the Facts, Mathes Papers.

Bs2,835,312.22 in 1956–1957. The true stockholders of companies like EVICSA were difficult to ascertain. Stock certificates were usually issued to the bearer only, so there were no registers of shareholders. Presidents and directors of the companies testified that they did not know who owned the shares.[22]

Pérez Jiménez was implicated in the EVICSA web of ownership because his minister of the interior and minister of development owned shares. EVICSA was originally formed with a capital of one-half million bolivares in 1954. Minister of the Interior Laureano Vallenilla Lanz put up 40 percent of the capital, and engineer Dr. Francisco J. Sucre, Dr. Luis Malaussena, and Inversiones Orinoco each had invested 20 percent of the original capital.[23] Inversiones Orinoco had been organized in 1948 as a land development corporation; its founders were Dr. Silvio Gutiérrez, Leopoldo Romero Sánchez, Hijo; Henry F. Rodner,[24] and Dr. Carlos Daboin. The same four men also held stock in Oficina Técnica Gutiérrez. Inversiones Orinoco also had shares in various other companies in addition to EVICSA: Inversora de Venezuela, FAISA, and Urbanizadora Caracas.[25] Extant records did not allow investigators to determine who the shareholders of Inversiones Orinoco were, but the Venezuelan government assumed that Pérez Jiménez had held shares in that corporation as well as in EVICSA.

The question of the identities of the shareholders in these corporations was delicate, as was the question of which foreign companies had offered bribes to facilitate business with the Venezuelan government. Although investigations in the United States

[22] Plaintiff's Memorandum on the Facts; Plaintiff's Evidence, 7:168, 187–189, Mathes Papers.

[23] Plaintiff's Evidence, 7:168; Plaintiff's Memorandum on the Facts, Mathes Papers.

[24] Henry F. Rodner, born in Annapolis, Maryland, and a graduate of the U.S. Naval Academy, was a naval engineer who had lived in Venezuela since 1945. He worked for and became a director of the Oficina Técnica Gutiérrez and was also a director of Inversiones Orinoco, Inversora de Venezuela, Urbanizadora Caracas, Almacenadora Caracas, and the Hotel Avila Company. He was a friend and business associate of Silvio Gutiérrez, who was Pérez Jiménez's minister of development.

[25] Plaintiff's Evidence, 7:168, 175, Mathes Papers.

and Venezuela in the 1970s revealed that many U.S. corporations commonly did offer bribes to foreign governments, none of the evidence against Pérez Jiménez implicated any U.S. corporations. One can only assume that Betancourt decided, or was required, to expunge evidence relating to U.S. corporations for the extradition hearings in the United States. Similarly, Betancourt did not wish to probe too deeply into the links between Venezuelan business-men and the Pérez Jiménez government for fear of alienating valu-able political allies. Even Betancourt's minister of justice, Dr. Andrés Aguilar Mawdsley, had had his name appear on some of the EVICSA shares, although he testified that he had never paid for the shares and had never received dividends; he had allowed his name to be used to accommodate his friend Dr. Leopoldo Romero Sánchez, Hijo.[26] The dance of the millions no doubt touched many people who chose to stay in Venezuela during the 1950s. Acción Democrática's majority was not stable enough to risk the thorough investigation that might have clearly outlined the details of Pérez Jiménez's graft.

Ironically then, the strongest charges against Pérez Jiménez for graft were those that involved the use of state workmen and mate-rials on his private estates. Termed petty peculation, these charges would probably have been insufficient for extradition in themselves but did add bulk to the case against Pérez. Rafael Polidoro Rodrí-guez, for example, testified that he had helped to build a wooden pavillion with a thatched roof, a ball court for *bolas criollas*, and two little round kiosks at Pérez's country estate, El Peñón. As an employee of the state, Polidoro Rodríguez had been paid with public funds.[27]

Pérez Jiménez was also charged with using his influence to benefit from land speculation. He had presided over numerous government contracts for highways and other urban improvements that spurred a boom in urban construction, especially in Caracas. The case of C.A. Industrial del Cartón was illustrative. On July 22, 1955, the government designated the land of Elías Issa Chejin

[26] Ibid., p. 36.
[27] Ibid., 8:9–10.

and David E. Issa Espinoza for government use. Although the decree was published in the *Gaceta Oficial*, the owners of the land testified that they had not known of the proposed government purchase of the land. One of Pérez's intermediaries, Fortunato Herrera, offered the Issas Bs30 per square meter for a purchase-sale option, which his corporation, Polinversiones, took over. Herrera subsequently had the property appraised at Bs120 per square meter and sold it to the government. He made a profit of over Bs3 million on the deal.[28]

Angel Saldivia, who had worked for Industrial del Cartón, stated that Herrera had threatened them with the SN if they refused to sell. Herrera had also alluded to serving as an intermediary for one he called "My General." Saldivia concluded: "It must be assumed that this referred to the Dictator Pérez Jiménez, since it is very clear to all Venezuelans that there were no other Generals in this country than the Usurper."[29] Saldivia's testimony, it might be noted, was taken by officials of AD after. Pérez Jiménez had fled Venezuela; the Issas had registered no protest about the land deal until after Pérez had been overthrown.

Other witnesses also stated that Pérez Jiménez had shared profits with Herrera or Dupouy or other intermediaries. In none of the cases in the court record, however, was Pérez Jiménez's documented involvement any more overt than in the Industrial del Cartón or EVICSA cases. The Venezuelan government could only point to the rather weak link of testimony by people who had heard the intermediaries say that Pérez Jiménez had some interest in the business at hand.

The evidence which implicated Pérez Jiménez in several alleged murders was similar in nature, but even more tenuous. The chain of command ran from the SN agent who killed someone to Pedro Estrada, head of the SN, to Laureano Vallenilla Lanz, the minister of the interior, to President Pérez Jiménez. Pérez Jiménez also had direct links with the SN officer through daily breakfast meetings and direct telephone connections between the presidential

[28] Ibid., 6:19; 7:114, 123–125, 138.
[29] Ibid., 7:115.

mansion and limousine and the SN headquarters. Witnesses testified that it was "common knowledge" that Pérez Jiménez directly
ordered the SN to do his bidding.[30]

The Venezuelan attorney general accused Pérez Jiménez of
ordering four men killed: Leonardo Ruíz Pineda on October 21,
1952; Germán González on October 24, 1952; Antonio Pinto Salinas
on June 11, 1953; and Luis Hurtado Higuera about March 13, 1954.
Ruíz Pineda, a lawyer and clandestine general secretary of AD,
was killed in a shoot-out with SN agents when the SN tried to arrest
him and his friends. González, the owner of the car in which Ruíz
Pineda had been riding, was arrested on October 21 and was killed
on October 24 by a military policeman on duty at the SN jail, allegedly in an escape attempt. Pinto Salinas, a lawyer and an AD
leader, had also been beaten and killed by SN agents in a fabri-
cated escape attempt. Luis Hurtado, a labor leader arrested to ensure tranquility for the Tenth Interamerican Conference, was presumably beaten to death, although his body was never recovered.[31]

In none of these cases was the person who actually did the
killing clearly identified. Testimony existed that President Pérez
Jiménez was immediately notified of the death of Ruíz Pineda,[32]
but no statement established that Pérez had ordered the death of
any of these individuals. Hurtado's body was never found, and no
witnesses claimed to have seen him dead; the details of that murder
were provided in two anonymous telephone calls to Judge Guillermo Tell Aveledo. Judge Tell Aveledo quoted the telephone informant's account of a statement made to him by an employee of the
SN: "He says that he knows by actual experience that on that
night more or less identified, they put the body of a dead man
into a vehicle that he believes was an automobile."[33] One is left to
wonder how the unidentified informant could readily recognize the

30 Ibid., 3:159, 224; 10:40.
31 Ibid., 1:2; 10:1–10, 27, 34–35; 11:5; Plaintiff's Memorandum on the
Facts, Mathes Papers.
32 Plaintiff's Evidence, 1:2.
33 Ibid., 11:5.

dead body as Hurtado's but be uncertain whether the vehicle in question was an automobile.

In short, common sense would lead one to conclude that Pérez Jiménez knew of, condoned, and probably ordered the violent acts of the SN, but the courts of law required substantial evidence beyond that of "common knowledge." Counsel for the Venezuelan government further had to demonstrate that the crimes were not political and did not occur during a political struggle for power. Acción Democrática and the Communist party had indeed been outlawed in 1948 and 1950, and they feebly continued some underground activity, but as Howard Westwood, of Covington and Burling, argued, it was ridiculous to claim that a struggle for power had existed during the whole ten years of Pérez Jiménez's government. The murders charged had occurred in 1952, 1953, and 1954.

Thus, the earliest of these crimes was committed almost four years after the decree to outlaw the parties cited by the defendant, and there is no evidence that any violent revolutionary activity was carried on or continued after the issuance of the decree. The defendant's attempt to imply that a struggle for power existed during the ten years of his regime from the fact that he entered and departed from power by military coups d'etat cannot seriously be considered as bearing upon the murders committed in the fourth, fifth, and sixth years of the defendant's regime when he was at the height of this power.[34]

The lawyer allowed that there was some underground activity at the time of the fraudulent election of 1952; the political opposition was necessarily clandestine because of the nature of Pérez's dictatorship. "There is not a suggestion," Westwood added, "that the Acción Democrática or any other group was engaged in a violent struggle for power with the defendant."[35]

Counsel for the Venezuelan government minimized the underground activities of AD and the Communist party during the 1950s. He obviously did not want to leave Pérez Jiménez an opening to argue that he had merely defended his government from subver-

[34] Memorandum in Reply to Defendant's Memorandum on the Facts, Mathes Papers.

[35] Plaintiff's Memorandum on the Facts, Mathes Papers.

sion. Such defensive actions, if crimes at all, were clearly political ones. The Venezuelan government was anxious, however, to document the repression and violation of civil rights that had taken place under Pérez's regime. Such testimony was not necessary, and indeed may even have been prejudicial to the charge that Pérez was guilty of common crimes. It was important though for the Acción Democrática government to continue to place in the record testimony which implicitly compared the repressive dictatorship with the new, democratic government. For example, they solicited a statement for the court record from Rafael Caldera, leader of COPEI: "I am fully convinced that General (ret.) Marcos Pérez Jiménez is personally responsible for all the acts committed against the public liberties, against the Venezuelan people and against the funds of the people during his term of office, as well as, in great part for the outrages committed in the periods when, although not President, he exercised influence in the Government."[36]

Such statements supported Betancourt's international strategy and his efforts to use the proceedings as an international forum to establish the legality and credibility of his own government. The contrasts between Pérez Jiménez's government and that of Betancourt also reminded the Eisenhower government of the resentment caused when the United States so uncritically supported dictators in Latin America.

The Venezuelan government had completed its case by June, 1960, and Pérez Jiménez's attorneys began to outline an elaborate defense. Judge William Mathes overrode the objections of the Venezuelan counsel and allowed the defense attorneys to seek depositions in Venezuela and Europe. By fall, the court procedings were at a standstill while David Walters and the other defense attorneys prepared for their work abroad.

In September, however, the Judicial Council of the Fifth Circuit intervened to halt the case. After a mid-September conference with Chief Justice Earl Warren and others at the Judicial Conference of the United States in Washington, D.C., Chief Judge of the Judicial Council Richard Rives notified Judge William Mathes

---

[36] Plaintiff's Evidence, 2:113, Mathes Papers.

that he was to be removed from the case "as a result of their conference."[37] Mathes in letters of September 30 and October 4 relinquished all pending matters in the Florida district, noting his regret at "being compelled to 'desert the ship' in this case."[38] The Judicial Council for the Fifth Circuit affirmed his removal at their meeting of October 7, "to avoid doubt as to jurisdiction or power to act," and stressed that "the proposed order involves no reflection upon Judge Mathes or upon the Chief Judge or other Judges of the Southern District of Florida."[39] Howard Westwood, of Covington and Burling, explained that the removal of Mathes was simply a matter of judicial housekeeping; no one had expected the case to last so long, and the delays and inconveniences caused by Mathes's shuttling from California to Florida were many.[40]

The timing of Mathes's removal must arouse suspicions that more than "judicial housekeeping" was at stake. It may have been considered expedient to neutralize the case as a potential political issue between Richard M. Nixon and John F. Kennedy. Or the Venezuelan government may have feared that the Eisenhower administration in its lame duck days might have allowed the case against Pérez Jiménez to be dismissed. Whatever the reasons for Mathes's removal, they did not appear to be related to a speedy conclusion of the case. Not until March, 1961, after the inauguration of John Kennedy, was Judge William Whitehurst assigned to the case.

Betancourt must have taken heart at the opportune delay in the case and certainly at the election of Kennedy. The stirrings of a new U.S. Latin American policy that had been observed in the last years of the Eisenhower government might well develop into a new, and ostensibly more sympathetic, approach to democratic governments in the Americas. The new mood in Washington should have alarmed Pérez Jiménez but apparently did not alter his resolve to remain in Miami and to rely on his lawyers' efforts to defend him.

[37] *Pérez Jiménez v. Aristeguieta and Maguire*, 10:2793.
[38] Ibid., 2798.
[39] Ibid., 2795–2796.
[40] Interview with Howard Westwood, November 18, 1969.

5

The Extradition Hearings,
January, 1961–August, 1963:
Perez Jiménez's Defense and Appeals

Pérez Jiménez's defense fell into three overlapping phases. First, his counsel David Walters argued that the legal evidence was insufficient for an indictment against the former president. Secondly, Walters took advantage of all procedural appeals and delays available to Pérez Jiménez. Finally, Walters mounted a campaign to establish the political nature of the charges against Pérez and to demand that the U.S. secretary of state honor the principle of political asylum. The procedural delays provided the time for Pérez Jiménez to press the political argument upon President John Kennedy and the State Department directly through petitions and indirectly through U.S. groups which lobbied on his behalf. The delays worked against him in the long run, however, since they allowed the Acción Democrática government in Venezuela to gain more credibility as a stable democratic ally of the New Frontier.

The first line of defense, then, aside from protesting the latitude allowed the Venezuelan government in amending complaints and seeking new evidence, was to attack the inferences drawn from the evidence presented.[1] Walters maintained that President Pérez Jiménez had been engaged in a struggle against AD and Communist terrorists for the entire time that he was in power. The struggle was not necessarily violent during the entire period, but the alleged murders did occur during a climate of tension between the government and the illegal opposition. A government must defend itself

[1] Precedent in extradition hearings forbade the defense from offering contradictory evidence or impugning the plaintiff's witnesses; the defense had to accept the plaintiff's evidence as valid, but could then rebut inferences drawn from that evidence. See *Pérez Jiménez* v. *Aristeguieta and Maguire*, 19,507 (5th Cir., 1962), 12:3329; and Marjorie Whiteman ed., *Digest of International Law*, VI, 1000.

from attacks, and any deaths which result must be termed political.[2]

Walters presented a number of depositions to testify to the political climate in Venezuela during the 1950s. The most striking assertions were advanced by Pedro Estrada, hardly an impartial witness. Estrada charged that Pérez Jiménez's opposition had tried to overthrow the government through bombings, sabotage, and assassination attempts. Moreover, AD and the Communists had combined forces with other revolutionary groups in the Caribbean in order to sweep all of the military governments from power. The Venezuelan revolutionaries had scorned no allies, the former head of SN revealed; they sought help from Mexican and Cuban communists, and they recruited some of the most beautiful women in the Caribbean to go to Venezuela to try to subvert the army officers. Mixing the trivial with the transcendental, Estrada tried to discredit the AD leaders and to portray Pérez's government as a respectable and normal one.[3]

In refuting the evidence which implicated Pérez in four murders, counsel for the defense assumed that Pérez's police force had legally maintained law and order. Naturally, this assumption altered the inferences which the plaintiff had drawn from the same evidence. Thus, Ruíz Pineda was killed when he resisted arrest; he might even have been killed by his friends since he had been standing between his friends and the SN agents during the exchange of gunfire. Germán González had lied when he identified the car used by Ruíz and his friends as stolen; arresting him on suspicion of aiding terrorists surely was reasonable. If he tried to escape from jail, the guard on duty had been justified in firing at him. Luis Hurtado and Pinto Salinas might have provoked their guards to beat them.[4]

More telling than the traditional "escape attempt" justification

[2] Memorandum in Support of Defendant's Motion to Dismiss, Mathes Papers, Zimmerman Library, University of New Mexico, Albuquerque.

[3] *Pérez Jiménez* v. *Aristeguieta and Maguire*, 10:2183, 2865–2867; Attachments to the Affidavit of Pedro Estrada, Mathes Papers.

[4] Memorandum in Support of Defendant's Motion to Dismiss, Mathes Papers; *Pérez Jiménez* v. *Aristeguieta and Maguire*, 9:2613; 11:3238–3239; 3252–3253.

for murder was the defense's argument that the evidence was incompetent or insufficient to convict Pérez Jiménez for these deaths. Some depositions had been taken out of context. Statements had been lifted from the trials of other persons, and the witnesses had not intended to testify against Pérez Jiménez. Much of the testimony, coming from members of AD, or at their prompting, was partisan. For example, two investigations had been conducted in the murder of Pinto Salinas: one at the time of his death and one later by AD. Since the plaintiff had only submitted the later version, Walters assumed that the earlier evidence favored his client. Other depositions had also come from political enemies of Pérez Jiménez. Some of the witnesses had died since giving their statements.[5]

Additionally, most of the testimony was also insufficient under Florida law to prove the crimes alleged, Walters continued. Most of the evidence in the Luis Hurtado case was hearsay; the murder weapon had not been identified in the Ruíz Pineda case; the military policeman who had allegedly killed González had never been identified;[6] and similar hard evidence was lacking in the case concerning Pinto Salinas. But most importantly, Walters argued, there was no hard evidence to implicate Pérez Jiménez in any of the murders. The documentation did not even establish that Pedro Estrada had ordered the deaths of the four men. The plaintiff had assumed that Estrada (or ultimately Pérez Jiménez) was responsible for all criminal actions of his employees. Although Estrada and Pérez Jiménez had met frequently, no one had recorded any of the conversations between the two men. "What connivance or crimes can we attribute to the frequent conferences that Eisenhower had with Allan Dulles and J. Edgar Hoover?" Walters concluded.[7]

---

[5] *Pérez Jiménez* v. *Aristeguieta and Maguire*, 4:1046; 9:2613–2615; 11: 3208–3211; Memorandum in Support of Defendant's Motion to Dismiss, Mathes Papers.

[6] Memorandum in Support of Defendant's Motion to Dismiss, Mathes Papers; *Pérez Jiménez* v. *Aristeguieta and Maguire*, 11:3238–3239.

[7] Memorandum in Support of Defendant's Motion to Dismiss, Mathes Papers.

Pérez Jiménez's defense arguments again made it clear that a dictatorial regime's repressiveness and violations of human rights do not lend themselves well to charges of murder in the regular courts. Even when people can safely charge a regime with criminal abuse of power, these allegations are too grand for the plodding nature of judicial procedure. Worse, if there is insufficient evidence to convict for the common crime, then the defendant can magnify the decision to excuse himself from culpability in the greater crime.

Less successfully, Pérez Jiménez's defense tried to discredit the witnesses and the evidence in the financial crimes. The evidence, however, was more damning, and counsel could merely point out omissions and challenge inferences. For example, Walters charged that no evidence had been advanced to suggest that any of the government contracts from which Pérez might have benefited were improper or illegally granted. Some of them appeared to have been awarded on the basis of competitive bids. Moreover, evidence relating to the alleged commissions was incomplete. The Venezuelan government had not questioned extensively the officials of the companies that had given bribes, nor had they instigated proceedings against the supposedly guilty companies. The counsel for the Venezuelan government conceded that they had been unable to secure records from the powerful international companies and had insufficient evidence to bring the companies to trial. Pérez Jiménez's defense attacked the veracity of the spokesmen for international companies who had testified that other companies had given bribes, but not their own.[8]

On the charges of land speculation, Pérez again argued that the Venezuelan government had not provided some key evidence. There was no documentation to indicate that the prices paid by Pérez's government for the land parcels had been inflated or unjust; no appraisals had been submitted to support the inference that the president had illegally manipulated prices for his own benefit. If the Issas had not known that their land was designated

---

[8] Ibid.; Memorandum in Reply to Defendant's Memorandum in Support of His Motion to Dismiss, Mathes Papers; *Pérez Jiménez* v. *Aristeguieta and Maguire*, 10:2819–2820.

for government use, their ignorance could hardly be used against Pérez Jiménez. Other people who had sold land to the government had read the *Gaceta Oficial* and had been aware that their land had increased in value. The defense further classified Fortunato Herrera as a name dropper. Herrera's remarks about "My General" and the SN did not prove that "his General" had ordered the business or even knew of it.[9]

David Walters, for the defense, dismissed as inconsequential the charges of petty peculation:

The terminology "petty" is indeed appropriate. It describes not only the nature of the charges but the *motives* behind the charges. It serves to emphasize the *personal and political* malice that motivates these extradition proceedings. . . . May society be protected from actions of this sort which seek to convert accepted conduct on the parts of heads of state to criminal acts to serve the political and personal objectives of the accuser. In order to place these charges in their proper perspective, visualize President Eisenhower's successor seeking his indictment for having taken vacation trips on Government transportation or for the construction of practice golf greens and the like. We trust that decisions of such grave international moment will not be predicated on such *petty* accusations. [Emphasis in the original][10]

Both the financial crimes and the violent deaths, then, Walters characterized as normal occurrences in Venezuela. President Eisenhower's putting greens and conversations with J. Edgar Hoover were placed in the same category as Pérez Jiménez's bowling greens and conversations with Pedro Estrada. Doubtlessly, in the pre-Watergate perception of the appropriate norms of behavior for administrative officials, there was some validity to the analogy.

After attacking the inferences drawn by the plaintiff, Pérez's defense argued persuasively that the crimes charged were not in the extradition treaty. Outlining the relationship between malversation, embezzlement, bribery, and extortion, Walters insisted on a strict construction of the treaty. Using the *Corpus Juris Secundum*

[9] Memorandum in Support of Defendant's Motion to Dismiss, Mathes Papers; *Pérez Jiménez* v. *Aristeguieta and Maguire*, 9:2653.

[10] Memorandum in Support of Defendant's Motion to Dismiss, Mathes Papers.

as a basis for his definitions, he then showed how they corresponded to Venezuelan law:

Bribery, an offense against public justice, may be defined as the voluntary giving or receiving of anything of value to influence a public officer
in the discharge of his official duties. [*C.J.S.*, II, 840]

. . .

Extortion is the unlawful act of an officer in exacting money or property from another under color of official right by the wrongful use of
force or fear; bribery, on the other hand, involves a voluntary rather than
coerced payment and may consist of either the offering or receiving of
property to influence official conduct. Further, in bribery it is assumed
that the bribe-giver is engaged in the doing of some unlawful act as to
which the officer is influenced in regard to his official duty, whereas
extortion may be committed against one regardless of the lawfulness of
the act in which he is engaged. [*C.J.S.*, II, 841]

. . .

Embezzlement is broadly defined as the fraudulent appropriation of
another's property by a person to whom it has been entrusted or into
whose hands it has lawfully come. [*C.J.S.*, I, 670]

. . .

To make out a case of embezzlement it is generally necessary to show
that the property was within the protection of the statute, belonged to
someone other than accused, that accused acquired it lawfully, and occupied a fiduciary relationship, and a conversion of the property with a
fraudulent intent. [*C.J.S.*, V, 674]

Walters quoted from the Venezuelan Penal Code of 1863 to argue
that Venezuelan lawmakers had considered criminal malversation
to be the same as embezzlement. The defense attorney further
asserted that the treaty phrase "embezzlement or criminal malversation" illustrated the synonymous use of the two terms. Bribery
and extortion clearly differed from embezzlement. A person who
appeared to be guilty of bribery and extortion should not be surrendered for embezzlement. If the United States and Venezuela
had wanted to include bribery and extortion in the list of extraditable crimes, they would have specified them either in the original
treaty or in an amendment to it. In 1902, the United States and
Mexico had added bribery to the list of crimes in the extradition
treaty between them. The addition indicated that they had not

considered the crime of embezzlement or malversation to be the same as bribery, Walters argued. A narrow reading of the treaty would not allow the United States to surrender Pérez Jiménez if his illicit enrichment had come from bribery and extortion.[11]

In April, 1961, with the filing of a series of documents and depositions which depicted Pérez Jiménez as a strong ally in the hemispheric fight against communism, the defense rested. These documents as well as the evidence intending to show that President Betancourt was arbitrary, vengeful, and soft on communism were largely irrelevant to the judicial hearing, since the federal judge would only consider sufficiency of evidence. The determination of whether the crimes alleged were political and whether the U.S. interest would be served by extraditing Pérez Jiménez would be left to the U.S. secretary of state after the conclusion of the *prima facie* hearing.

As noted earlier, Judge William Mathes had been removed from the case in October, 1960. On March 6, 1961, the chief judge of the Southern District of Florida, Judge William Whitehurst, assigned himself to the case. Mathes had presided over the presentation of most of the evidence and arguments of both sides; Whitehurst had only to read the considerable record, to hear final arguments, and to decide whether sufficient cause had been shown to extradite Marcos Pérez Jiménez for malversation and murder.

Howard Westwood for the plaintiff filed a memorandum to guide the judge to the evidence and arguments. Counsel for the defense refused to file such a memorandum and insisted that Judge Whitehurst should read the entire court record. Whitehurst absorbed the bulky record quickly and announced his decision on June 16, 1961. Insufficient evidence existed, he ruled, to extradite Pérez Jiménez on the murder charges; the plaintiff had not established the former president's complicity in the crimes. Judge Whitehurst did certify, however, that sufficient evidence existed for indictment in the financial crimes.[12]

The decision carefully avoided the issue of whether or not the

[11] Walters's arguments and definitions are found in ibid., Annex No. 6. See also this volume, Appendix D.
[12] Certification to the Secretary of State, Mathes Papers.

murders were political crimes. Thus, Pérez Jiménez had less cause to appeal the decision by arguing that the financial crimes had been mixed with political ones and were thus not subject to extradition.

Numerous other avenues of appeal existed, however, and Pérez Jiménez's attorney kept the case in the courts for the next two years through a flurry of petitions and pleas that several times went to the Fifth District Court of Appeals and to the U.S. Supreme Court. The appeals challenged the jurisdiction of Judge Whitehurst and alleged that he had never called for the evidence from the clerk's office and had not read all of the court documents. Also, since Pérez Jiménez would be tried in Venezuela for each one of the offenses alleged, Walters demanded that the judge rule on the competency of the evidence in each incidence instead of delivering a general ruling.[13] Pérez Jiménez's defense counsel also continued to insist that the offenses charged against Pérez were not listed in the extradition treaty.

Agencies of the U.S. government intervened more directly in Pérez Jiménez's case after the June, 1961, decision. Although bail was not immediately revoked after the court finding, surveillance of Pérez Jiménez increased. One day after Whitehurst's decision, the U.S. Border Patrol stepped up their guard at his home on 4609 Pine Tree Drive in Miami. When Pérez left his estate, two Border Patrol squad cars preceded him and two followed him. Bond was increased to $100,000 after the failure of one appeal on August 23, 1961.[14] Walters succeeded in keeping Pérez Jiménez out of jail on bond, but the failure of each appeal brought closer that day in December, 1962, when bail was revoked.

Pérez's attorney charged that the U.S. government hoped that Pérez would cut short his appeals if he were in jail.[15] There may have been some truth to the charge, but Irving Jaffe of the Justice Department replied that the effort to revoke bail reflected U.S. in-

---

[13] *Pérez Jiménez* v. *Aristeguieta and Maguire,* 1:78–79, 169, 172, 274; 2:322–330.

[14] *Miami Herald,* June 18, 1961; *Pérez Jiménez* v. *Aristiguieta and Maguire,* 1:134.

[15] *Pérez Jiménez* v. *Aristeguieta and Maguire,* 1:206.

terest. If Pérez should escape before being surrendered, the U.S. would be embarrassed. Pérez should be jailed, Jaffe argued, until the secretary of state made his final decision. Incarceration would not harm Pérez Jiménez's dignity. Jaffe warned that the kid gloves were off: "The importance of this man in his own eyes, if nowhere else, is one of the factors that increases the possibility of embarrassment. . . . The United States Government does not view him as such an important character. As it stands now, he is a subject of treaty obligation. If Venezuela regards him as important—and he obviously regards himself of some importance—these are matters which we must take into account."[16] He added, "We are concerned not so much with this petitioner or with the sufficiency of the evidence in this case as we are with the proper interpretation or the interpretation that conforms to the Government's view of provisions of this treaty."[17]

Jaffe and the Justice Department finally won in December, 1962, after one of Pérez Jiménez's key appeals was rejected. The chubby former dictator was marched off to jail like any garden-variety pickpocket, and there he would remain until Dean Rusk finally disposed of the case in August, 1963.

Clearly, the Kennedy administration had less sympathy for Pérez Jiménez than had the Eisenhower government. Latin American policy had become more crucial to the United States with the perceived threat from Fidel Castro's Cuba. Significantly, the June, 1961, decision against Pérez followed one month after the Bay of Pigs invasion of Cuba, and Pérez was jailed only one and one-half months after the missile crisis of October, 1962. The extradition proceedings thus expressed the Latin American policy of the United States as unequivocally as did the more publicized Cuban events.

The Bay of Pigs fiasco suggested to John Kennedy that force might wisely give way to persuasion in the Caribbean. Kennedy courted Rómulo Betancourt, whose progressive administration could be a model for the Alliance for Progress. Both Kennedy and

[16] Ibid., pp. 226–227.
[17] Ibid., 2:390.

Betancourt held up the Venezuelan democratic government as the best defense against both dictatorship and communist subversion. The model simultaneously needed U.S. support and advanced U.S. goals in Latin America. In December, 1961, Betancourt reminded Kennedy that "In the decade of the 1950's, one of the most ominous for Latin America, dictators silenced with generalized terror the muffled and passioned call for a better life for the multitudes without bread, without shelter, without land, without schools. And from the economically most powerful country of the continent, the United States of America, came medals to decorate despots but not consistent cooperation for the economic development and social improvement of Latin America."[18]

Kennedy subsequently affirmed that interpretation and complimented Betancourt: "You personify all that we admire in a political leader. Your liberal leadership of your country, your persistent determination to achieve a better life for your people, your long fight in favor of democratic government not only in your own country but also in all the Caribbean, your camaraderie with other progressive liberal leaders of this hemisphere—all that has converted you, for us, into a symbol that we desire for our own country and for our sister republics."[19]

Betancourt's attitude toward Fidel Castro's Cuba further gratified the U.S. government. Like the United States, the Venezuelan government criticized Fidel Castro's relationship with the Soviet Union, and Betancourt denounced violations of human rights in Cuba. So strong were Betancourt's attacks on the Cuban government that Ché Guevara characterized the Venezuelan president as a prisoner of his own repressive forces. Cuban Foreign Minister Raúl Roa charged that the U.S. Department of State and the Central Intelligence Agency dictated Betancourt's policies. Insulted at the Cuban allegations and reiterating his distaste for Cuba's evolution away from liberal democratic patterns, Betancourt broke rela-

[18] Rómulo Betancourt, *La revolución democrática en Venezuela 1959–1964: Documentos del gobierno presidido por Rómulo Betancourt*, II, 199.
[19] Ibid., III, 317.

tions with Cuba in November, 1961.[20] Betancourt was promptly rewarded for his action when President John F. Kennedy and his wife visited Venezuela in December, 1961.

Subsequently, in 1963, Betancourt more explicitly drew the connections between dictatorships such as that of Pérez Jiménez and the condemnation of the leftist Cuban government: "We will have greater moral authority, greater militant backing of our people with their incorruptible and deep desire for liberty, to combat the Sovietized danger of Cuba when the personalistic dictatorships which use power for the illicit enrichment of pirates and of gangs who are partners in the illicit gains obtained from the usurped power have disappeared from the political map of the continent."[21]

Hence, the two years which Pérez Jiménez took for his appeals coincided with a growing trust and respect between John Kennedy and Rómulo Betancourt. Pérez's public relations campaign in the United States and his efforts to influence U.S. officials had some success. It seemed, however, in 1962 and 1963 to be anachronistic to argue that dictators were the best friends of the United States and the best defense against the spread of communism in the Western Hemisphere. As time passed and Betancourt validated his own noncommunist credentials, Pérez Jiménez's bargaining position worsened in the United States. Any cynic could see that the former dictator no longer had anything to offer in exchange for preferential treatment from the Kennedy government. Betancourt had all the cards.

Pérez Jiménez stolidly continued to believe that the United States would not extradite him if he could only hold out long enough. His efforts to influence public and official opinion appealed to two groups: civil libertarians in the United States, and the people who remained convinced that only a firm, indeed repressive, dictator could maintain order in Latin America. He won more allies

[20] República de Venezuela, Ministerio de Relaciones Exteriores, "Exposición de la Cancillería," November 5, 1961, *Libro amarillo de la República de Venezuela, 1962*, pp. 11–14.

[21] Ministerio de Relaciones Exteriores, "Discurso de Betancourt en Consejo de la OEA," February 20, 1963, *Libro Amarillo de la República de Venezuela, 1964*, p. lii.

after he was unceremoniously jailed, but he failed to convert policy makers who saw more advantages in appeasing Betancourt. Nor could he expect a general show of sympathy from the majority of the U.S. citizens who had probably never heard of him.

Pérez tried to convince the courts and the public that the request for his extradition was politically motivated and malicious. Moreover, his actions as president of Venezuela had been well within the accepted norms for Venezuela, or indeed for most countries. Pérez's attorneys and public relations agents further characterized Betancourt's administration as an unstable one which could not guarantee Pérez's safety, even if it wanted to. If Secretary of State Dean Rusk surrendered Pérez Jiménez, Rusk would be sending him back to certain death.[22] The obvious conclusion followed that Pérez Jiménez should receive political asylum in the United States.

Some of the material that Pérez used to establish the nature of the Betancourt government had been gathered by his attorneys in early 1961, over the objections of the attorneys for the plaintiff. Judge Mathes had allowed David Walters to journey to Venezuela and to Europe to take depositions from people who had had knowledge of Pérez's or of Betancourt's administration. These depositions included the lengthy statement from Pedro Estrada as well as comments from people still living in Venezuela. Walters used the visit to Venezuela and the depositions taken there to the hilt.

Before leaving, Walters had announced to the court that he feared for his life and safety in Venezuela. Counsel for the Venezuelan government quickly objected to Walters's implication but agreed to ask the Venezuelan attorney general to facilitate the work of the defense attorneys.[23]

Edward N. Moore, Walters's legal partner, testified that even the official cooperation had not made his job an easy one:

As soon as I arrived in Caracas, it was perfectly obvious that there was an air of excitement about my visit. I became an object of curiosity—I

[22] *Pérez Jiménez* v. *Aristeguieta and Maguire,* 2:443–444.

[23] Ibid., 10:2768; Howard Westwood to David Walters, October 26, 1960, Mathes Papers.

was pursued by newspaper reporters, and statements were attributed to me which were never made. Each day the situation became increasingly worse. Government officials, employees, clerks, and former clients whom I represented, were afraid to talk with me on the streets for fear that their cordial attitude to me would be construed as an indication of friendliness toward our client, GENERAL MARCOS PÉREZ JIMÉNEZ. As a matter of fact, I received many calls from individuals who stated that they wanted so much to help me but were afraid for their lives, and for that reason would not be in a position to speak with me or give me information which we sorely needed.[24]

Other events, he noted, made him feel even less welcome. The newspapers termed him a *persona non grata*. Anti-American demonstrations were held in front of the National Congress, and the U.S. flag was burned. An AD senator, Estanislao Mejias, suggested that Moore should be lynched or beaten in the streets of Caracas. Moore's response typified much of his testimony: "I am not a timid person, yet, recalling how the Communists of Venezuela were so bold and unrestrained as to stone and spit in the face of Vice President Nixon and his wife, when they visited that country, I began to be concerned about my own position which then appeared to be quite precarious.[25]

Moore played up the alleged Communist threat as much as possible. He implied that Pérez Jiménez had persecuted the Communists, and now in league with AD the Communists wanted revenge. The defense offered excerpts from the notorious "Red Book," which purported to document Communist influence in Venezuela; letters that Betancourt had written in his more radical youth were entered in the court records to suggest his Communist affiliations. Some of the prisoners that Moore was permitted to talk with also alleged that Venezuela was full of Communists. Luis Enrique Torres, in jail for three years without a trial, fatalistically expected a "Communist" judge to find him guilty. Daniel Augusto Colmenares, a former agent of the SN, said that a Communist's false complaint of assault and battery against him had landed him in jail. And Benjamin Núñez Escobar, who represented Miguel Sanz Añez,

[24] *Pérez Jiménez* v. *Aristeguieta and Maguire*, 11:3026.
[25] Ibid., pp. 3046–3048.

another SN agent, warned Moore that his life was in danger. Núñez said he had been attacked and beaten by Communists when he undertook Sanz Añez's defense.[26]

Pérez Jiménez's defense also charged that the Venezuelan legal system was inhumane. Stories were told of people who had been in jail for years without a trial; the examples of Gregorio Gonzáles Gómez, Luis Enrique Torres, and Daniel Augusto Colmenares were given. Pérez's lawyers also emphasized the Venezuelan Federal District Bar Association's resolution which prohibited lawyers from representing any former member of the SN. Luis Enrique Torres complained that his public defender did little for him.[27]

These principal themes of the defense, presented for the court record, also made their way into U.S. newspapers and into the hands of groups thought to be sympathetic to Pérez's cause. The publicity hit the mark in several instances. Some members of the U.S. Congress opposed Pérez's extradition. Congressman William C. Cramer of Florida, Henry Schadeberg of Wisconsin, and James B. Utt of California praised Pérez for his battle against the Communists and worried about the gains that the Communists had made under President Betancourt.[28]

Some radical fringe groups also tried to defend Pérez. In January, 1963, five men filed a self-styled petition to intervene in the extradition proceedings. The petition called for alertness against the world Marxist, Communist conspiracy in which Washington officials were involved. The conspiracy had begun in 1933, the group asserted.[29]

The press continued to keep the issues before the public, especially in Miami. Don Shoemaker of the *Miami Herald* conducted the traditional poll of Caracas cab drivers. According to them, Pérez Jiménez had been more provident to Venezuelans than

[26] Defendant's Exhibit B, Mathes Papers; *Pérez Jiménez v. Aristeguieta and Maguire*, 11:3036–3038, 3041, 3049. For a more realistic view of Pérez Jiménez's relations with the various Communist groups, see Robert Alexander, *The Communist Party of Venezuela*, pp. 26–42.

[27] *Pérez Jiménez v. Aristeguieta and Maguire*, 11:3036.

[28] *Miami Herald*, October 14, 1962; *New York Times*, July 26, 1963.

[29] *Miami Herald*, January 16, 1963.

Betancourt had. The chauffeurs and Mr. Shoemaker concurred that Betancourt was at the same time unpopular with the oil interests and too far to the political right for some other Venezuelans. Venezuelans, however, despite their more forgiving attitude toward Pérez Jiménez, did not want him back as president, Shoemaker reported. Another *Herald* journalist, John Pennekamp, speculated on whether Pérez Jiménez was receiving a fair trial. He wrote: "Maybe Pérez Jiménez should stay in jail. I don't know. But I keep wondering about the failure of *habeas corpus* to be available in making the decision." The *Arizona Republic* also thought that the odds were stacked against Pérez: "When the ex-president first sought freedom on bail, Chief Justice Earl Warren—who seldom seems to worry that an accused Communist spy might jump bail— turned down Jiménez's appeal."[30]

Columnist Drew Pearson more objectively remarked that Betancourt faced the same opposition in the United States that he did in Venezuela: the far left and the far right. And those who disliked Betancourt often took up Pérez Jiménez's cause. The State Department, for example, received about six hundred letters a week after the John Birch Society called for a letter-writing campaign on behalf of Pérez Jiménez. On the other hand, the American Civil Liberties Union also supported asylum for Pérez. The executive director, John de J. Pemberton, Jr., wrote to Dean Rusk that granting asylum would serve U.S. interests better than extradition. The ACLU opposed extradition because the principle of political asylum had been such an integral part of the U.S. civil liberties structure, and the extradition of a former head of state for alleged abuse of power would be unprecedented. The ACLU added that the suspicion that Pérez would be a victim of political persecution if surrendered had also prompted their plea. Although Venezuela had no death penalty, the former president faced a long prison term. Moreover, the Venezuelan government might try him for the murders, even though the U.S. court had found insufficient evidence for these crimes.[31]

[30] Ibid., October 16, December 20, 1962; *Arizona Republic*, July 13, 1963.
[31] *Miami Herald*, February 23, March 10, June 17, 1963.

After Pérez's bail was revoked and he took up residence in the Dade County Jail, his wife, Flor, assumed more visibility in the media effort to drum up sympathy for him. At Christmastime when Pérez had just gone to jail, Mrs. Pérez Jiménez held a press conference, accompanied by four public relations men and her three oldest daughters. As a wife and mother, she appealed to the people of the United States to grant her family the same consideration that refugees from Communist China had received. Several *Herald* articles portrayed the sad Christmas the four Pérez Jiménez children would have with their father in jail. At another press conference in February, 1963, Flor told newsmen that Pérez Jiménez's life would be in danger if he were surrendered. As evidence, she pointed to the jailing and harassment of Venezuelans who had expressed sympathy for her husband. President Betancourt, she charged, was behind the intimidation efforts. In May, Flor wrote President Kennedy to ask him to cancel the extradition order.[32]

After Pérez was in jail, the newspapers around Miami made much of the conditions of his imprisonment. Visits were limited, the heat was excessive, and the food was not to Pérez's liking. The former dictator shed forty-five pounds in his eight months in jail, a not unbecoming loss. He was indeed treated like the common criminal depicted in the charges before the U.S. courts.

Betancourt's government continued to press the United States for the surrender of Pérez Jiménez and to object to Pérez's defamation of the democratic government. Ironically, by 1963, Betancourt's three goals of isolating *de facto* governments in the Americas, ending corruption in Venezuela, and developing institutional norms of due process were meeting with mixed success. To counter the guerrilla activity from the right and the left, Betancourt several times suspended constitutional guarantees in Venezuela. Criticized for the emergency measures, Betancourt retorted that a democratic government had even more obligation to remain in power than an illegitimate one; he refused to see his popularly elected government fall as the one in 1948 had. Nor was his international thesis of a

[32] Ibid., December 13, 18, 1962; February 16, May 16, 1963.

cordon sanitaire to isolate *de facto* governments enthusiastically supported by other American governments. It soon became apparent that the United States deplored leftist ideology more than unconstitutional status; Castro's Cuba was isolated, but the irregular maneuverings which brought Fernando Belaúnde Terry to power in Peru in 1963 were accepted, over Betancourt's strong protests to Kennedy.[33] The United States continued routinely to recognize the military governments that came to power in the mid-1960s.

Even Betancourt's campaign against administrative graft was not going well. More powers were granted to the Investigating Commission against Illicit Enrichment by the Constitution of 1961, but in February, 1963, Betancourt admitted:

It is possible, and I am not unaware of it, that in subordinate sectors of the public administration the disgraceful custom of peculation can persist. But the way to fight these remainders of traditional vices in the country, for those who really want to fight them and not just to discredit the democratic regime, is not to cast indiscriminate and vague accusations, without names or surnames, but to publish with all possible details the fraudulent actions of all those who are not loyal to the ethics and the refinement of state functionaries or to send me all the data and evidence in confidence that they will not remain buried in Miraflores but that they will be sent immediately to the General Comptroller's office and to the investigating police bodies.[34]

Still, Betancourt continued to believe in the importance of Pérez Jiménez's extradition. As he had stated in March, 1962:

We believe that we are offering a service to international political ethics when we begin before the courts of the United States the trial of the former Venezuelan dictator for assassination committed in Venezuela and for plunder of the public wealth of Venezuela. Now the judges in the United States have found that he stole at least thirteen million dollars. It is much more. And this is very important, because only leaders

---

[33] República de Venezuela, Fiscalía General de la República, *Informe al Congreso Nacional, 1960*, pp. 154–159; *Informe del Fiscal General, 1961*, pp. 15–110; Betancourt, *Revolución democrática*, III, 19–20; IV, 156.

[34] Betancourt, *Revolución democrática*, III, 308–309.

who are ready to submit to public trial can assume such a position. I am surely convinced that we are doing the world a great service in this matter.[35]

After June 17, 1963, when the U.S. Supreme Court refused to rehear one of Pérez Jiménez's appeals, Betancourt must have sensed imminent victory. As Secretary of State Dean Rusk began to consider the record, however, there was still a possibility that the U.S. government would suffer a last-minute loss of nerve. The Venezuelan government sent several attorneys to Washington to help reassure Rusk that Pérez Jiménez would be treated fairly if he were surrendered.[36]

Much of the burden of dispelling the secretary of state's concerns fell to the Venezuelan ambassador to the United States, Enrique Tejera París. On July 19, 1963, Dean Rusk wrote to Ambassador Tejera París to ask for more reassurances; Rusk had met with Pérez Jiménez's lawyers and was concerned about some of the possible dangers to Pérez if he were surrendered.

Tejera París impatiently dismissed as absurd the contention that Pérez would be in physical danger. The Venezuelan government had already outlined the security measures which would be taken to ensure the former president's safety. Venezuela, jealous of its new international reputation for judicial regularity, had more of a stake in Pérez Jiménez's security than did the United States. "Also," added the ambassador, "I am sure that your Excellency is fully informed that my Government does not torture prisoners as happened in my country before the month of January of 1958." Nor should Secretary Rusk question the Venezuelan legal process. The trial would be speedy unless Pérez Jiménez chose to prolong it through persistent interlocutory appeals and other tactics "as

---

[35] Ibid., pp. 15–16.

[36] *Miami Herald*, July 1, 1963. The U.S. government argued that the two months allowed the Venezuelan government to complete their case only began to run on June 17; to have held that it had begun earlier than that date would have denied time for appeals. The extradition treaty stipulated that the accused should go free if the sixty-day grace period expired without his surrender. See Memorandum for Intervenor M. Aristeguieta, Mathes Papers.

the accused do with success at times in all countries." Of course, Pérez Jiménez would receive appropriate legal assistance. Some prominent members of the Venezuelan bar had already offered to defend him.[37]

Tejera París concluded reproachfully by recalling the delays in the United States and by hinting that Venezuelan confidence in the United States would be shaken if the prisoner were not surrendered:

Said tribunals [of the United States] have correctly insisted that no one is above the law. Only to reaffirm that principle, and in spite of exasperating procedural obstacles, such as the many that have obstructed the trial until now, has my government carried this process forward. I hope Your Excellency, as well as the Courts of your country, will value the vital importance of recovering that principle and that you will not allow the groundless objections of the lawyers of the accused to continue to obscure a principle that ought to be kept sound if the Governments of this Hemisphere are to have a mutual respect for each other.[38]

On August 12, Dean Rusk made his decision. Pérez Jiménez would be surrendered to be tried for peculation or malversation; for having received money or negotiable valuables, knowing of their illicit origin; and for fraud or prevarication. In a note to Ambassador Enrique Tejera París, Dean Rusk reminded the ambassador of the guarantees that had been offered. The secretary of state reiterated that Pérez Jiménez might be tried only for the crimes specified.[39]

Two lower-court cases involving Pérez Jiménez provided a last-ditch effort to avoid surrender. Illona Marita Lorenz filed a suit in Florida to force Pérez to support her and her infant daughter, and Enrique García sued to collect a fee that Pérez allegedly owed

---

[37] Enrique Tejera París to Dean Rusk, July 22, 1963, Archive 59-95, Archives of the Corte Suprema de Justicia, Caracas, Venezuela.

[38] Ibid.

[39] Dean Rusk to Enrique Tejera París, August 12, 1963, Archive 59-95. Whiteman's *Digest of International Law* (VI, 1051) states that when a treaty says that the accused may not be tried for offenses other than those for which he was surrendered, it is usually unnecessary to remind the requesting government of its obligations.

him for acting as an intermediary in a business deal.[40] Pérez fought both suits, and the cases entered the courts. Pérez Jiménez's counsel then filed a last-minute motion before the U.S. Supreme Court on August 14, asking that the extradition be postponed until the Fifth Circuit Court of Appeals in New Orleans could hear appeals from the two lower-court rulings against Pérez Jiménez. Supreme Court Justice Arthur Goldberg heard the arguments and denied the appeal on August 16. The justice noted that "The only effect of granting his application for a stay would be to preserve the jurisdiction of this court to review a procedural ruling which, however determined, could only delay but not prevent extradition. . . . At some point all litigation must end. I see no compelling reason for further delaying this one."[41]

On Saturday, August 17, Pérez Jiménez was taken from the cell where he had been for eight months and was escorted to the airport by a six-car convoy of U.S. marshals and metropolitan police. At 11:47 A.M. they arrived at an apron of Miami International Airport where a Venezuelan plane waited. The plane, double crews, guards, officials, a doctor, and a nurse had been ready for five days, at the suggestion of the U.S. State Department. Pérez's car sat at the airport for thirty-five minutes while the federal officials telephoned Washington to make sure that they should really let Pérez out of their custody.[42]

At 12:25 P.M. the former president walked a double row of thirty U.S. and Venezuelan guards to the plane, where he was told he could have any seat he wanted. Twelve Venezuelan detectives accompanied him. Pérez's daughter Margot had driven to the airport to wave good-by; the other three daughters and his wife were at home. Illona Marita Lorenz arrived at the airport too late to see him depart.[43]

Thus, all of the weapons in Pérez's apparently invincible de-

[40] *Miami Herald*, August 1, 7, 8, 14, 1963.

[41] Ibid., August 15, 16, 1963.

[42] Ibid., August 17, 1963; Memorandum for M. Aristeguieta, Mathes Papers.

[43] *Miami Herald*, August 17, 1963.

fense arsenal failed him. He could not obtain a ruling of insufficient evidence from the courts. He did not gain enough time through procedural delays to develop a strong political groundswell for him in the United States. Nor could he persuade Dean Rusk that he was being surrendered for political crimes to a political enemy. His defense failed not so much because it was insufficient or weak as because some glimmers of Camelot remained in mid-1963 to cast luster on an idealistic plea to bring presidents to trial for their abuses of power. The idealism coincided with a realistic appraisal of Betancourt as a valuable Caribbean ally in the campaign against Fidel Castro. Moreover, in the summer of 1963, Venezuela was conducting a presidential election, only the second since the overthrow of Pérez Jiménez. Acción Democrática could use the Pérez Jiménez trial as a symbol of 1958 campaign promises kept and as a reminder that citizens' grievances against the democratic government could not match those against the former dictatorship.

The puzzling question remains: Why did Pérez Jiménez not leave the United States when he saw the court decisions going against him? There is the bare possibility that he welcomed the chance to defend his regime before the Venezuelan courts and people and thus did not try to subvert the formal extradition hearings by fleeing. On the other hand, his abhorrence of political gestures, his concern for his safety in Venezuela, and his suspicions of the AD courts would hardly have encouraged him to cooperate with his enemies. It is more likely that Pérez underestimated the differences between the Eisenhower and Kennedy governments and was caught by surprise by his arrest in December, 1962. His political intuition had not been good in appreciating the changes in Venezuela that had allowed a popular, democratic movement to unseat him in 1958. In his efforts to convince the American public and politicians that dictators served U.S. interests better than democrats, he also misjudged U.S. politics in the early 1960s. Ironically, if he could have held out for another year, John Kennedy's death and the new wave of military governments in Latin America might have provided a more sympathetic environment for his arguments.

It would be slight consolation for Pérez to see that the time that had worked against him in the United States had perhaps worked for him in Venezuela by softening some of the public hostility toward him. He would have plenty of time to contemplate such quirks of fate when he returned to Venezuela in August, 1963. He would not leave the country again until August, 1968, at the conclusion of the Venezuelan government's case against him just before another election.

6

The Nonpartisan Politicians Again: Pérez Jiménez's Apologia and the Election of 1963

Pérez Jiménez returned to Venezuela to stand trial at the same time the new Venezuelan democracy was also being tried. Civilian politicians made ready for the December election, while leftists, inspired by the Cuban example, threatened that the elections would not take place. President Betancourt found his AD government under attack by revolutionaries at the same time the political coalition he had carefully nurtured with COPEI also faltered. COPEI, dissatisfied with AD's determination to press Raúl Leoni as their presidential candidate, broke away to nominate their own Rafael Caldera. Acción Democrática's woes were compounded further when one of its own former members, Raúl Ramos Giménez, chose to head up a leftist presidential ticket.[1]

The vital questions of whether elections would even be held and whether Acción Democrática could maintain its popular majority overshadowed another political phenomenon. Two presidential candidates advanced campaign themes that were vaguely reminiscent of Pérez Jiménez's New National Ideal. Germán Borregales, relatively unknown and without substantial campaign funds, could easily be dismissed, but Arturo Uslar Pietri, a respected author, teacher, and former cabinet minister, was a force to be reckoned with. Uslar had both the money and the wit to conduct a sophisticated media campaign that appealed especially to *caraqueños*, often suspicious either of AD's emphasis on rural issues or of Betancourt's unyielding persecution of young leftists. Uslar, a politi-

---

[1] The full slate of candidates with their parties was: Raúl Leoni (AD); Rafael Caldera (COPEI); Jóvito Villaba (Unión Republicana Democrática); Arturo Uslar Pietri (Independientes Pro-Frente Nacional); Wolfgang Larrazábal (Frente Democrática Popular); Raúl Ramos Giménez (Acción Democrática en Oposición); and Germán Borregales (Movimiento de Acción Nacional).

cal independent, criticized the divisiveness of political parties and called for a rapid development of industry and agribusiness in Venezuela. He also insisted that Venezuela should conduct an autonomous and sovereign foreign policy which would not interfere with other nations' rights to select the form of government that best suited them. With these issues Uslar subtly evoked the unity of the past at the same time he criticized AD's domestic and international initiatives.[2]

Less subtle efforts to revive Pérez Jiménez himself as a political contender failed. The newly formed Nationalist Authentic Party nominated him as a presidential candidate, but the former dictator was declared ineligible since he was a prisoner on trial.[3]

With the imminence of elections, Pérez Jiménez was hustled out of sight to a high-security prison in San Juan de los Morros. He had his own private courtyard apart from the general prison yard, six houses for family and friends were available close to the prison, and an apartment at the nearby military hospital had been reserved in case he should need medical attention.[4] Even with such luxury compared to his Dade County jail cell, Pérez Jiménez complained that the accommodations were inadequate for a former president. He protested that visiting hours were too short, that he should not have to conform to all prison rules since he was not a condemned criminal, and that he did not have a refrigerator, a television, or a typist to help him prepare his court statements.[5] His lawyers compared Pérez's treatment with that of Gustavo Rojas Pinilla in Colombia during a similar trial. Former president Rojas Pinilla had been permitted to live in a special residence during the court process. As a Venezuelan former president, Pérez Jiménez should receive no worse treatment. After all, "our defendant has been President of the Republic and as such he has been Com-

[2] Institute for the Comparative Study of Political Systems, *The Venezuelan Elections of December 1, 1963* vol. 2, *Candidate Biographies and Candidate and Party Platforms*, Election Analysis Series No. 2, pp. 36–46.

[3] *New York Times*, August 22, 1963.

[4] Ibid., August 17, 18, 1963; *Miami Herald*, August 18, 1963.

[5] Segunda pieza principal, p. 512, Archive 59-95, Archives of the Corte Suprema de Justicia, Caracas, Venezuela.

mander in Chief of the National Armed Forces; he is likewise General of Division of our Army and for all these reasons deserves treatment more consonant with his high rank."[6] The Supreme Court found no merit in the argument that Pérez was being dishonored but did allow some of the minor niceties that he requested.

The Supreme Court informed him upon his arrival that he was to name his defense attorneys, to study the court record to date, and to render his *declaración indagatoria* (preliminary statement) so that the *sumario,* or *prima facie* stage, of the trial might be concluded.[7] The trial, or *plenario,* might then commence.

Pérez noted that his defense would be limited by his lawyers' having to travel from Caracas, but he named Rafael Naranjo Ostty, Morris Sierralta, and Rafael Pérez Perdomo as his defense attorneys.[8] The willingness of the three to serve the former dictator suggested that the height of public hostility against the *perezjimenistas* had passed. During the earlier trials against the Seguridad Nacional, most of the lawyers were court-appointed lawyers; attorneys had hesitated to defend the *perezjimenistas* because of sincere repugnance or because of fear of popular reprisals. Nor were Pérez's lawyers without stature in Venezuelan legal circles. Nicknamed "the Old Fox," Naranjo Ostty claimed seldom to have lost a case in nearly a half-century of legal practice.

Although Naranjo Ostty thought that the Pérez Jiménez trial was at heart political, he denied that his own politics had led him to defend the former president. The old lawyer had not previously known Pérez Jiménez and feigned surprise that people should criticize him for taking the case:

This case is not only a political trial, but it is a political trial and a half, as I will demonstrate. In my firm and in those of my companions in the defense, we have defended prominent members of the Republican Democratic Union party accused as presumed authors of political crimes, and we have not been called urredistas; we have defended prominent members of the Communist party accused of political crimes and we have

[6] Ibid., p. 530.
[7] Primera pieza principal, p. 183, Archive 59-95.
[8] Ibid., pp. 196, 199.

not been called Communists and, now, because we defend General
PÉREZ JIMÉNEZ, accused as the presumed author of the *common
crime of peculation*, we are called perezjimenistas. [Italics in original][9]

"The Old Fox" could hardly have been sincerely surprised at
the criticism, but apparently he decided that the challenge of the
case would outweigh any public censure he might receive.[10] Cynics
noted that the case would also be a remarkably lucrative one.

After selecting his defense attorneys, Pérez Jiménez began to
record his opening statement. An unsworn declaration in the defendant's own words, the *declaración indagatoria* might be compared to Fidel Castro's defense after the attack on the Moncada
Barracks. Pérez Jiménez, too, hoped that history would absolve
him, and he interpreted the meaning of the proceedings against
him for the record. Loosing the bitterness that had accumulated
during the years of U.S. hearings, Pérez Jiménez began to turn his
trial for peculation into an apology for his political beliefs and
actions. His statements lauded his own government as a nationalistic and prosperous one and characterized Rómulo Betancourt's administration as one which had accomplished little of note and had
compromised national honor to obtain Pérez's extradition. Although
strong in his denunciation of the AD government, Pérez Jiménez
did not limit his invective to domestic politics. The former dictator
excoriated the U.S. government of John Kennedy specifically for
conceding his unprecedented extradition and generally for its new
policy toward Latin America.

Pérez Jiménez's declaration played on a popular theme in
Venezuela: that material gain and personal vengeance flavored
partisan politics more than purity of principle did. Thus, only
governments such as his which remained above politics could encourage the economic development that Venezuela needed.

Pérez Jiménez began by rejecting the AD assertion that his
trial was part of a regular and impartial judicial procedure. Speaking of the law under which he was charged, Pérez pointed out that

[9] Rafael Naranjo Ostty, *La verdad de un juicio trascendental*, p. 180.
[10] Interview with Rafael Naranjo Ostty, Caracas, Venezuela, February
12, 1970.

the Constitution of 1953 had repealed Article 65 of the Law against Illicit Enrichment. That law had authorized the Federal Court, later the Supreme Court, to hear accusations against the president. Even though the 1961 constitution revived the law, it should not be applied to any actions committed between 1953 and 1961. Thus, the Supreme Court did not have the jurisdiction to try him. Nor did it have the authority to delegate the jurisdiction to the judge at San Juan de los Morros, where the *sumario* was taking place. The Supreme Court might try presidents, but it could not try former presidents.[11] Pérez's argument illustrated again the logical problems which accompanied the effort to hold an arbitrary ruler responsible for unconstitutional, or illegal, actions.

Moreover, Pérez stated for the record that Venezuela's judicial system could hardly be called independent and nonpolitical. Some of the judges on the Supreme Court, elected by partisan votes in Congress, were his political enemies. It was ridiculous to expect that the AD judges would not do the bidding of the AD president: "In other words, it is deplorable that at times the Judicial Power, for example, becomes a flawless subordinate of the Executive Power; or, for example also, the Legislative Power is spectacularly trampled by the Executive Power, without provoking the chorus of objections that in this case would indubitably be justified. And most deplorable of all is that these things happen under the authority of a regime whose democratic nature has been boasted to the four winds."[12]

The collusion of Venezuelan and U.S. politicians had also violated the integrity of international law, according to Pérez Jiménez. The former president had been irregularly surrendered for crimes which did not exist in Venezuelan legislation and for crimes which he could not have committed. For example, the minister of the treasury was responsible for the treasury funds; the president could not then be charged with wrongfully appropriating treasury funds over which he had no direct official responsibility. The judge

---

[11] Declaración Indagatoria, 1 pieza principal, p. 307; 2 pieza principal, p. 440, Archive 59-95.

[12] Ibid., 1 pieza principal, p. 307.

in the United States who had issued the decision on his case had not read the court record.[13]

Politics had prevailed over principle in both Venezuela and the United States because of simple greed. The Venezuelan government had been willing to spend any amount to secure his extradition, and U.S. politicians had accepted the money in exchange for the extradition. Pérez estimated that the Venezuelan government had spent more than the thirteen million dollars that it had charged him with misappropriating. Unfortunately, Pérez lamented, the Venezuelan people would never know the exact figure spent because the comptroller general would release no records of the expenses.[14] Pérez elaborated further:

Up to now from the information that I have been able to analyze properly, there was an indubitable expenditure of seven million dollars to the North American lawyers. A sum greater than one hundred thousand dollars has also been spent to pay and compensate specified Venezuelan officials who have traveled to the United States because of this process. All these expenditures have gone out through disbursements not subject to review, disbursements which are intended for the security of the State. This is the only way to be able to spend large sums without being subject to control by State agencies which have such a function.[15]

Touching on a motif made famous in Latin America by Enrique Rodó's *Ariel*, Pérez Jiménez said that Venezuelan national honor had been damaged when money had purchased the disrespectful treatment of one of her former presidents. The Venezuelan nation should have been ashamed to have seen Pérez Jiménez unceremoniously lodged in the Dade County jail along with common criminals. The U.S. government was known for its prejudicial treatment of people of Hispanic background, but President Betancourt

[13] Ibid., 2 pieza principal, pp. 357, 466.

[14] One estimate held that Pérez Jiménez had had to spend three times as much as the Venezuelan government in the U.S. proceedings. Whether this was true or not, Pérez Jiménez should have been able to estimate the governmental expenses from knowing what his own had been. Unfortunately, his estimates could not be entirely trusted, since they included such undocumented expenses as "millions of dollars" to bribe U.S. officials. Ibid., 1 pieza principal, pp. 276, 343; 2 pieza principal, p. 419.

[15] Ibid., 2 pieza principal, p. 416.

should not have allowed his quest for vengeance to outweigh his responsibility for upholding the national honor:

Although the present government will win, the Nation will be the loser in the long run because her honor will be damaged in the honor of one of her sons, who held one of the highest ranks in the Armed Forces. In the best of cases—which can be the worst of cases—if the Government wins the suit, the Nation will have gained in a shame that will have been paid for with the price of gold. This litigation is not a moral lesson, especially if one takes into account the morals of those who have intervened in it to inspire and urge it on. This litigation is marked with hatred, and a lesson of shame cannot be a moral lesson.[16]

The U.S. officials who had abetted Betancourt in his mission of vengeance had acted not from principle, but from self-interest, Pérez Jiménez charged in his unsworn statement. Dean Acheson, that "notable merchant of influence," had simultaneously advised the U.S. president, the State Department, and the Venezuelan government, clearly a conflict of interest; nor had he reported on his income tax return all of the fees he had earned in the Pérez Jiménez case. Furthermore, the Kennedy family had held grudges against Pérez Jiménez because they had not secured business contracts with his government when he was in power; thus, Robert Kennedy's enthusiasm to extradite Pérez Jiménez was comprehensible, if not ethical. Governor Nelson Rockefeller, too, had traded an advantageous petroleum contract for promises that he would facilitate the extradition of Pérez. Even Richard Nixon had borne a grudge against Pérez Jiménez because a company in which he had an interest had failed to receive a construction contract from the Venezuelan government in the 1950s. Pérez Jiménez offered no evidence to support his charges.[17]

Widening his attack on the Calibanlike United States, Pérez Jiménez speculated on the economic motivation behind the Alliance for Progress. The alliance, Pérez stated, obeyed the typical Yankee notion that all Latin American countries were alike, had the same problems, the same idiosyncrasies, the same kinds of people, and

---

[16] Ibid., 1 pieza principal, p. 344.
[17] Ibid., pp. 297, 298, 350, 353; 2 pieza principal, pp. 416, 427.

would benefit from the same remedies. The plan clearly intended to make Latin American nations the economic colonies of the United States. What better symbol of that intent than the choice of Puerto Rican Teodoro Moscoso as administrator of the program? "And no one moderately clear-sighted could not know that the Yankee ideal is to 'puertoricanize' Latin America and finally to have twenty Free Associated States." Puerto Ricans did not have a sovereign nation, were second-class citizens in the United States, and held no status to which other Latin Americans might aspire.[18]

Unfortunately, Pérez Jiménez continued, the U.S. plan was working. Latin America was more "puertoricanized" in 1963 than it had been in 1960. No country had strengthened its monetary exchange. No country had lessened unemployment. No country had seen real per-capita income grow, although statistics sometimes distorted the truth. On the other hand, many countries had seen their real per-capita public debt rise. Many countries had seen the rise of social disturbances and the appearance of Communist sympathizers. All countries had experienced the growth of anti-Yankee sentiment. All countries had come closer to becoming true economic colonies of the United States. The former dictator lamented that Latin American leaders had not seized upon Pérez Jiménez's plan for economic development, proposed at the Panama Conference in 1956. If they had, the program might have prevented the United States from so thoroughly dominating Latin America in the name of economic development.[19]

One of the first to criticize the Alliance for Progress in these terms, Pérez Jiménez argued that U.S. economic aid increased rather than decreased Latin American economic dependency. Although Pérez had not in fact obtained economic aid from the United States when he was president, some Venezuelans might find his newfound nationalism at variance with some of his other actions in office. He had, after all, received the Legion of Merit from the U.S. government, had given U.S. entrepreneurs free rein in Venezuela, had sold new oil concessions to foreigners, and had per-

[18] Ibid., 1 pieza principal, 291.
[19] Ibid., pp. 293–295.

mitted the signing of the decidedly disadvantageous commercial treaty with the United States in 1952. Nonetheless, the thesis that economic aid increased Latin American dependency was gaining credence all over the continent, and Pérez Jiménez joined his leftist compatriots in the argument.

Having criticized the Venezuelan and U.S. politicians who negotiated his extradition, Pérez Jiménez took the opportunity afforded by his opening statement to defend his regime as a whole. He had an advantage over the Venezuelan government's prosecutors here, since the terms of the extradition specified that their case was to be limited to consideration of the common crimes of embezzlement or malversation. Pérez, however, could address the unspoken, but more consequential, issues of the merits of different forms of government. His administration, he summarized, had been one of action, of visible accomplishments, of no debts, of no more than normal corruption and concentration of power. He had spent less and had built more roads than had the AD government. He had achieved at least as much in agrarian reform, although he had operated under a different philosophy than did the AD government. Betancourt divided the land among the rural poor, an unproductive measure that had not even measurably helped the *campesinos*. Pérez Jiménez had preferred a more modern and developmentalist approach, "expropriating" land from Venezuela's greatest landlords, the desert and forest. His programs might have yielded even more results if they had not been halted in January, 1958, he added.[20]

Maladministration and mishandling of funds occurred in all administrations, and his was no worse than any other, Pérez noted. People had charged, and Betancourt had acknowledged, that corruption continued in the AD government. For example, the financial statements of the Venezuelan consulate in Miami were being examined to ascertain the validity of the charges that the consulate had mishandled the funds allotted to pay for Pérez Jiménez's extradition.[21] Moreover, Pérez had left Bs2,384 million in the public trea-

---

[20] Ibid., pp. 280–281; 2 pieza principal, p. 477.
[21] Ibid., 2 pieza principal, pp. 481–484, 455.

sury on January 23, 1958, and the nation had no external nor internal debt:[22] "This brings us to the following consideration: How can it be explained that a government made up of maladministrators, of peculators, with admittedly less income can present the Venezuelan Nation with tangible works of collective good, surpassing by at least five times the works of a so-called democratic government, the former without contracting debts and leaving in the National Treasury the cited sum?" Answering his own question, Pérez Jiménez reflected that robbers left great works and democrats, perhaps without robbing, left little. Maybe, he suggested, thieves and embezzlers benefited the nation more than self-proclaimed honest and ethical politicians.[23]

Pérez Jiménez spoke bitterly of his trial and of Betancourt's driving and unprecedented urge for revenge on his political enemy. On the topic of political vengeance, Pérez recalled a popular Mexican saying about the day of San Miguel: "Today is the day of that formidable Archangel who cast the Devil from the Heavens; if the Devil had cast out San Miguel, today would be the fiesta of the Devil."[24] Pérez elaborated on the relationship between justice and politics in Venezuela:

Persecutions against an overthrown Chief of State and the functionaries of the old regime are always for political motives, no matter how they are disguised. Can it be that law then, as Fichte said, is only the politics of force and the idealized statement of force? It is simple because the law is clear, and complicated in a country where everything is political and the judges also are politicians and the judges become ministers and legislators, and, reciprocally, the ministers and the legislators, judges; and the legislators and the judges exercise executive functions and legislate and judge and all scoff at all the virtues without being concerned for the jurisdictions of the institution to which they belong or for the credit or honor of the Republic.[25]

[22] In fact, Pérez's "surplus" reflected bills which the dictator had postponed; the governing junta paid most of them off rapidly, and to the tune of considerable criticism, in 1958. See James A. Hanson, "Cycles of Economic Growth and Structural Change Since 1950," in *Venezuela: The Democratic Experience*, ed. John D. Martz and David J. Myers, pp. 74–76.

[23] Declaración Indagatoria, 2 pieza principal, p. 381, Archive 59-95.

[24] Ibid., pp. 358–359.

[25] Ibid., p. 462.

Pérez Jiménez as a political figure was still far from rehabilitation in 1964 as he completed his *declaración indagatoria*. Nevertheless, his assessment of Venezuelan political mores and behavior was shared by a number of Venezuelans. In particular, his assertions that his extradition had compromised Venezuelan sovereignty, that political parties were self-interested and divisive, and that Venezuelan justice was highly politicized rang true in the tumultuous political climate of 1963–1964. A lawyer's efforts to nullify the extradition treaty, the 1963 election returns, and the disqualification of prejudiced Supreme Court judges in the Pérez Jiménez case partially corroborated some of former dictator's opinions.

The attempt to nullify the extradition treaty with the United States at first glance appears to be a frivolous suit brought by one who had been linked to the Pérez Jiménez dictatorship. Tito Gutiérrez Alfaro was a brother of Pérez Jiménez's minister of health, Pedro Antonio Gutiérrez Alfaro, and he filed before the Supreme Court on May 21, 1963, a petition to nullify Article 14 of Title II of the treaty. The offending clause stipulated that persons charged with peculation or malversation might be extradited. Gutiérrez argued that the crime of peculation or malversation by an official of the state was a political, not a common, crime. He traced the history of the crime in various Venezuelan penal codes and constitutions. The treaty in question had violated the Venezuelan constitution because it treated peculation like a common crime. Since treaties had to be passed into law by Congress, the Supreme Court had the authority to review the laws which enacted treaties to determine whether they conflicted with the constitution. If they did, the constitution must take precedence, and the offending treaty article must be declared null and void.[26]

The petition began before Pérez had been extradited. The decision was issued after he had been surrendered, after the election of 1963, and after the election of the new Supreme Court judges. In a split decision, the court refused to hear the case, then moot. The majority argued that the court had no competence to decide on the legality or constitutionality of an international treaty

---

[26] *Gaceta Oficial de la República de Venezuela*, May 21, 1965, pp. 1–2.

because the decision would have extraterritorial effect. Moreover, Venezuela had apparently renounced unilateral abrogation of a treaty in the preamble of the 1961 constitution, which called for cooperation among the nations of the Western Hemisphere.[27]

Two judges considered the issues raised to be serious ones and dissented from the majority ruling. José Gabriel Sarmiento Núñez and José Román Duque Sánchez objected to the decision that the court could not review the constitutionality of Venezuela's international treaties; they feared that the majority had subordinated Venezuelan sovereignty to international law. Sarmiento's twenty-three pages and Duque Sánchez's two pages of dissenting opinion indirectly took issue with Rómulo Betancourt's aggressive efforts to press the democratic governments in the Western Hemisphere to coordinate their foreign policies. Beneath the legal language lay an uneasiness with and a suspicion of Betancourt's staunch internationalism.[28] Few Venezuelans probably heard of the court case or of the dissents. It was significant, however, that two members of the judicial elite believed that some of AD's foreign initiatives compromised Venezuelan national sovereignty.

Another elite group in Venezuela apparently appreciated Tito Gutiérrez Alfaro's argument. The prestigious Venezuelan Academy of Political and Social Sciences subsequently elected the attorney to membership; the essay which supported his candidacy recapitulated his research and arguments on the authority of the Supreme Court to review international treaties.[29] Gutiérrez Alfaro, then, was a respected legal authority whose Supreme Court petition was not viewed as a frivolous gesture. Some Venezuelan legal experts have judged the Gutiérrez case to be of greater theoretical interest for an international lawyer than the extradition case itself.

The 1963 election returns further suggested that others shared Pérez Jiménez's mistrust of political parties. Although AD's Raúl Leoni won the election, the AD majority slipped badly from the

---

[27] Ibid., p. 4.

[28] Ibid., pp. 7–9, 13–16, 30–31.

[29] Tito Gutiérrez Alfaro, *La inconstitucionalidad de los tratados internacionales.*

1958 victory. Leoni won 32.8 percent of the national vote, compared to Betancourt's 49.2 percent in 1958. Some of AD's loss may have been picked up by the other major candidate, Rafael Caldera of COPEI, who won 4 percent more of the national vote than he had in 1958.[30] Acción Democrática's electoral strength was probably more affected, however, by splits in the party, by the lesser appeal of Raúl Leoni as a candidate, by some hackneyed platforms and programs, and by Betancourt's handling of the urban terrorism. More significant than AD's possible loss to COPEI or to URD's Jóvito Villaba was the increase in the percentage of Venezuelans who voted for men who might generally be termed "nonparty" candidates. In 1958, for example, only 5 percent of the voters chose a candidate who was not affiliated with one of the three major political parties; in 1963, that percentage rose to a substantial 28.1 percent of the electorate.[31]

Arturo Uslar Pietri won the greatest number of the "nonparty" votes in 1963. Coming in fourth, Uslar Pietri received 469,240 votes, or 16.1 percent of the national total.[32] Uslar's campaign was one of the few that diverged fundamentally from the program of the major political parties, and he criticized the inefficiency and divisiveness of AD in particular. He advocated a change to nonpartisan, independent government, investment in the industrial and agricultural infrastructure, a more neutral foreign policy, and amnesty for political opponents of the existing government.

Uslar had portrayed the advantages of an independent government in glowing terms:

The government would not be the weapon of one political group to gain advantage over other political groups. If an independent candidate, unattached to party positions, were to be elected, he would neither favor

30 Institute for the Comparative Study of Political Systems, *Venezuelan Elections of December 1, 1963*, vol. 3, *Final Provisional Election Returns, Presidential and Legislative, Broken Down by Region and State*, Election Analysis Series No. 2, pp. 9–11.

31 John Martz, *The Venezuelan Elections of December 1, 1963*, vol. 1, *An Analysis*, Election Analysis Series No. 2, pp. 23, 38–39, 40–42.

32 Institute for the Comparative Study of Political Systems, *Venezuelan Elections*, III, 9.

nor fight any political party. The successful independent candidate would need the support of the largest possible number of electors to work effectively in facing the grave problems which threaten the very foundations of the nation. Not only the stability of the nation's institutions, but the very possibility of future national development is endangered.

The nation does not want another program of vague doctrinaire proclamations about democracy, rights, equality or promises of vague resolutions from the independent candidate.[33]

Uslar's program for economic development, especially his proposals for agriculture, could have been lifted from some of Pérez Jiménez's speeches on the New National Ideal:

One of the factors which conditions the potentialities of Venezuela is her huge territory, with its immense resources of water, land, forest, and mineral deposits. . . . The "potential Venezuela" requires an agriculture totally developed by both traditional and new methods. With this agriculture we should be able to produce great quantities of food and fiber at low prices; thus the cost of living would not go up but we should also be able to export. Warehouses, highways, silos, and refrigerators will have to be provided to ensure a good and sure distribution of agriculture products. Rapid and direct communications throughout the country must be established. Even today half of Venezuela is still land for conquest: the whole expanse of land surrounding the Orinoco River—which we call the Guayanas and which politically is the Amazonas and the state of Bolívar—is unconquered territory which must be incorporated, civilized, and used.[34]

Uslar proposed a simple and neutral foreign policy:

A policy of sovereignty does not have to be one of hostility or fear, much less one of isolation in international relations. Venezuela should adopt a policy of understanding with the rest of Latin America. She should seek closer affinity with the Caribbean nations and with continental America for the advance of their common interests. She should not agree to pacts or bargains that imply the delegation or diminution of her own faculties. Venezuela must follow the policy of her own interests and not that of the interests of other nations. The preservation of her supreme right of decision is fundamental. She must not be led into a contradiction of her traditional principles of peace, non-intervention, and self-determination.

[33] Ibid., II, 36.
[34] Ibid., p. 37.

All communities have the right to advance and defend their independence and to choose the form of government which suits them best,
without foreign interference or coercion.[35]

Finally, Uslar spoke out on the issues of politicized justice as
he saw it. The issue was a personal one to him, for he had been
tried for peculation by the AD government in 1946–1947. In 1963
he sought to appeal both to the young leftists who were being imprisoned by Betancourt's government and to the *perezjimenistas*.
A system of justice which divided the country into persecutors and
persecuted should be ended. A real democracy would have neither
political prisoners nor exiles; nor should public employees be dismissed because of their political party affiliations. Public employment should be awarded solely on the basis of merit.[36]

Although Uslar had not served the Pérez Jiménez government,
he indicated that his call for political amnesty should extend even
to Pérez Jiménez. After the December elections, Congress voted
for the judges who would sit on the Supreme Court to hear the
charges against Pérez Jiménez. Uslar led his parliamentary delegation to abstain from the voting as a protest against the trial.[37]

The antiparty sentiments appeared to appeal principally to
residents of Caracas and the surrounding area. The heaviest vote
for Uslar in 1963 came from Caracas, where he received 39.9 percent of the total Federal District vote. Conversely, AD received
only 13.65 percent of the Caracas vote, running behind both Uslar
Pietri and Wolfgang Larrazábal (20.5 percent).[38] In the interior,
with the metropolitan vote excluded, Raúl Leoni of AD received
38.9 percent of the vote to Uslar Pietri's 8.9 percent.[39] The so-called
Caracas Question, in which the major parties received fewer votes
in Caracas than they did nationwide, began to appear in the elec-

---

[35] Ibid., p. 45.

[36] Ibid., pp. 38, 39.

[37] Acta del Congreso, 2 pieza principal, pp. 593–594, Archive 59-95.

[38] Institute for the Comparative Study of Political Systems, *Venezuelan
Elections*, III, 9.

[39] The metropolitan vote here includes that from the states of Aragua
and Miranda as well as the Federal District; ibid., p. 25.

tion of 1946 but became much more extreme in the 1958 and 1963 elections.[40]

Several factors may explain the "Caracas Question" in general and Uslar's Caracas vote in particular. First, Uslar Pietri, as a member of the sophisticated urban elite, clearly appealed to urban instead of rural voters, and he exploited that appeal through a well-planned media campaign.[41] No political leader had come from the Caracas elite since Laureano Vallenilla Lanz, Hijo, had called on the Venezuelan mandarins to govern the nation.

Second, many *caraqueños* were concerned that urban problems were worse than they had been in 1958. The city's rapid growth from 414,802 inhabitants in 1941 to 1,501,802 in 1961 and from 10.8 percent to 19.9 percent of the national population during the same timespan strained urban services.[42] Housing, public transportation, and public utilities such as water and electricity became increasingly inadequate. Daily traffic jams frustrated the majority of *caraqueños*, and terrorism in the early 1960s made the urban environment even more insecure. President Betancourt made a bad situation worse by stubbornly refusing to allocate money to the capital city for improvement of services; he reasoned that the city had prospered at the expense of the countryside during the Pérez Jiménez years, and one way to redistribute Venezuelan wealth was to reverse the spending patterns of the 1950s. Some city planners hoped that a city full of discomforts would discourage the flood of rural migrants to the capital.[43] Small wonder that *caraqueños* began nostalgically to recall Pérez Jiménez's benevolence to the city, displayed in freeways in the city and to the beach, modern apartments and government buildings, a new racetrack, a new university, and even a contract to begin construction on a metropolitan subway system.

[40] Martz, *Venezuelan Elections*, p. 40; Boris Bunimov Parra, "Las fluctuaciones electorales en la ciudad de Caracas," in *Estudio de Caracas*, vol. VIII, part 1, *Gobierno y política*, pp. 719–742.

[41] Martz, *Venezuelan Elections*, p. 32.

[42] David J. Myers, "Policy Making and Capital City Resource Allocation: The Case of Caracas," in *Venezuela: The Democratic Experience*, ed. John D. Martz and David J. Myers, p. 284.

[43] Ibid., pp. 286, 299.

Finally, the metropolitan core of Venezuela probably held an unrepresentative concentration of people who most naturally would have opposed political parties, or at least AD. Entrepreneurs had willingly joined in the revolt against Pérez Jiménez but had retained a suspicion of AD's socially progressive programs. They feared that urban terrorism and disorder, the cause of which they laid at AD's door, would scare away foreign investment and curtail Venezuela's economic progress. Some of the growing middle classes would also have been concerned about the violence, about the arbitrary arrests and suspension of constitutional guarantees, and about the health of the economy that provided them with their jobs. Uslar appealed to middle-class urbanites who were not members of AD or Copei when he promised that government jobs should be awarded on merit rather than on party affiliation. Moreover, many of the new arrivals to the middle class might have been anxious about their new status in a period of rapid change and might well have vented their frustration on the party in power. Middle sectors in Latin America have also been said frequently to identify with reference groups whose status is clearly superior to their own. Uslar's elite status would have attracted the socially insecure more than Raúl Leoni's middle-class origins. Even the lowest ranks of Caracas society, the thousands of unemployed and underemployed slum dwellers, might have seen cause to vote against the AD candidate. Their life chances had not measurably improved under the democratic government. It is difficult, however, to see what appeal Uslar's platform would have had for them, and their votes may well have gone to another antiparty candidate like Wolfgang Larrazábal. On the other hand, there is some evidence of a preference for authoritarianism among the Venezuelan poor, so Uslar Pietri may have picked up some of the antiparty vote in the barrios.[44]

In sum, a significant number of people in Caracas believed

[44] Martz, *Venezuelan Elections*, p. 29; Institute for the Comparative Study of Political Systems, *Venezuelan Elections*, II, 39; Enrique Baloyra and John D. Martz, *Political Attitudes in Venezuela: Societal Cleavages and Political Opinion*, pp. 62–64. See Talton Ray, *The Politics of the Barrios of Venezuela*, for a discussion of the impact of partisan activities in the barrios.

that political parties, especially AD, fomented dissension in the Venezuelan body politic. Additionally, some groups thought that the governing party was particularly damaging to their interests.

Following the election of 1963, the effort to select judges to hear Pérez Jiménez's case before the Supreme Court began. The difficulty in finding unprejudiced judges who were willing to participate in the trial probably further fed the minority's belief that AD justice was politicized. The 1961 constitution had divided the Supreme Court into three tribunals: the Political-Administrative Tribunal; the Tribunal of Civil, Mercantile, and Labor Abrogation; and the Tribunal of Penal Abrogation. Each tribunal had five judges elected by Congress in joint session to serve for nine-year terms. Congress also chose alternate judges (*suplentes*) for each chamber. When the court heard a case against a Venezuelan president, the three chambers met jointly, and an absolute majority of the fifteen magistrates was required for conviction. After the installation of the new Congress, new judges were elected to the Supreme Court on April 2, 1964.[45] Shortly after being elected to the court, some of the judges began to disqualify themselves from hearing the Pérez Jiménez case.

Three judges voluntarily asked to be excused from the case. Saul Ron Troconis and Miguel Landáez explained that they had already issued an opinion on the case. As members of Congress, the two had approved the transitory dispositions of the new constitution; the twentieth disposition had confiscated Pérez Jiménez's Venezuelan property. Troconis and Landáez considered that that clause, based on decree twenty-eight of February, 1958, had punished Pérez Jiménez for the same crimes which the current trial would consider. Dr. Ignacio Luis Arcaya disqualified himself because the Code of Criminal Procedure precluded an enemy of the accused from hearing the case. Dr. Arcaya explained that his hatred of Pérez Jiménez was public knowledge because of the persecution he had suffered from December, 1952, until January, 1958.[46]

---

[45] After the election, AD claimed 21 of 45 senators and 64 of 177 deputies, so they were unable to block the election of judicial candidates from other parties, even if they had wanted to.

[46] Acta del Congreso, 2 pieza principal, pp. 635, 636, Archive 59-95.

Pérez Jiménez, through his lawyers and the press, called for other judges to resign from the case. On September 17, 1964, the president of the court, José Manuel Padilla, excused himself from the case after a newspaper campaign had accused him of a conflict of interest. One of his relatives, Dr. Ramón Pinto Salvatierra, had, as president of the National Agrarian Institute, sold the property named El Deleite to Fortunato Herrera through a third person. Dr. Padilla suspected that some underhanded maneuvers had forced the disclosure, but he admitted that it was true.[47]

On September 24, 1964, Pérez Jiménez wrote to the Supreme Court to exhort four other judges to be honorable enough to admit their animosity toward him. Dr. Hugo Ardila Bustamante, as a member of the AD hierarchy, could not be impartial, Pérez charged. He had publicly stated that Pérez Jiménez was responsible for the crimes charged against an SN agent. Other AD members, Jonas Barrios, Carlos Ascanio Jiménez, and Rafael Rodríquez Méndez, should also withdraw because they were political enemies of Pérez Jiménez and claimed to have suffered under the Pérez government. The four judges ignored Pérez's charges except to request that the slurs against their honor be struck from the court record. The acting president of the court complied with their request.[48]

The search for alternate judges took about six months. Of the *suplentes* invited to join the court for the case, eleven refused. Each judge who declined gave an apparently credible reason, but one is left to wonder whether, like Arturo Usler Pietri, they disapproved of the judicial action and wished to have nothing to do with it. Of the judges who refused, one pleaded poor health, and four said they were too busy to give the case the time it would require. Two others reported that they could not be impartial in a case against Pérez Jiménez and they had publicly expressed an opinion on the case.[49] Three men disqualified themselves because

[47] Despacho, June 23, 1964, 2 pieza principal, pp. 678–679; Despacho, September 17, 1964, 2 pieza principal, p. 758, Archive 59-95.

[48] Despacho, September 25, 1964, 2 pieza principal, pp. 758-759, Archive 59-95.

[49] Luis Crespo Flagel—poor health; Federico Cisneros Bertorelli, Alejandro Urbaneja Achelpohl, Reinaldo Rodríguez Navarro, Tomás Polanco—too

they had acted on the case at an earlier stage: Dr. José A. López Borges had been a coordinator between the attorney general's office and the Investigating Committee against Illicit Enrichment; Dr. René De Sola had been the minister of foreign relations in the provisional government that had initiated the case; and Dr. Orlando Tovar had been associate legal advisor and director of the secretariat of the governing junta in 1958. Moreover, as a congressional deputy from the Federal District from 1958 to 1964, he had commented on the former president's guilt. One magistrate, Dr. Rafael Clemente Arráiz, accepted in July but begged to be excused in October when he was offered a judgeship in Miranda State and the Federal District.[50]

Not until December, 1964, was the Supreme Court ready to open the trial of Pérez Jiménez. The wheels of justice moved slowly in democratic Venezuela, but they did move.

Venezuelan democracy, then, in 1963–1964 survived a severe testing. The crisis could hardly be said to be over, however, as Raúl Leoni assumed the presidency with the narrowest of electoral majorities. Guerrilla activity slacked off somewhat immediately following the election but subsequently increased again. Also, a grave political problem was the realization that a significant number of people, principally in Caracas, continued to be hostile to the two major political parties and preferred what they defined as "independent" candidates.

Pérez Jiménez's trial had had a low priority during the months

---

busy; Jesús Diez and José Enrique Machado—could not be impartial. See 2 pieza principal, pp. 645–795, Archive 59-95, for the letters from the judges who refused to hear the case.

[50] López Borges to Supreme Court, July 1, 1964, 2 pieza principal, p. 647; De Sola to Supreme Court, July 11, 1964, 2 pieza principal, p. 660; Tovar to Supreme Court, October 22, 1964, 2 pieza principal, p. 795, Archive 59-95. In December, 1964, the regular magistrates who served on the case were Hugo Ardila Bustamente, Rafael Rodríguez Méndez, José Gabriel Sarmiento Núñez, Federico Meleiro, José Agustín Méndez, Carlos Ascanio Jiménez, Pedro Espinoza Viloria, Jonas Barrios E., J. R. Duque Sánchez, and Carlos Trejo Padilla. The four alternates were Luis Torrealba Narváez, César Tinoco Richter, José Jacinto Faria De Lima, and Francisco Meaño. Carlos Acedo Toro was a regular magistrate but did not attend the first hearing.

that directly preceded and followed the election. Left to himself in confinement, Pérez prepared his opening court statement and attacked the prejudice of his judges. His *declaración indagatoria*, a pastiche of attacks on AD and apologies for his own administrative achievements, expressed his views of what was normal and regular behavior for a political leader. Refusing to limit his statements to a consideration of the common crimes with which he was charged, Pérez played on a traditional theme in Venezuelan politics: that political parties set neighbor against neighbor and threatened Venezuelan national harmony and economic development. Many of the critics of Acción Democrática voiced the same opinions that Pérez Jiménez did. It remained to be seen whether Pérez or any other independent could benefit from a political movement founded on the rejection of partisanship.

7

The Supreme Court Trial of Pérez Jiménez: An Uncommon Proceeding

The extradition order which authorized Pérez Jiménez's surrender stipulated that he could only be tried for actions which the U.S. magistrate considered common crimes: peculation, malversation, and related felonies. Judge William Whitehurst's decision, which characterized all the crimes against persons as political and all financial crimes as common, did not, however, resolve the perplexing dilemma for the Venezuelan courts and lawyers. If Pérez Jiménez were only an ordinary citizen indicted for embezzlement, he would not be appearing before the Supreme Court. On the other hand, if he was accused of political crimes, he would not have been extradited. Unfortunately too for those who wished to make an example of Pérez Jiménez's actions, the common crime of embezzlement was less serious than the political one of mismanagement of the nation's fiscal affairs. Thus, the Venezuelan judicial proceedings suffered from an unavoidable ambiguity.

Other democracies had also grappled with the problem of how to hold an executive accountable for his actions in office. One of the founding fathers of the U.S. Constitution, Alexander Hamilton, believed that impeachment was intended to apply to the abuse of a public trust, or a political crime. When President Andrew Johnson was impeached by the House of Representatives in 1868 and absolved by a close vote in the Senate, it was for "high crimes and misdemeanors in office." His crime, apparently political, had been to dismiss Secretary of War Edwin Stanton against the wishes of Congress. The U.S. House of Representatives appeared to agree with Alexander Hamilton, while the majority of the Senate took the opposing view that impeachable crimes should be statutory ones. The argument was renewed in 1974 when the House Judiciary

Committee conducted hearings to determine whether President Richard M. Nixon had committed impeachable crimes. Although Nixon's resignation in August, 1974, evaded a clear resolution of the question, some congressmen had argued that Nixon might be impeached for his abuse of the public trust, while others contended that he had first to be judged guilty of statutory crimes.[1] Both Pérez Jiménez's peculation and Nixon's obstruction of justice had at the very least been related to the larger accusation of administrative irresponsibility and immorality.

Former president Pérez Jiménez could strike no bargains to avoid his trial, so the Venezuelan Supreme Court finally had to reach a decision on the nature and the seriousness of Pérez's crimes. It would be a leisurely process. Pérez Jiménez's *declaración indagatoria* and the selection of the Supreme Court judges had already consumed sixteen months by December, 1964; another two years would pass before the court ordered verification of the evidence in November, 1966. Pérez Jiménez accused the magistrates of delaying the case in 1964 because officials in the U.S. Departments of State and Justice feared that Pérez Jiménez's sentence might have repercussions on the U.S. elections. Pérez's attorneys subsequently charged that the AD government purposely avoided a quick trial so that they might keep Pérez in jail for a longer period of time, regardless of the sentence to come.[2] Whatever the reason, Pérez remained in jail, and the trial continued until August, 1968, just as another presidential election campaign was in full swing.

From the first hearing in December, 1964, the court set aside Tuesday and Thursday mornings to consider the case. Pérez had been moved from the jail in San Juan de los Morros to the public jail in Caracas at the end of May so that he could more easily attend the Supreme Court hearings.[3] Two prosecuting attorneys conducted the government's case: Antonio José Lozada and José Díaz

---

[1] John M. Blum et al, *The National Experience*, II, 367, 811–813.

[2] Visita, September 25, 1964, 3 pieza principal, pp. 763–764; Señalamiento no. 6, November 17, 1964, 3 pieza principal, p. 39, Archive 59-95, Archives of the Corte Suprema de Justicia, Caracas, Venezuela.

[3] Visita, September 25, 1964, 3 pieza principal, pp. 763–764, Archive 59-95.

Andara. Lozada, as the solicitor general (*fiscal general*) and head of the Public Ministry, was the chief prosecutor, and he appointed Díaz Andara as special prosecutor before the Supreme Court to represent the Public Ministry as a defender of the constitution and the rights of the state. Lozada had been elected by Congress at the same time the court's magistrates had been chosen. The attorney general, defined as the representative of the executive by the 1961 constitution, had surrendered the role of chief prosecutor of Pérez Jiménez to the solicitor general. The dual prosecution before the Supreme Court, confusing at times, was protested by the defense but continued throughout the trial. Two sets of accusations and two sets of arguments were employed, although they differed little in content or emphasis. It might be noted that few common criminals merit special prosecutors whose major responsibility is to ensure the defense of the constitution.

The opening statements of the prosecutors repeated in large part the charges and summaries of evidence from the U.S. hearings. Indeed, the U.S. extradition itself became a bit of new evidence, as the prosecution asserted that Pérez's crimes were common because the United States would not have surrendered him for political crimes. The solicitor general characterized Pérez Jiménez's crimes as continuous while he was in office and asked for a maximum penalty of thirteen years and four months in the penitentiary.[4]

Although the U.S. contribution to the case was noted, the arguments acquired a slightly different tone in Venezuela. It was now necessary for the prosecution to establish that malversation or peculation existed in the Venezuelan penal code, that Pérez Jiménez's actions amounted to those crimes, and that the crimes were not political ones in Venezuela. It was no easier in Venezuela to establish the illicit means by which Pérez had enriched himself than it had been in the United States. Lozada sought a liberal interpretation of the Venezuelan statutes when he contended that the legal definition of "to peculate" was "to steal [*substraer*] money from the public administration." The verb *substraer*, the prosecutor argued,

[4] Escrito de cargos de Fiscal General, March 18, 1965, 3 pieza principal, pp. 73–75, 110, Archive 59-95.

should be seen in its generic sense to cover direct withdrawal of funds or their procurement through fraud and artifice. Peculation (*peculado*) and embezzlement (*malversación*) were synonymous, and although they were given distinct names in some countries, the meaning remained the theft, withdrawal, diversion, appropriation, or fraudulent robbery of funds belonging to the state. Lozada concluded that Pérez Jiménez had robbed the national treasury because the nation had paid the sums from which his commissions, or bribes, had come.[5]

Solicitor General Lozada sometimes referred to Pérez's crimes as though they were political ones, although he continued to insist that they were common. For example, he quoted a legal expert who had held that peculation was an offense against the public faith because it had compromised administrative morality more than it did the material wealth of the nation.[6] Characterized thus, peculation appears to be an abuse of public trust, a political offense. On the other hand, Lozada argued persuasively that a crime committed for personal benefit was a common and statutory one, no matter who executed it. Pérez Jiménez's motives, Lozada continued, had not been political: "The economic activities of Pérez Jiménez and his accomplices until 1958 show that he executed his unlawful operations to satisfy his initial resolution to accumulate wealth at the expense of the Public Treasury, since with the violation of different penal provisions on various dates, the accused only wanted to take the Nation's wealth fraudulently. . . ."[7]

Díaz Andara's court statement also reflected the ambiguity of having to accuse a political figure of a common crime. Díaz Andara traced the long history of administrative peculation in Venezuela and the shorter history of the efforts to check such fiscal irresponsibility. Using an image popular with the prosecution, Díaz Andara compared Pérez Jiménez's fortune to that amassed in the *Thousand and One Nights* of Arabian mythology or by medieval alchemists. No rational explanation had been put forward to account for those

[5] Ibid., pp. 97, 101–105.
[6] Ibid., p. 110.
[7] Ibid., pp. 93–94.

fantastic riches, either. Turning to world history, Díaz saw the same miracle accomplished by the Florentine Medicis and contemporary Latin American heads of state. Simón Bolívar had set a good example for Latin America, regrettably not often followed. The historian Vicente Lecuna had recorded that Bolívar had had four million pesos in 1804; most of that sum had disappeared by the end of the Wars for Independence. At one point, Bolívar had refused to participate in a speculative venture with Francisco de Paula Santander because he believed that a political leader should not use his influence to increase his own wealth. In Lima on January 12, 1825, Bolívar had decreed the death penalty for embezzlers of public funds.[8]

Malversación and its most serious form, peculation, had long existed and had been punished severely in other countries, Díaz Andara continued. Unfortunately, in Venezuela public reaction had not been strong enough against such malefactors: "Among Venezuelans it is a common and current thing to see those spectacular fortunes among functionaries of high and low rank appear overnight, at the cost of the national wealth and even more lamentable, instead of evincing a healthy and redeeming reaction in favor of administrative honesty, today people follow the Spanish proverb which says 'Who steals from the public robs no one.'"[9]

The defense also employed many of the same arguments that had been used in the extradition hearings or in Pérez Jiménez's *declaración indagatoria.* Since they continued to charge that the extradition had been illegal, their defense attacked the U.S. courts and procedures. Thus, for both the prosecution and the defense, the U.S. participation in the trial still bore significance.

Naranjo Ostty and the other defense attorneys also argued that the extradition order was being violated because Pérez was not being tried for the same crimes for which he had been surrendered. The United States had surrendered the former president for embezzlement or malversation, for receiving money or negotiable

[8] Escrito de cargos de Fiscal del Ministerio Publico, March 25, 1965, 3 pieza principal, pp. 5, 12, Archive 59-95.

[9] Ibid., p. 293. Peculation consisted of the theft of state funds by one who had custody over the administration of the funds. See Appendix D.

valuables with knowledge of their illicit origin, and for fraud or breach of trust. The Venezuelan government had added extortion, corruption of officials, and infraction of the duties of public functionaries to the list of charges; these crimes did not appear in the extradition treaty or in the U.S. secretary of state's certification for extradition.[10]

The defense, rather naturally, was less enamored of the long history of peculation in Venezuela than it was with the history of political persecution. Persecution of former presidents and confiscation of their property without legal evidence or formal trials had been prevalent in Venezuela. The greatest crime that a Venezuelan could commit, the defense commented, was to fall from power: "Our history, as we see it, says that the only ones brought to trial are the 'fallen,' the 'overthrown,' the 'overpowered.' Also we see that many of the 'fallen' rise again and pass from 'condemned' to be seen as heroes. The law of vengeance grows and turns with more impetus against the one who uses it. The insults and diatribes against Napoleon during the hundred days lasted just that long: one hundred days. Because, on returning to Paris, he was again the great Emperor, Napoleon I, the winner of great battles and the genius of Europe."[11]

The nineteenth and twentieth centuries of Venezuelan history were full of examples of Venezuelan presidents who had persecuted their predecessors, Naranjo related. The only nineteenth-century president who had been above such vengeance had been Juan Falcón, who came to power in 1863. Other presidents had accused the fallen leaders of instigating revolution and treason and had applied penalties which ranged from exile to confiscation of property to death. The trend had continued into the twentieth century. Juan Vicente Gómez had considered the extradition of Cipriano Castro from the United States in 1909 for abuse of power. Upon Gómez's death in 1935, Eleazar López Contreras allowed Congress

[10] Señalamiento no. 2, October 20, 1964, 2 pieza principal, pp. 782–784, Archive 59-95.
[11] Contestación a los cargos, April 8, 1965, 3 pieza principal, p. 262, Archive 59-95.

to confiscate the former president's property. The AD government in 1946–1947 had conducted trials which, with slight show of evidence, had decreed the confiscation of the property of López Contreras and Isaías Medina Angarita. Obviously, the AD indictment of Pérez Jiménez was part of the history of reprisals against the powerless, not a regular judicial process. Continuing, Naranjo Ostty said, "One cannot, on the pretext that someone has supposedly violated the law, punish that person with a violation of the law." The prosecution was not even considering the defendant innocent until proven guilty; in fact, the Law against Illicit Enrichment assumed the guilt of the accused and required him to prove his innocence.[12]

The defense objected to the prosecution's cavalier use of evidence. The prosecutor Díaz Andara had argued that since Pérez Jiménez could only have accumulated his vast fortune through illicit use of his official influence, specific evidence need not be provided.[13] Not so in a court of law, countered Naranjo Ostty. The court still had the responsibility to consider the specifics of the case and could not properly assume Pérez's guilt on the basis of hearsay evidence. The only difference between Pérez Jiménez's case and those cited from the nineteenth and twentieth centuries, the defense alleged, was that the Venezuelan government had taken their charges before foreign courts. In short, a foreign nation had helped Venezuelan leaders carry out an act of political vengeance.[14]

Having summed up its case in an opening statement, the defense asked that the case be dismissed because the Supreme Court had no jurisdiction over crimes of an ordinary citizen like a former president. The trial was a political one, it was not based on specific evidence necessary to convict on the crimes charged, and, finally, it placed Pérez Jiménez in double jeopardy. The Supreme Court

[12] Ibid., pp. 295–296, 321–334.

[13] Escrito de cargos de Fiscal del Ministerio Publico, March 25, 1965, 3 pieza principal, p. 251, Archive 59-95.

[14] Contestación a los cargos, April 8, 1965, 3 pieza principal, pp. 295–296, Archive 59-95.

would consider the same criminal actions that the governing junta had in 1958 when it had confiscated Pérez's property.[15]

The Supreme Court responded to the plea to dismiss the case on August 11, 1966. The majority found no merit in any of the defense pleas. They ruled that the Supreme Court did have the competence to hear a case against a former president when the crimes had been committed during his term of office. The prosecution did not have to supply exact names, dates, and places for the crimes charged; such citations had the purpose of determining which court had territorial jurisdiction but had no relevance before the Supreme Court, which had jurisdiction throughout the nation. Earlier confiscatory actions taken against Pérez Jiménez had been legislative or executive and did not preclude a trial because no concrete crime had been imputed to Pérez Jiménez in the earlier actions. Thus, the majority persisted in the ambivalent argument that Pérez was being charged with common crimes, but normal judicial procedure might be waived because of the high rank he had previously enjoyed.[16]

Three magistrates wrote dissenting opinions. José Román Duque Sánchez, Francisco Meaño, and Marco-Antonio Quintero Saluzzo questioned the majority's arguments. As in the decision involving the constitutionality of the extradition treaty, Duque Sánchez's opinion was brief. The court could not hear a case against a former president; the competence to hear cases against presidents and high officials had been granted the court not because of the court's hierarchical importance, but because of the rank of the functionaries indictable before it. Therefore, the competence did not extend to former presidents, who were no longer important officials. The president and high government officials must be subject to special trials or hearings because of the functions with which they were entrusted. To try a former president in regular courts, however, did not threaten the stability of the state. He should be

15 Despacho, November 16, 1965, 1 pieza de la incidencia, p. 1, Archive 59-95.
16 Sentencia, August 11, 1966, 3 pieza de la incidencia, pp. 70–71, 90–92, 103–104, 123–127, Archive 59-95.

judged by his natural judges, Duque Sánchez thought; Pérez Jiménez's case should be sent to a competent lower court. To recognize the incompetence of the Supreme Court to hear the case did not nullify the whole judicial process, as the defense had pleaded. The Supreme Court had not usurped any functions and could simply declare itself without jurisdiction and pass the record on to the competent court.[17]

Marco-Antonio Quintero Saluzzo dissented on other grounds. He thought that the confiscation of Pérez Jiménez's property by the constitution and the junta indeed did amount to a trial for the same deeds that the former president was being charged with before the court. It would be illogical to believe that the Constituent Assembly had penalized Pérez Jiménez without considering him guilty of the crimes imputed in decree twenty-eight. The Supreme Court had earlier allowed two magistrates to withdraw from the hearings on the grounds that they had already given a decision on the same case when they signed the constitution, which had confiscated Pérez Jiménez's property. The Supreme Court, therefore, logically should declare valid the defense plea that Pérez Jiménez had already been condemned for these crimes. Pérez Jiménez should go free.[18]

Shortly after the majority decision had been handed down, Marco-Antonio Quintero Saluzzo withdrew from the court. The magistrate said that his recent dissent had stated that Pérez Jiménez should be freed. Since he had spoken on the substance of the case, any opinion that he would give in the definitive sentence necessarily would be repetitious. On these grounds, the Code of Criminal Procedure required that he disqualify himself.[19] Once more the search for an alternate magistrate began. Seven judges refused to hear the case; finally José Araujo Ortega accepted the

[17] Sentencia, Voto salvado de Dr. José Román Duque Sánchez, 3 pieza de la incidencia, pp. 15, 17–22, Archive 59-95.

[18] Sentencia, Voto salvado de Dr. Marco-Antonio Quintero Saluzzo, 3 pieza de la incidencia, pp. 6–7, 15, Archive 59-95.

[19] Escrito, September 20, 1966, 3 pieza de la incidencia, Archive 59-95.

court seat.[20] Quintero Saluzzo had withdrawn on September 20, 1966; José Araujo Ortega replaced him on November 9, 1966.

The defense attorneys on October 13 again protested the delays in the case and requested that hearings be held daily instead of twice a week and that no halts be called to find new magistrates when one withdrew.[21]

Solicitor General Antonio José Lozada laid the delays at Pérez Jiménez's door. After all, Pérez had taken six months to prepare his *declaración indagatoria,* and he had been the one who had tried to disqualify prejudiced judges. His court statements were too long, and his requests to dismiss the case also took up more time. The court should exercise its privilege to set hearings as often as it wished and should reject the defense petition.[22] The court did so.

After it was determined that the Supreme Court did have jurisdiction in the case, the magistrates turned to a consideration of the evidence. The Tribunal of Substantiation ruled on the admissibility of evidence which the prosecution and the defense wanted to introduce, and various subordinate courts examined the admissible evidence for validity. Little of note was added to the evidence summarized in the U.S. hearings; there were a few more details, and there was a difference in emphasis, but there was no wholesale effort to reconstruct the case. In fact, in several instances, the prosecution's case was weaker than it had been in Miami. One valuable piece of documentation had disappeared from the state archives, and several witnesses changed their earlier testimony or alleged that AD had forced it from them.

The case of the purloined letter was most embarrassing to the government. The letter in question was that of October 24, 1958, which Pérez Jiménez had written from Miami to Consul Diógenes

[20] José Araujo Ortega to Supreme Court, November 3, 1966, 3 pieza principal, Archive 59-95. Five judges gave virtually the same reasons for declining that they had given earlier; they were Alejandro Urbaneja Achelpohl, Jesús Diez, René De Sola, Reinaldo Rodríguez Navarro, and Luis Crespo Flegal. César Naranjo Ostty declined because his father was one of the defense attorneys. Gabriel Parada Docovich gave no reason for his refusal.

[21] Escrito, October 13, 1966, 3 pieza principal, pp. 2–6, Archive 59-95.

[22] Despacho, November 9, 1966, 3 pieza principal, pp. 4–7, Archive 59-95.

Peña to acknowledge the ownership of the suitcase which contained the documents verifying much of his wealth. The letter had been of key importance since it established Pérez Jiménez's ownership of the suitcase and documents. In October, 1963, after Pérez had been extradited, it was discovered that the original of the letter had disappeared from the official archives. An investigation began on October 28, 1963, and concluded that the document had disappeared from the archive of the Ministry of Foreign Relations after November, 1959. The solicitor general concluded the investigation on March 5, 1964, although Díaz Andara told the Supreme Court that he thought the investigation should be continued in an attempt to determine responsibility for the theft or loss of the letter. Most of the witnesses who had seen the original letter testified that the existing photostatic copy was a true and faithful one, so the prosecution continued to use the document, although over the protest of the defense.[23]

It appeared in 1967 that some witnesses were less eager to aid the AD case than they had been in 1959. The Issa family, for example, changed the emphasis of their testimony. As they had testified earlier (see chapter 4), David Elías Issa Espinoza and his father had sold land to Pérez Jiménez's intermediary, Fortunato Herrera, who had subsequently sold the land to the government at a greatly inflated price.. The Issas first claimed that official pressure had been brought to bear on them to sell the land at the lower price. Under cross-examination, David Elías Issa changed his story and denied that he had been threatened by Fortunato Herrera. When he had testified that he had been intimidated, he had given his own subjective analysis of the political situation. When asked whether he had been coerced by the Technical Judicial Police in 1959, he replied:

I don't know if there was an intentional coercion, but when we went to testify to the Technical Judicial Police, the political situation in Venezuela, which was a situation of change from one system of government to another, was effervescent, so when a person, or at least when we, went

[23] Escrito de cargos de Fiscal del Ministerio Publico, 3 pieza principal, pp. 72–77, Archive 59-95.

to testify, especially if the fact is taken into account of spending many hours in the headquarters of the Technical Judicial Police, or rather in the outer offices before going to make the statement, we were a little terrified; besides, I should observe that in spite of their courteous treatment of me, there were some responses that were insinuated.[24]

In short, without really changing the content of the testimony, Issa deemphasized Pérez Jiménez's relations to Herrera in the first case and implied, without making any charges, that his statement in 1959 had not been rendered entirely freely. Elías Issa Chejin, David's father, still insisted that Fortunato Herrera was Pérez Jiménez's right-hand man but denied that Pérez Jiménez had had anything to do with the land transaction. He added that he had not been dissatisfied with the selling price, since he had bought the land for two bolivares per square meter and had sold it for thirty bolivares per square meter.[25]

Beltran Cecil Blechinberg Gordon, who had earlier testified that Pérez Jiménez had received commissions on some Vickers-Armstrong contracts, refused to ratify his previous statements because "they were forced from me by a lawyer who said he was from the attorney general's office and by five persons." The prosecution promptly requested an investigation of his earlier statements.[26] Other witnesses changed testimony only in minor, and unimportant, details. The defense attorneys occasionally challenged the reliability or the identity of a witness or cited his animosity for Pérez Jiménez, but no major revelations came from the other cross-examinations.

The court did not permit the defense to offer some of the evidence that it wished to. For example, the attorneys were not allowed to examine documents in the Ministries of the Interior, Foreign Relations, and Justice to determine how much the nation had spent on Pérez Jiménez's extradition. They could not force the prosecution to produce documents to show that Pérez had directly ordered his ministers to grant a number of cited contracts. They

[24] José Agustín Catalá, ed., *Proceso a un ex-Dictador*, II, 262.
[25] Ibid., p. 276.
[26] Ibid., pp. 284, 290.

could not search the archives of the Ministry of Defense to discover reports of technical commissions in regard to acquisitions of defense material referred to in the indictment. Nor could the defense offer evidence to show that Presidents Rómulo Betancourt and Raúl Leoni also employed state workmen on their private estates.[27] The court thus ruled that three points of the defense were irrelevant to the case: the cost of the extradition in the United States, the charge that Pérez Jiménez's ministers had executed contracts without his express orders, and the defense that the so-called petty peculation was normal, rather than exceptional, behavior of Venezuelan presidents.

In addition to the changes in witnesses' testimony prompted by cross-examination, then, the defense offered only one new bit of evidence. They were allowed to question the minister of defense on the nation's business with firms which had allegedly paid bribes to Pérez Jiménez. The attorneys found that the destroyer *Aragua* had been returned to the Vickers-Armstrong shipyards for repairs after the 1958 coup. Noting that the Venezuelan government continued to deal with firms which had broken the law by bribing Pérez Jiménez, the defense typified such action as immoral, inconsistent, or both. Either AD felt no compunctions about dealing with firms that had been engaged in illicit business, or the charges against Pérez Jiménez were not valid, they argued.[28] The defense reached the same conclusion that had intrigued Judge William Mathes in the U.S. hearings: accepting a bribe had usually been considered a greater crime than offering one.

The final hearings were held in November and December, 1967, and January, 1968. Obviously more than the statutory thirty days had passed since the court began to admit and evaluate the evidence on November 8, 1966. The Supreme Court had granted several extensions of the time period, over the protests of the defense attorneys and Justice José Román Duque Sánchez. Duque Sánchez held that the time period for the introduction and ratifica-

27 Ibid., pp. 223–227.
28 Ibid., p. 335.

tion of evidence could not be extended.[29] The majority of the court again ruled most liberally in favor of the prosecution.

José Díaz Andara's concluding statements asserted that the evidence was conclusive enough to establish Pérez Jiménez's guilt. He referred to Elías Issa Chejin and David Issa Espinoza as "people excessively coercible" since they had claimed first to have been coerced by Fortunato Herrera and later by the Technical Judicial Police. He reiterated the prosecution's view that the evidence need not be any more specific:

> The defense had tried hard to sustain, after examining each of the persons who was called to testify, that that testimony does not prove the existence of the crime of peculation or establish the responsibility of General (r) Marcos Pérez Jiménez in its commission. It is clear that no witness in particular has said, or could say, that he saw the accused take with his own hands money and valuables from the Public Treasury of the Nation, whose direction and administration he exercised in virtue of the high charge that he held of President of the Republic; but the number of concordant indications, grave and precise, that involve the contracts and commissions, sustains the truth and probatory force of the accusations from the broadest point of view. . . .[30]

The defense's summation was divided into two parts: a statement by Pérez Jiménez himself and a concluding statement by his attorneys. On December 5, Pérez Jiménez covered much of the same ground that he had reviewed in his *declaración indagatoria*. He condemned the mistreatment of Hispanic minorities in the United States and U.S. efforts to keep Latin America in a state of economic subservience. He again denied that leaders such as Rómulo Betancourt, with their international outlooks, could help Latin America to shake off the ties of dependency to the United States. As evidence of AD's antinational stance, Pérez noted that the case against him had been constructed for U.S. courts instead of Venezuelan ones: "The advice of foreign professionals in a point as specifically Venezuelan as is a trial against a former president of our country demonstrates something that is injurious to the dignity

---

[29] Disiente de José Román Duque Sánchez, September 28, 1967, 6 pieza principal, Archive 59-95.

[30] Informe, November 8, 1967, 6 pieza principal, p. 78, Archive 59-95.

of our jurists if it is interpreted one way or highly flattering if it is interpreted in another way. The first would be if they had shown an incapacity to carry the work forward within strictly legal limits; the second would be if the Attorney General could find no professionals here malleable and immoral enough to manufacture a case outside the law."[31] In reference to the prosecution's case against him, Pérez Jiménez said that he had been framed. The famous suitcase of documents had not been forgotten, but stolen, then ransacked and filled with false documents that had never belonged to Pérez Jiménez. The former president also criticized the looting of his home and other properties after his departure.[32]

Pérez Jiménez concluded that the Supreme Court had three reasons to find him guilty: first, the expediency of confirming the U.S. government's judgment in granting his extradition; second, the necessity to satisfy Betancourt's desire for revenge; and third, the necessity for the Venezuelan government to justify the money spent on his trial. On the other hand, the magistrates might consider the merits of finding Pérez innocent. Many political groups had called his trial a political one; if any of these groups came to power in the approaching 1968 elections, they could release Pérez Jiménez from jail and implicitly suggest that Pérez's trial had been irregular. The magistrates might also consider the possibility that the dignity of the court would be damaged if it were considered an instrument of political persecution and executive vengeance. Pérez warned the judges that his condemnation could be divisive at the time of another bitterly contested presidential election: ". . . it is necessary to take into account the circumstances that Venezuela is going through. Each day more symptoms of division and conflict among Venezuelans appear, and each day more hatreds are accumulated whose overflowing in any given moment can mean a national catastrophe. All the sectors of the country show restlessness about this and cry out for efforts to be made to pacify the nation. I don't know how much a condemnatory sentence might contribute to in-

[31] Intervención, December 5, 1967, 6 pieza principal, p. 5, Archive 59-95.
[32] Ibid., pp. 20–22.

tensify factors of disunity and hatred that bring closer the outbreak that we good Venezuelans are pledged to avoid."[33]

The defense attorneys in their summation dwelt on the legal and logical problems of holding the president solely responsible for all of the deeds of his administration:

It is a grave and faulty simplification to try to make the President of the Republic responsible for the activity of the whole Government, as the prosecution tries to do, when it concerns a penal action of a strictly personal nature. It is the official who is in charge of the administration of the Public Treasury who should bear the penal responsibility in the case of appropriation or theft. It is absurd to think that any theft or appropriation of public funds by subordinate officials and in any part of the country can cause the President of the Republic to bear penal responsibility for peculation, and it is to this incredible conclusion that the thesis of the Solicitor General leads us.[34]

The defense also restated their view that Pérez had not exceeded the limits of regular and normal presidential actions. They charged that the nation had paid butlers, stewards, cooks, waiters, chambermaids, ironing women, laundresses, gardeners, and the person in charge of the swimming pool at Los Núñez, the private estate of Rómulo Betancourt in 1960–1961:[35] "Why does the construction of a well and the work of gardeners constitute a crime on that house which was the residence of the former president Pérez Jiménez, and why are the expenses of repairs on the *quinta* 'Los Núñez' and the payment of salaries to gardeners and other workers who rendered services at 'Los Núñez,' paid with the Nation's money, not characterized as crimes?"[36]

Fiscal General Antonio José Lozada could not resist responding to the concluding statements of the defense. He denied the relevance of the charges that the nation had spent too much to secure Pérez Jiménez's extradition and the validity of the allega-

---

[33] Ibid., pp. 70–71, 73.
[34] Informe [Defense], January 1, 1968, 6 pieza principal, p. 25, Archive 59-95.
[35] Ibid., pp. 57–59.
[36] Ibid., p. 58.

tion that Pérez Jiménez was being tried for crimes that had not been specified in the U.S. order of surrender. Lozada contended that although Pérez Jiménez had been surrendered for peculation, extortion and corruption of officials had been the means by which Pérez had committed the crime of peculation; the means of commission of the crime helped to determine criminal responsibility and could properly be included in the trial. Moreover, Lozada said, the length of the trial was Pérez Jiménez's fault, since he had first obstructed justice by fleeing to the United States.[37]

The question of the length of time that Pérez Jiménez had spent in jail could affect the length of his ultimate sentence. The penal code specified that one day of detention was worth two days of sentenced time. If Pérez's detention were calculated from December, 1962, he had spent five years in jail at the time of Lozada's summation; thus, his sentence would have to exceed ten years if he were to remain in jail after the court decision. Lozada argued that Pérez's detention had only begun in August, 1963, when he was returned to Venezuela.

Lozada also inserted a supplementary memorandum into the record in January, 1967. Inadmissible because it referred to the alleged murders and political persecution under Pérez Jiménez's rule, the memorandum read in part:

The 24th of November of 1948, the accused as head of a military rebellion, overthrew the government presided over by the illustrious Venezuelan Don Rómulo Gallegos. With this act of force he attacked the sovereignty of the people, deposed a regime of law, and set in its place one of the most terrible dictatorships that this country has suffered. In order to support it, he created instruments of political repression that were the terror of the citizenry. Its members committed all kinds of crimes against persons and their property, for which they were tried after the 23rd of January 1958. . . . Illegal arrests were the rule. Neither age, sex, nor social condition was respected. General (r) Marcos Pérez Jiménez gave precise orders for the director of the Seguridad Nacional and the subordinate officials of the so-called Political-Social Section to

---

[37] Escrito de replica, January 10, 1968, 6 pieza principal, pp. 4, 5, 68–74, 83–84, Archive 59-95.

carry out all those deeds against liberty and the physical integrity of persons. . . . Not even the companions of the accused, the members of the Armed Forces, escaped this notorious political persecution; they were also subjected to strict surveillance, and many were jailed or exiled from the country.[38]

To justify the inclusion of the supplementary memorandum, Lozada added:

Because of respect for the United States court sentence and the U.S. State Department's order of surrender, the prosecution had not, until now, alluded to the crimes against persons, against the public faith and the national powers perpetrated by the accused during the time of his long public actions. But the fact that the accused has converted these hearings into a public tribunal to praise his arbitrary and usurping system of government and to revile the democratic government has obliged us to point out to the country the evil effects of his administration and to emphasize, in contrast, the extraordinary work which the legal, democratic government has realized and continues to realize for the collective benefit of all Venezuelans.[39]

Lozada finally refused to bow to the strictures of the extradition order and the fiction that Pérez Jiménez was only a common criminal. His outburst reflected his resentment at Pérez's criminal political actions, actions which had cast Lozada's political party from power in 1948 and had subjected its members to a decade of exile and persecution. More, Lozada apparently feared that Pérez Jiménez's grand defense was not only abetting his historical absolution but also reviving his political appeal.

Lozada's statements were rendered on January 10, 1968, and the court began to consider its decision after that date. In May, Pérez Jiménez's defense attorneys resigned from the case in protest at the length of time which had lapsed without a sentence. The case should have been concluded by February 28, at the latest, Rafael Narranjo Ostty told the press. The defense attorneys had other business to attend to, and besides, there was no point in their continuing like "toads, beating their heads against the wall." The attorneys refused to complain of the irregular delays to the U.S.

[38] Escrito adicional de la replica, January 10, 1968, 6 pieza principal, pp. 2–3, Archive 59-95.

[39] Ibid., pp. 22–23.

government because "as Venezuelans . . . we cannot . . . at any time complain before a foreign government of the deficiencies or irregularities that Venezuelan authorities might commit."[40]

The long-awaited decision finally came on August 1, 1968. Of the fifteen judges, only eight made up the simple majority. Finding him guilty only of the minor crime of continuous profit from public office (*lucro de funcionarios*), the court sentenced Pérez Jiménez to four years, one month, and fifteen days in prison. Since the former president had already passed more than that time in jail, he was free to leave Venezuela immediately. On August 1, the same day as the sentence, Pérez boarded a plane for Spain.[41]

In subsidiary parts of the decision, the majority saw no reason to require Pérez Jiménez to restore to the nation the wealth he had derived from his years in power, since the 1961 constitution had already confiscated his Venezuelan property. He was enjoined, however, to pay the court costs of his trial.[42]

The majority had heeded the defense arguments in their weighing of the evidence. They had accepted the evidence that demonstrated Pérez's enrichment through use of his official position but had rejected the material which did not specify the concrete actions through which the enrichment was effected. They had not considered any evidence which had related to third persons when it had not clarified the deeds of Pérez Jiménez.[43]

The court rejected the prosecution's liberal interpretation of peculation or embezzlement. They ruled that Pérez Jiménez, since he had not had direct custody over the treasury, could not be found guilty of the specific crime of embezzlement: "The taking of money or other goods does not appear configured in the deeds proven, since it has been made evident only that the accused, in the exercise of public functions, obtained personal benefit from acts of public administration in which he participated. It was not proved that the crimes of extortion, corruption and benefit from function-

[40] Rafael Naranjo Ostty, *La verdad de un juicio tracendental*, pp. 211, 213.

[41] *New York Times*, August 2, 1968.

[42] Catalá, *Proceso*, II, 408.

[43] Ibid., pp. 390–398.

aries had been used as devices to commit the crime of peculation and therefore, . . . this Court diverges from the juridical qualification of the deeds imputed to the accused by the representative of the Public Ministry and the prosecuting party. . . ."[44]

Five justices dissented in favor of a more stringent penalty, and two justices separately argued that the long trial had indeed exceeded the statute of limitations and that Pérez Jiménez should be freed without judicial condemnation. Rafael Rodríguez Méndez, Carlos Ascanio Jiménez, Jonas Barrios, César Tinoco Richter, and Martín Pérez Guevara contended that Pérez Jiménez should be found guilty of more than the minor crime of benefiting from public office. The crucial point of conflict between the majority and the minority centered around the interpretation of peculation, the crime which carried the greatest penalty. The minority thought that the majority had skirted the issue by ruling that the president could not commit peculation. "From that inexplicable omission comes, however, the conclusion that from now on the most notorious criminals of peculation will be able to invoke the authority that emanates from a Supreme Court decision in order to try to elude the penalty established in Article 195 of the Penal Code, whose hope of application, according to the sentence, is reduced to those cases in which the agent of the crime appropriates to himself unduly the money or other goods available because they are materially within reach of his hands, because of his official functions." According to the minority, "taking money with which he was entrusted" should cover more than the goods in one's physical possession. The official should also be responsible for the value by which the national patrimony was reduced because of his abuse of powers even when the valuables were not within his physical custody.[45]

In Venezuela, continued the minority, the president and the cabinet ministers who administered the national wealth could enrich themselves without directly withdrawing funds from the treasury:

[44] Ibid., pp. 397–398.
[45] Ibid., pp. 416, 418.

. . . the power with which the President of the Republic and the cabinet ministers are invested permits them to manage the resources of power and to dispose legally of the national patrimony in a form so ample and at times so free of obstacles that in order to maintain administrative morality, the effective protection of penal justice is required.

Although it is painful to admit it, this protection ought to be particularly vigorous in our country, where public office is considered by many as an opportunity to enrich oneself, using the innumerable means that circumstances or legal situations offer to facilitate the commission of illegal acts.[46]

The minority conceded that it might appear absurd to hold the president responsible for each and every one of the irregularities committed by lesser officials, but when the president deliberately abused the power of office to enrich himself, he betrayed the confidence of Venezuelans. If peculation could only be charged against minor officials, the magistrates excluded from punishment the very one who had the greatest opportunity to undermine administrative honor and responsibility. Pérez Jiménez should have been condemned to fifteen years, eight months, and twenty days, plus the corresponding accessory penalties.[47]

The majority and the minority differed, in essence, on the same issue that divided U.S. constitutional authorities when a presidential impeachment was considered. Can the president be charged only with statutory crimes, defined strictly, or may he be held responsible for the political crime of maladministration?

Justices José Román Duque Sánchez and Luis Torrealba grappled directly with the logical dilemma in their separate dissenting opinions. Duque Sánchez had consistently taken an independent view in the court decisions that touched on the Pérez Jiménez case: the nullification of international treaties, the jurisdiction of the Supreme Court in the case, and now the final decision. His opinions carefully weighed the complex issues involved. Torrealba and Duque Sánchez said that Pérez Jiménez should be freed without a condemnation because the period of judicial proscription had

[46] Ibid., p. 419.
[47] Ibid., pp. 422–423, 425.

lapsed. The two also agreed with the majority that Pérez Jiménez could not have stolen funds from the treasury because the funds were beyond his direct physical and material control.[48]

Duque Sánchez's contribution to the legal arguments went further than the simple consideration of the specific crime and the lapse of time. A president could not be guilty of embezzlement from the public treasury, but, unfortunately, it was easy for a president to become wealthy, not by embezzlement but by abusing the power of his office. The penalties in the penal code did not appear equitable; the president, who had greater possibilities to enrich himself, was liable for a lesser penalty than the minor official who slipped a few bolivares from public funds. The solution lay, however, not in the deformation of the definition of peculation, but in a modification of the penal code which would increase the penalty for the graver crime.[49]

The issue of whether the court should have passed a condemnatory sentence or a stay of proceedings because of delays was of theoretical interest only. Pérez Jiménez would have gone free on August 1 in either case. The real issue lay in whether the court should admit embarrassment at having unjustly prolonged the trial or whether Pérez Jiménez should be dishonored by a public declaration of his guilt, even though that declaration carried no further penalty. Duque Sánchez thought that the trial had been delayed through no fault of the defendant and that the defense appeals could not be termed unnecessary delays in the trial. To call for a stay of proceedings did not benefit the accused, but only the public interest, Duque wrote. Courts and magistrates should support a rapid and efficient administration of justice.[50]

In sum, the prosecution tried to confine their animus toward Pérez Jiménez to ordinary statutory definitions and procedures. Nonetheless, the extreme definition of peculation, the wide range of poorly documented crimes attributed to Pérez, the presumption of guilt, and Lozada's final outburst revealed that the trial bore more

48 Ibid., p. 429.
49 Ibid., pp. 431–433.
50 Ibid., pp. 433–438.

than a trace of vengeance. The bitterness was natural under the circumstances, and the AD prosecution did make a commendable effort to treat their old enemy as an ordinary criminal. The AD government sincerely wanted to establish a legal precedent, to develop the independence of the judicial system, and to promote administrative morality, but they also wanted to see Pérez Jiménez receive as severe a punishment as possible.

The divided Supreme Court decision was a tribute to AD's intention to develop an independent judiciary. If a unanimous decision had been rendered, one might have concluded that the trial had been a vengeful farce. Yet the majority decision adhered to the letter of the law, if Pérez Jiménez were to be considered a common criminal. The sentence found him guilty of the specific crime of profiting from public office and ignored the fact that the penalty was relatively minor. The five-man dissenting minority came closest to the prosecution's contention that Pérez's offenses had been so great that the law should be stretched in order to punish him more severely. Duque Sánchez pointed out that if one wished to punish the president severely for illicit enrichment, the penal code must first be amended to make such enrichment a major crime. The three opinions represented three different judgments on the limits of a former president's penal responsibility for the misdeeds of his administration.

The lack of agreement among the justices also mirrored the changes in the Venezuelan political climate since 1958. In that year Venezuelans had been nearly unanimous in their rejection of Pérez Jiménez and in their approval of the three major political parties, as demonstrated by the January revolt and the December election. Some of that consensus began to slip away, however, as political tactics and philosophies began to diverge in the democratic environment. In 1963 a total of 28.1 percent of the electorate voted against the major parties, and leftist guerrillas tried to overthrow the government by force. These divisions continued, if somewhat abated, in 1968 as a new national election approached. In regard to Pérez Jiménez, some Venezuelans had forgiven and forgotten his crimes by 1968; others considered his punishment irrelevant to the important issues facing Venezuela; and still others nurtured a lingering bitterness toward him and the type of government he had represented. Some speculative analogies with U.S. history might again be illuminating. Would the actions of President Andrew Johnson have been judged as harshly ten years after he left office? Or will Richard Nixon be as widely condemned for abuse of presidential power in 1984 as he was in 1974? Presidential reputations often appear to be more closely related to changing national moods and priorities than to historical deeds.

In any event, the trial of Marcos Pérez Jiménez clearly was an uncommon trial. Pérez was an important figure in the Venezuelan political spectrum—and would continue to be for the immediate future following his conviction.

8

Politics and Perezjimenistas
in the 1960s and 1970s

It took Betancourt and the Acción Democrática hierarchy ten
years to throw Pérez Jiménez out of office and another ten years to
secure a court sentence which condemned him for his crimes. The
AD leaders would spend yet another ten years trying to prevent
Pérez Jiménez from returning to power through an open, democratic election. Pérez eventually lost this battle with AD for many
of the same reasons he had lost the first two: a lack of political
astuteness and perhaps a lack of courage or will. From 1968 to
1978, Pérez Jiménez became increasingly ineffective in countering
the AD moves against him. His ineffectiveness stymied the 20–30
percent of the population who were willing to vote for him in the
expectation that he could duplicate the feat of Juan Perón, who
returned to power in Argentina in 1973 after eighteen years of
exile.[1]

The struggle to declare Pérez Jiménez ineligible to hold public
office again actually began as part of the case against him before
the Supreme Court. As a subsidiary part of the decision, Pérez
Jiménez was prohibited from holding political office for the period
of his penal sentence, in accordance with Article 14 of the penal
code. In referring to the penal code instead of the Law against
Illicit Enrichment, the court majority opted for the less rigorous
penalty. Moreover, the sentence considered that the period of political proscription began when Pérez began to serve the time of his
sentence. In effect, the majority said that Pérez Jiménez could not
hold office for four years, one month, and fifteen days of his time
in jail, a period already lapsed by August, 1968.[2]

[1] *Latin America*, November 24, 1972.
[2] *New York Times*, August 2, 1968.

The five magistrates who had argued for a more stringent penalty—Rafael Rodríguez Méndez, Carlos Ascanio Jiménez, Jonas Barrios, César Tinoco Richter, and Martín Pérez Guevara—also took issue with the majority's ruling on Pérez Jiménez's political future. The dissenting magistrates, reflecting the views of the AD hierarchy, thought that the political prohibition should extend from the moment in which the sentence was dictated. One who had been condemned for robbing the public coffers should not pass directly from jail to public office, they reasoned. Pérez Jiménez should be barred from holding public office for five years after the expiration of the corporal penalty.[3]

The men who wanted to prevent Pérez Jiménez from holding public office in the immediate future tried again in October to force the issue. José Antonio Lozada as solicitor general petitioned the court to accept the prosecution's interpretation that the political ineligibility be applied to the future rather than to the past. He cited the Law against Illicit Enrichment to substantiate his thesis that Pérez Jiménez should receive the greatest possible period of disqualification because of the gravity of his continuous criminal actions. The court replied in a decision published on October 9, 1968, that they could not revoke or reform a sentence but could clarify a ruling or clear up doubtful points. In response to Lozada's plea, the majority said that the penalty of political disqualification had been applied properly according to the penal code. Six judges dissented, arguing that disqualifications should apply to the future and that the court could so rule under its power to clarify doubtful points.[4]

The question of Pérez Jiménez's disqualification from political office was not a moot one. In 1967, Pérez Jiménez had founded from jail a political party, the Cruzada Cívica Nacionalista (CCN). That party, with his help, was waging an effective campaign in 1968. The CCN's platform was simple; it announced that it was the "political capital of Marcos Pérez Jiménez" and "political arm of

---

[3] José Agustín Catalá, ed., *Proceso a un ex-dictador*, II, 424–425.
[4] Ibid., pp. 448–451.

Pérez Jiménez" and that its sole mission was to do his bidding.[5] CCN's major issue appeared to be Pérez Jiménez's treatment at the hands of the AD government and the most important campaign document was probably Pérez Jiménez's book *Frente a la Infamia*, published early in 1968. The book reproduced many of Pérez's arguments and statements before the Supreme Court, including part of the *declaración indagatoria*. Those who were weary of AD's alleged partisanship, mediocrity, wastefulness, and political vengeance were urged to vote for the CCN ticket. His continuing detention and his subsequent disqualification for office made Pérez less than a viable candidate for the presidency, so the Cruzada offered only a slate of congressional candidates and left their followers free to vote for whichever presidential candidate they chose. Pérez Jiménez, did, however, head up the list of senatorial candidates for the Federal District.

AD made a final effort to remove Pérez's name from the ballot in November when the Junta Principal of the Federal District met to validate the congressional lists. An AD member of the junta, Héctor Carpio Castillo, demanded that Pérez's name be struck from the list because he was a condemned criminal and because he had not registered to vote. The COPEI and URD representatives on the junta rejected the plea, and Pérez's name remained on the list. Carpio Castillo reserved the right to appeal the decision to the Supreme Electoral Council.[6]

COPEI's presidential candidate, Rafael Caldera, welcomed independent voters' support in 1968. He sensed a real possibility of victory and could not afford to offend any potential voters, including *perezjimenistas*. COPEI had spent the ten years following the 1958 revolt in carefully building up their party machinery and in gaining prestige and some political patronage by acting as AD's loyal opposition. The cooperation with the AD congressional majority had been firmest between 1959 and 1963, but the subsequent opposition had stayed within the bounds of acceptability. COPEI

[5] RIC Universales, *Año Político 1968*, pp. 72, 157.
[6] Ibid., p. 165.

had maintained party unity, had grown stronger, and hoped to exploit their position as the second major party in the face of recent AD divisions.

Most Venezuelans continued to perceive COPEI as a party to the right of AD. The more conservative stance proved particularly attractive to some of the business community. Additionally, in 1968 Rafael Caldera hoped to pick up some support from the left by calling for amnesty for all opponents of the democratic government, including the guerrillas if they agreed to lay down their arms. During the past two years, some members of the Movimiento de la Izquierda Revolucionaria (MIR) and the Venezuelan Communist party had indicated their willingness to forego the unsuccessful guerrilla action in favor of a return to legal parliamentary opposition. Caldera made it clear that he would accept their support as well as that of the conservative *perezjimenistas*; early in the campaign, Caldera had advocated unconditional liberty for Pérez Jiménez himself. Echoing a theme which Arturo Uslar Pietri had used in 1963, Caldera renounced the use of law to settle political grudges. The reference to political grudges and spurious judicial actions may have been intended to counter AD spokesman Carlos Andrés Pérez, who proposed to initiate a series of trials to compensate people who had spent time in Pérez Jiménez's concentration camps of Guasina and Sacupana. In another appeal for unity which was similar to Uslar's 1963 platform, Caldera promised that he would also renounce the Betancourt doctrine of distinguishing between legitimate and de facto governments in the Americas.[7] Uslar Pietri had apparently discovered a valuable source of political support in 1963. Whether characterized as antiparty, conservative, independent, or *perezjimenista*, a substantial number of voters could be attracted by candidates who opposed AD.

The evidence that that body of iconoclastic voters existed tempted two other major contenders to join the presidential race in 1968, thus dashing Caldera's hopes for a united opposition to

[7] *Latin America*, July 14, 1967; February 9, 1968; Aníbal Oliveres, "Con quien se irá el perezjimenismo?" *Elite* 2238 (August 17, 1968): 3–4; Demetrio Boersner, *Venezuela y el Caribe: Presencia cambiante*, p. 100.

AD. The candidate who promised to be the more serious threat at the polls was Luis Beltrán Prieto Figueroa, who headed a new party, the Movimiento Electoral del Pueblo (MEP). Prieto loomed large on the electoral horizon for two reasons: he was attractive to the left and the labor movement, and he represented the most serious defection that AD had yet experienced.[8] Commanding a majority of the AD rank and file in 1967, Prieto was nonetheless outmaneuvered by Betancourt and the party hierarchy, who preferred and nominated Gonzalo Barrios. AD leader Carlos Canache Mata tried to denigrate Prieto's defection by terming it a Communist plot, but Prieto denied the charge and struggled to maintain a leftist, but non-Communist, appeal throughout the campaign. Political opinion polls in November, 1968, showed him running neck and neck with the AD and COPEI candidates, with special strength among the poor in the Caracas barrios.[9]

Prieto's candidacy might be seen more as an AD candidacy of the left than as an antiparty appeal. The fourth presidential candidate, however, openly sought to gain from the hostility toward the two main parties. After months of discussion, negotiation, and rejection of possible candidates, the "unified opposition" of Jóvito Villaba (URD), Arturo Uslar Pietri (FND), and Wolfgang Larrazábal (FDP) reached an agreement. In June, 1968, they announced that they would all support Miguel Angel Burelli Rivas for the presidency while putting forward their separate congressional lists. The coalition was a minor miracle, considering the ideological diversity represented and the ambitions of the three party leaders. Nonetheless, they had not missed the significance of the 1963 election results and, in the face of the AD split, saw a possibility for success against the establishment parties. Jóvito Villaba explained in a newspaper interview why victory was certain for Burelli: ". . . the three parties which make up the Victory Front obtained in 1963 a total of 1,355,000 votes; that is, of each 10 voters, 5 voted for us.

---

[8] *Latin America*, November 3, 1967; John D. Martz, "The Party System: Toward Institutionalization," in *Venezuela: The Democratic Experience*, ed. John D. Martz and David J. Myers, p. 96. See also José Rivas Rivas, *Las Tres Divisiones de Acción Democrática*.

[9] *Latin America*, January 12, November 29, 1968.

In the meantime, Acción Democrática, which was the triumphant minority with the candidacy of Dr. Leoni, obtained 951,000 votes, and COPEI, the second minority, only won 589,000. This means . . . that in 1963, of each 10 votes, 5 went to the parties which are backing Burelli, 3 for Acción Democrática and 2 for COPEI. . . . The country . . . wants new faces, new methods, a new style." COPEI had no chance of winning, he added, because it was a noisy and isolated minority with fascist tendencies. Moreover, Caldera's costly political campaign, calling for change, would not help him: "Caldera created the image of change, and this will turn against him because the people don't want to change one sectarianism for a worse one or to substitute Nazi totalitarianism for Venezuelan democracy."[10]

Aside from the "independent" voters, the Victory Front, as the coalition called itself, hoped to exploit the anger of the business community at AD for pushing Venezuela's entry into the Andean Pact and for passing the law to negotiate service contracts instead of new petroleum concessions. They also spoke of according amnesty for opponents of the democratic regime and promised to do away with sectarianism in the government. There was some appeal to women voters, as Uslar had tried in 1963, and a popular independent theme: that jobs and ministerial positions would be awarded on the basis of ability rather than party allegiance.[11]

The December election results surprised many, including the opinion polls, which had predicted a near tie among Caldera, Barrios, and Prieto. A total of 3,723,710 voters distributed their presidential votes among four major candidates. A comparison of the 1968 returns with those of 1963, as shown in the table below, suggests some trends. First, the AD split probably contributed to that party's defeat, since the combined totals of Prieto and Barrios would have represented 44.8 percent of the vote. Second, both major parties improved their electoral strength. Third, both major

[10] See RIC Universales, *Año Político 1968*, for photographs of the news articles. See Enrique Baloyra and John D. Martz, *Political Attitudes in Venezuela: Societal Cleavages and Public Opinion*, pp. 110–151, for a discussion of the ideological characterizations of the parties.

[11] RIC Universales, *Año Político 1968*, pp. 74, 77, 80, 109, 161.

parties also improved their showing in metropolitan Caracas; the Federal District still preferred candidates other than the AD or COPEI nominees, but the margin was not as great as it had been in 1963. The Caracas Question seemed to be fading slightly as an electoral phenomenon.[12]

Presidential Votes, 1963 and 1968

	1963		1968	
	National	Caracas	National	Caracas
AD	957,699	65,333	1,051,870	141,387
COPEI	588,372	50,665	1,082,941	161,717
URD	551,120	62,669		
IPFN (FND)	469,240	191,028	829,397	185,194
FDP	275,304	98,129		
MEP			719,733	150,495

The appeal of allegedly independent candidates continued, but Burelli Rivas must have been chagrined to find that their election mathematics had not produced victory. Burelli's vote did not come close to the combined total of the three independent parties in 1963. He did receive the largest vote in Caracas, but that figure did not match Uslar Pietri's Caracas vote in 1963. The ideological diversity of the coalition may have confused, or alienated, some voters, and Burelli probably did not have the same popular appeal as the better-known Villaba, Larrazábal, and Uslar Pietri. One study of the voting in different urban precincts suggests that the middle- and upper-class voters preferred Uslar Pietri in 1963 but turned to Caldera in 1968. Burelli did better with the lower class than with the upper and middle groups, although he was also less popular with the poor than Uslar had been.[13] One might speculate

[12] Ibid., no page numbers, for 1968 figures; for 1963 figures, see Institute for the Comparative Study of Political Systems, *The Venezuelan Elections of December 1, 1963*, vol. 3, *Final Provisional Election Returns, Presidential and Legislative, Broken Down by Region and State*, Election Analysis Series No. 2.

[13] John D. Martz and Peter B. Harkins, "Urban Electoral Behavior: Caracas, 1958–1968," *Comparative Politics* 5 (July, 1973): 543.

that the middle- and upper-class voters were sophisticated enough to see through the opportunistic coalition; the ideological and personal differences apparent within the coalition were bound to produce squabbling and a lack of direction after the election. If one wished to oppose the government party, he would do better with a recognized leader who had dependable party support. Moreover, in 1968 COPEI still had not held the presidential chair and might more seriously have been seen as an opposition, rather than a government, party.

If people were mildly amazed at Burelli's showing, many were astounded at the size of the CCN legislative vote. The Cruzada pulled in 400,093 votes (11.1 percent) nationwide and captured 26.6 percent of the Caracas vote. Their showing at the polls entitled them to four senators and twenty-one deputies, the fourth largest congressional delegation. Pérez Jiménez himself, as the head of the senate list, was elected to the representative body.[14]

Analysts of the election termed the Pérez Jiménez vote a "non-leftist protest" of "disenchanted voters" and noted that the vote for Pérez was the strongest in urban lower classes, although Pérez also captured over 20 percent of the middle- and upper-class urban vote. Another study speculated that the vote might reflect the political socialization of many Caracas barrio dwellers who came to political consciousness when Pérez Jiménez was attempting to extinguish the strength of AD in the city; thus, these voters had less commitment to the democratic parties. A Venezuelan psychoanalyst, Hernán Quijada, thought that a number of Venezuelans must be suffering from split personalities when they voted for democratic candidates for the presidency at the same time they chose former dictators for Congress.[15]

Since it composed one of the major parts of the CCN cam-

[14] *New York Times*, August 2, 1968; David J. Myers, "Urban Voting, Structural Cleavage, and Party System Evolution: The Case of Venezuela," *Comparative Politics* 8 (October, 1975): 140.

[15] Martz and Harkins, "Urban Electoral Behavior," p. 540; Myers, "Urban Voting," p. 140; RIC Universales, *Año Político 1968*, p. 169. For more extensive coverage of the 1968 election, see David J. Myers, *Democratic Campaigning in Venezuela: Caldera's Victory.*

paign, Pérez Jiménez's trial before the Supreme Court may have had an impact on the voters. It publicized Pérez's regime and the prosperity that many urbanites had enjoyed during that time; the numerous construction jobs especially were remembered fondly by many who lived in the barrios. Additionally, many of the poor probably retained their hostility toward the law and a suspicion that lawmakers and courts acted arbitrarily. Their own suspicions of the courts may have prompted an empathy for Pérez Jiménez when he claimed that he was being unfairly prosecuted by his enemies.

From Madrid, Pérez Jiménez basked in his victory and accurately predicted problems ahead for COPEI: "Rafael Caldera has won the election with less than 30 per cent of Venezuelan votes; that means the other 70 per cent are against him, or at any rate not for him. We are about to see the emergence of a weakly based government, judging by these figures. . . . If Caldera wants to form an adequately stable and efficient government, he will have to carry out far-reaching reforms in the so-called 'democratic' system. Otherwise he will have trouble reaching the end of his term of office in peace."[16] The former dictator promised that he would return to serve in Congress as soon as he received his senator's credentials.

Pérez's comment proved prophetic, much to COPEI's dismay. AD, unused to the difficult role of opposition, obstructed and protested virtually every move COPEI made, especially in Caldera's first year. COPEI was not able, or chose not, to seek a stable coalition with any congressional party and had to improvise and rely on different groups at different times. It would be well into 1969–1970 before Caldera discovered some of the magic of nationalism and began to benefit from an increase in oil revenues due to the Middle East crisis and a new tax law. He also learned how to exploit the obstructionism of AD with the public and earned some public sympathy because of the recalcitrant Congress. Problems with labor strikes and student strikes continued to plague the regime for most of the five-year term, but the successful pacification of the guerrillas and the abandonment of the Betancourt Doctrine won over many.

[16] *Latin America*, December 20, 1968.

Indeed, in retrospect, some observers would term Caldera's foreign policy to be one of his greatest successes.[17]

AD, unhappily divided and in opposition, naturally resented the COPEI dominance and began immediately to examine the causes for their loss and the strategy for a return to power in 1973. The specter that proved to be most haunting to the AD leaders was the possibility that Pérez Jiménez might build upon his popular support and make a successful bid for the presidency in 1973. They would not welcome being edged out in votes by the pudgy retired general any more than they had enjoyed being thrown out of office in 1948. They worked tirelessly during Caldera's term to ensure that such an aberration could not occur.

The first line of defense was to ensure that Pérez would not return to Venezuela to assume his Senate seat. In his absence, the CCN would be less effective. AD did protest his election, as Carpio Castillo had threatened in November, 1968, by noting that he had not been a registered voter and thus was ineligible to run as a candidate. While that petition was being considered, a second attack was launched. The extradition order which surrendered Pérez Jiménez had stipulated that he might only be tried for the financial crimes; once he had left the country at the conclusion of his trial, however, if he returned voluntarily, he might be tried for other crimes. The family of one of the victims of Pérez's regime initiated a civil action against the former dictator which would call for Pérez's arrest and trial if he returned to Venezuela.[18] Whatever the real possibility of such a case actually being conducted and of Pérez's being arrested again, he cautiously chose not to return without assurances that he would not be imprisoned again.

The Cruzada's parliamentary delegation began their terms in hopes that their leader would return and in the meantime that they could exploit COPEI's need for political allies in the Congress. In March, 1969, they sided with COPEI to assure that Caldera's party would win the presidency of the Senate, in effect the vice-presi-

[17] Boersner, *Venezuela y el Caribe*, pp. 95–112.
[18] *Latin America*, January 31, 1969.

dency of the nation. Being able to strike no bargains in regard to Pérez Jiménez's return, the CCN later tried to threaten COPEI by abstaining or being absent from the quorum calls. CCN leaders frequently traveled to Lima, where Pérez Jiménez resided for part of the year, and kept the former dictator apprised of the party's tactics.[19]

Acción Democrática was as wary of the fractionalized Congress as the Cruzada had been hopeful for it. Betancourt's party attacked any party which sought out or dealt with the CCN. In October, the AD leaders accused COPEI of trying to revive Pérez Jiménez's reputation in order to achieve a majority in Congress. Even AD benefited, however, when the Cruzada began to splinter; one group of *perezjimenistas* aligned itself with AD against the ruling party.[20]

As Caldera's presidential term neared its halfway mark, the politicians began to plan for the 1973 election. AD led the way in seeking a way to prevent the Cruzada from building upon its newfound electoral strength to nominate Pérez Jiménez as their presidential candidate. In April, 1971, the AD leaders proposed that Venezuela adopt a new electoral system similar to that used by the French. If the winner were required to achieve a 51 percent majority, in a run-off election if necessary, the other parties could form a coalition to keep the former dictator out.[21]

The situation reached a climax when both Rómulo Betancourt and Marcos Pérez Jiménez returned to Venezuela in the same week of June, 1972. Pérez Jiménez registered as a presidential candidate and then quickly returned to Spain, where he would stay until he chose to begin his campaign. Bursts of violence accompanied the visits of the two former presidents. Civilians watched warily as former Defense Minister Martín García Villasmil called for a change of political procedures and hinted that he had been thinking about a military coup. Perhaps even more unusual than the thought

19 Ibid., March 14, October 24, 1969.
20 Ibid., October 17, 1969.
21 Ibid., April 23, 1971.

of a coup was the likely prospect that Pérez Jiménez and Betancourt would vie for the presidency in 1973.[22]

If some politicians wanted to prevent Pérez Jiménez from becoming president again, others were just as eager to see that Betancourt did not return to Miraflores. URD's Jóvito Villaba saw a perfect opportunity and seized it; he proposed that Congress pass a constitutional amendment which would prohibit anyone from holding a second term as president. The CCN and AD immediately joined forces to oppose the suggestion. COPEI initially endorsed the idea until the party leaders began to consider the possibility that Rafael Caldera might wish to run for the presidency again in 1978.[23]

The parties were in a quandary, weighing opportunism against a desire to keep Pérez Jiménez out. In July, 1972, URD continued to press the ban on second-term presidencies, while COPEI picked up on AD's earlier proposal to adopt a new electoral system like the French one. Then AD came up with yet another formula; the Congress should pass a constitutional amendment which would prohibit anyone who had been convicted of embezzlement of state funds from holding public office. As the discussion on the three possibilities continued, Rómulo Betancourt made the choice somewhat easier for his party when he announced that he would not accept the AD nomination for the presidency. AD leader Gonzalo Barrios then proposed a combination of the URD and COPEI plans; AD would support a revamped electoral system if COPEI would agree that a person could only serve one presidential term. Rafael Caldera's party naturally showed little enthusiasm for the so-called compromise.[24]

The entire issue was proving troublesome for COPEI's party unity. Some spokesmen wanted to ensure that Caldera's future presidential chances were not blocked. Others wanted to exclude Pérez Jiménez from the presidency at all costs. Still others, remem-

[22] Ibid., June 2, 9, 16, 1972.
[23] The constitution did not allow a president to hold two consecutive terms but did not prohibit nonconsecutive terms. *Latin America*, June 16, 1972.
[24] Ibid., July 21, August 4, 1972.

bering the comments of General García Villasmil, feared that tampering with the constitution might provide an excuse for aspiring *golpistas*. Finally, some iconoclastic thinkers opposed on principle the proposal to exclude Pérez Jiménez from public office; Luis Herrera Campíns believed that a healthy democracy should extend the privileges of that system even to those who had blatantly abused the public trust. Herrera's generous principles coincided with those of José Vicente Rangel, the leader of the newly formed Movimiento Al Socialismo (MAS).[25]

In spite of the wrangling, by October a deal was struck. COPEI agreed to support the AD amendment which would make anyone guilty of embezzlement ineligible to hold public office. Additionally, Foreign Minister Arístides Calvani announced that if Pérez Jiménez returned to Venezuela, he would be tried for his other crimes. By December 1, 1972, a new detention order had been registered for the former dictator. In their own strategy regarding the imminent presidential race, the COPEI leaders were determined to have the 1973 budget approved by Congress with a minimum of opposition. They had agreed to support the exclusion of Pérez Jiménez from the race in exchange for AD's promise to support the budget. An opinion poll which was released in November may have also influenced the sudden eagerness to prosecute Pérez Jiménez. The poll had shown COPEI and AD running about even in popularity; if Pérez Jiménez had run, however, he would have captured nearly 1 percent more of the electorate than either of the two major parties. COPEI's leadership may have suddenly recalled that some *perezjimenistas* had supported Caldera in 1968; perhaps presidential candidate Lorenzo Fernández might also pick up some of the former dictator's votes in 1973.[26]

In the face of the alliance between the two major parties—however temporary it might prove to be—the *perezjimenistas* quarreled over tactics and candidates. The Cruzada did appeal the constitutional amendment before the Supreme Court, but the court in August, 1973, denied the appeal. In December, 1972, Pérez Jiménez

[25] Ibid., September 29, 1972.
[26] Ibid., October 13, 27, November 24, December 1, 1972.

had advised his followers that he would choose a presidential candidate in due time but that in no case should any of his partisans support either of the two parties which had collaborated to block his return. He could not guarantee even that retaliation, however, and in April it was reported that some of the splinters of the old dictator's party were announcing support for Lorenzo Fernández of COPEI.[27]

In January, 1973, Pedro Tinoco, former minister of finance and leader of a *desarrollista* party, journeyed to Madrid to consult with Pérez Jiménez. Upon his return to Venezuela, he announced to the press that his followers and Pérez's would cooperate on a slate of candidates for Congress. Tinoco had money and a program which was appealing to some in the business community but did not have much of a popular base. He hoped that the *perezjimenistas* would provide that base and continued to hope that Pérez Jiménez would support his candidacy for the presidency.[28]

Former defense minister García Villasmil in January announced that his *perezjimenista* splinter group welcomed the Tinoco alliance. The general's own ambitions apparently intervened, however, and he made his own pilgrimage to Madrid in April. He returned with the news that Pérez Jiménez would announce his presidential preference in May. General García Villasmil broadly hinted that he was to be the favored candidate. The Cruzada tried to halt the appearance of new contenders for the right-wing vote by announcing that they intended to run Pérez Jiménez in spite of the constitutional amendment.[29]

The *perezjimenistas* took new heart from events in Argentina. Héctor Cámpora had been elected president in March, 1973, and then resigned and invited former dictator Juan Perón to return from Madrid to run in a new election. An estimated two million people greeted Perón and his wife, Isabel Martínez de Perón, when they arrived at the airport. In the September election, Perón won a smashing 62 percent of the votes.[30] The September assassination

[27] Ibid., April 13, 1973.
[28] Ibid., January 26, 1973.
[29] Ibid., April 13, 20, 1973.
[30] John Francis Bannon et al., *Latin America*, 4th ed., p. 372.

of President Salvador Allende of Chile and the accession of General Augusto Pinochet seemed an even more ominous sign that enthusiasm for civilian politicians was on the wane in Latin America.

Pérez Jiménez proved to be neither a Perón nor a Pinochet in his use of the opportunity provided by his apparent popularity in Venezuela. A *peronista*-inspired proposal to have his wife, Flor, or his oldest daughter, Margot Pérez Chalbaud, run as a congressional candidate was considered and rejected. The Cámpora solution to have either Flor or Pablo Salas Castillo run as a presidential candidate who would then resign in favor of Pérez Jiménez was also rejected. Pérez Jiménez instead chose another maneuver that had been popular with the *peronistas* when their chief was in exile in the 1950s and 1960s. At the end of October, Pérez Jiménez directed his followers to abstain from voting. Cruzada nominee Pablo Salas Castillo dutifully withdrew his name from the presidential list and announced that when the *perezjimenistas* won the majority of seats in Congress, they would repeal the constitutional amendment which prohibited Pérez's candidacy for the presidency.[31]

Even in the face of such political disarray, the Venezuelan government apparently expected some last-minute surprise from the *perezjimenistas*. To prevent such an eventuality, prominent *perezjimenistas* were arrested for subversion by Venezuelan security forces in the last week of November. The harassment lasted only for about a week.[32]

The election frenzy finally ended on December 9 when 4.6 million voters chose Carlos Andrés Pérez of Acción Democrática as the next president. The two major parties dominated the field of thirteen presidential candidates:

Carlos Andrés Pérez (AD)	2,122,427	(48.77%)
Lorenzo Fernández (COPEI)	1,598,929	(36.77%)
Jesús A. Paz Galarraga (MEP)	221,864	(5.09%)
José Vicente Rangel (MAS)	183,513	(4.21%)
Jóvito Villaba (URD)	132,829	(3.05%)

[31] *Latin America*, April 20, August 24, September 28, November 2, 30, 1973.

[32] Ibid., November 23, 30, 1973.

The seven candidates with the lowest numbers of votes, including conservatives Pedro Tinoco, Martín García Villasmil, and Miguel Angel Burelli Rivas, each polled less than 1 percent of the total vote. The two major parties won handily in Caracas as well as in the rest of the country.[33]

The legislative returns also dashed the hopes of the Cruzada Cívica Nacionalista. From the 400,093 votes which had represented 11.1 percent of the returns in 1968, the party fell to 178,089 votes, only 4.3 percent of the 1973 vote. Obviously the party divisions and Pérez Jiménez's lack of leadership had hurt the party.[34]

The election results may be explained both by the increasing sophistication of the two major parties and by the ineptness of the *perezjimenistas.* COPEI and AD spent about 50 percent of all campaign funds in 1968 and increased that percentage to 75–80 percent in 1973.[35] In 1973, AD had carefully oiled up the party machinery and had avoided catastrophic divisions; their candidate, Carlos Andrés Pérez, had a youthful and vigorous media image and had the confidence of much of the business community, which had contributed considerably to the campaign chest. By 1973 the oil bonanza produced by the problems in the Middle East promised great possibilities both for political patronage and for economic development. The new rush of oil wealth also changed the context of Venezuelan politics; the new president would be more concerned to spend the revenues wisely than to unite a population threatened by guerrilla action. In a sense, all had become *"desarrollistas"* by 1973, and both major parties had shown that they could be trusted to direct the fortunes of the capitalistic, activist state. AD's Carlos Andrés Pérez benefited from a more effective campaign and image, but COPEI's Lorenzo Fernández lost with more votes and a larger percentage of the national votes than Rafael Caldera had eked out in 1968.

On the other hand, Pérez Jiménez had not demonstrated that

[33] Embassy of Venezuelan Information Service, *Venezuela Up-to-Date* 15 (Winter, 1973–1974): 4; Myers, "Urban Voting," p. 130.

[34] Ibid., p. 142.

[35] Ibid., p. 143. For an account of election spending, see Domingo Alberto Rangel, *Elecciones 1973: El gran negocio.*

he could even hold together his diverse political party or organize an effective campaign. His party's divisions, the numerous opportunists who sought his endorsement, and his own wavering on tactics made him and his group appear ridiculous to the public. He had been outflanked and outmaneuvered by Rómulo Betancourt's policy in Congress and in the presidential campaign.

More, the intensified media emphasis on youth and energy portrayed Carlos Andrés Pérez as a vigorous fellow, with his flashy neckties, long sideburns, and political walks through the country. By contrast, Pérez Jiménez could only appear to be a rather short, chubby, and aging expatriate who was not noted for his dynamism. Acción Democrática sympathizers had begun publishing a series of books in 1969 to inform the youth of Venezuela of the horrors of the dictatorship that they could not remember.[36] The post-1968 *discoteca* generations may indeed have preferred political authoritarianism, but it is questionable whether Pérez Jiménez himself could have captured their imaginations or their loyalties for any length of time.

Pérez's vacillation and refusal to challenge the AD and COPEI constitutional amendment may also have convinced some voters that the former dictator was timid. He would not take the Senate seat that he had won in the elections of 1968, and he did not return to Venezuela to face yet another trial. The defiance that he had expressed in his trial and campaign publications in 1968 were missing in 1973; the 1973 publication *Marcos Pérez Jiménez: Diez años de desarrollo* contained great lists of numbers and graphs and some warmed-over speeches that Pérez had made in the 1950s. It did not stir the blood the way *Frente a la infamia* might have. Furthermore, Pérez Jiménez's well-touted nationalism was being undercut by President Caldera's nationalization of natural gas, the

[36] José Agustín Catalá's Ediciones Centauro published a series of court sentences delivered against various *perezjimenistas* as well as the sentence of Pérez Jiménez himself. These inexpensive volumes began to appear in 1969. In the introduction to *La denuncia: Crimenes y torturas en el regimen de Pérez Jiménez*, Catalá writes: "The publication of these documents and of others which will appear in different editions has as its object to teach the new generations the humiliating drama of a Venezuelan epoch whose repetition they will have the obligation of preventing" (p. 24).

oil reversion law, and the denunciation of the reciprocal trade treaty with the United States. Both COPEI and AD were nearing agreement on an early nationalization of Venezuelan iron and oil. Safe in Madrid, Pérez Jiménez had no part to play in these historic debates.

Nor did Pérez or the Cruzada improve their political position in preparation for the election of 1978. Pérez Jiménez remained in Madrid, and the CCN continued to be divided. In December, 1974, the party even expelled Pérez Jiménez for "betraying the party and deceiving the people."[37] By the time of the 1978 elections, the Cruzada was giving support to the AD candidate. The election returns in 1978, like those of 1973, showed an increasing tendency to a domination of the votes by the two major parties, an increasing expenditure on media campaigns, and less difference between the vote in Caracas and that of the rest of the country. Luis Herrera Campíns (COPEI) won with 2,482,853 votes, and Luis Piñerúa followed closely behind with 2,307,917 votes. The two major parties captured 89.96 percent of the vote. The candidate whom Pérez Jiménez had endorsed, Alejandro Gómez Silva of the Frente Unido Nacionalista (FUN), won only 8,641 votes, or less than 1 percent of the votes. Pablo Salas Castillo of the CCN did even worse with 6,617 votes.[38]

Pérez Jiménez from Madrid had issued a jeremiad just before the election, but he offered no solution to the ills he saw:

It pains me to see how we have lost the excellent opportunities that destiny has put in the hands of our leaders in these last 20 years; our politicians have thought more of their political groups than of Venezuela, and almost always the interests of the Nation have been opposed to party interests. The sense of patriotism has been lost. The sense of sacrifice has been exchanged for that of comfort and dissipation. Austerity does not exist. Corruption has risen to incalculable levels. Plans are not executed. Nobody obeys. The principle of authority has been lost. There is no responsibility among public functionaries. The governments create jobs

[37] *Latin America*, December 13, 1974.
[38] Embassy of Venezuela Information Service, *Venezuela Up-to-Date* 20 (Spring, 1979): 7.

for friends of the Party. The bureaucracy is bankrupting the Nation. Respect and morality have sunk to their lowest level, and the blame for this lies with those who have led the country badly.[39]

Many may have agreed with Pérez Jiménez, but they looked elsewhere to register a protest vote. Parties and candidates of the left, especially José Vicente Rangel's MAS, won more congressional seats in 1978 than they had in 1973. Rangel as a presidential candidate attracted 274,230 votes in 1978, compared with 183,513 in 1973. Municipal elections were held separately from the presidential elections for the first time, and the parties of the left gained even more in these elections held in June, 1979. It is difficult to state with certainty the meaning of voter abstention, but some Venezuelans may have chosen not to vote as a protest. The abstention rate in the presidential elections rose from 10.4 percent in 1973 to 12.9 percent in 1978 and an estimated 20–30 percent in the municipal elections of June, 1979. In 1979, dominance of election returns by the two major parties appeared to be accompanied by leftist protest votes and increasing rates of voter abstention.[40]

Pérez Jiménez and the *perezjimenistas* had been unable to construct a unified and durable political movement in the face of the prosperity of the 1970s. Never a politician, Pérez was clearly outclassed as AD and COPEI became increasingly sophisticated in winning votes. Pérez had come to political maturity in the last years of the Gómez reign but had remained isolated from the student political activity in Caracas and carried a lasting distaste for political maneuvering. His Argentine counterpart, Juan Perón, on the other hand, had grown up in a nation which had had a long tradition of political parties and democracy. Perón not only understood the traditional politics of the elitist parties, but also discovered that he could politicize the *descamisados* into a populist political base. Even at his advanced age and after eighteen years

[39] "Habla Pérez Jiménez: 'Hoy actuaría igual que en el golpe del 48,'" *Elite* 2774 (November 24, 1978): 63.

[40] Embassy of Venezuela Information Service, *Venezuela Up-to-Date* 20 (Spring, 1979): 7; *Latin America*, December 3, 1978; June 8, 1979; *Keesing's Contemporary Archives*, April 6, 1979.

of exile, Perón was ready to enter the fray again in 1973 when Héctor Cámpora invited him back. That gamble was a disaster, but it was a tribute to Perón's brashness and to the skill with which he had built the *peronista* movement.

Pérez Jiménez's support in the 1960s and 1970s, one suspects, was of a different stamp. The voters sympathized with Pérez's harassment (as they saw it) by the AD government and courts, they nostalgically longed for the relative prosperity and harmony of the 1950s, and they wished to protest the rule of the traditional parties who had not improved life, especially urban life, for many Venezuelans. Pérez Jiménez might have capitalized on this sympathy to challenge AD and COPEI, but he was rather easily removed from the political arena by their action to declare him ineligible for office. Some voters continued to vote for candidates designated as *perezjimenista*, but there was no consensus on what that term meant in 1978.

9

Conclusions

Marcos Pérez Jiménez and Rómulo Betancourt began their political careers under the shadow of Juan Vicente Gómez. Pérez Jiménez represented a modernizing tendency within *gomecismo* which wanted the benefits of economic development without disturbing the social structure of the country. Rómulo Betancourt sought modernization, too, but he was more radical. He wanted to replace the old caudillo personalism with an institutionalized political democracy which he believed would encourage the emergence of a strong middle class. He also hoped to terminate the elite's monopoly of national decision making and income. By the 1980s, the apparent maturity of Venezuelan democracy is a tribute to Betancourt's experience, his political skill, and his ability to take advantage of opportunities. Pérez Jiménez, too, was an opportunist, but a timid one who had no humane vision of the future; he was politically naive and unable consistently to exploit the chances that fate bestowed upon him.

Both the military man and the civilian quickly recognized the importance of organization and discipline. Each was instrumental in developing the modern institution that served as his main base of support: the army in Pérez Jiménez's case and Acción Democrática in Betancourt's case. Pérez had the initial advantage since he wanted to modernize an army that already existed; Betancourt had to create a political party from vague notions of reform and dissatisfaction with personalism and caudillism. Yet Pérez's army had only slight experience with an apolitical professionalism, and the strains and pressures of the 1950s provoked rifts between the president and the armed forces. As Pérez relied more on civilian advisors like Vallenilla Lanz and Pedro Estrada, he lost the loyalty of the armed forces, who turned against him in 1958. In exile he provided little leadership or encouragement for his followers. On the other hand, Betancourt single-mindedly kept to his goal of building a modern, disciplined political party. He worked toward that goal whether he was in Venezuela, in exile, in clandestine struggle, or in office. He could not prevent several divisions of his party, but his tenacious leadership ensured that AD, and incidentally the democratic system, would survive.

Betancourt had learned one lesson from Gómez better than Pérez Jiménez had. He determined to be just as tough in defense of his party and of democracy as Gómez had been in his own behalf. That toughness earned him considerable criticism, some enemies, and, ultimately, success in the Venezuelan political arena. Pérez Jiménez did not have the outgoing personality that gloried in a political battle. He was fairly easily bluffed and outmaneuvered. Ever the apolitical technocrat, Pérez Jiménez did not understand the need for or seek support from key groups or from the public at large.

Since 1928, public reaction had played a key role in the competition between the two groups. The 1928 rebellion encouraged Betancourt. The 1936 disorder shocked Pérez Jiménez. In 1948, no popular movement rose up to save Betancourt. In 1958, a popular movement did support the military action to force Pérez Jiménez into exile. After 1958, most of the popular acceptance or rejection of the two men has come in the voting booths. Throughout the fifty-year period under discussion, both men have continued to maintain some pockets of support even when they appeared to be at the lowest ebb of their fortunes. One might recall the image of Cipriano Castro's staunchest supporters giving homage to his bitterest enemy as Juan Vicente Gómez looked on. There is no doubt that a president who does not have the power or will to remain in office cannot reward his followers. So too, one might hypothesize that a momentary lauding of Pérez Jiménez, for example, might be intended as criticism of Betancourt rather than an enthusiastic wish for the return of dictatorship.

Pérez Jiménez may have retained some lingering popularity in

Venezuela because his trial allowed him to claim two of the most important issues in contemporary Venezuela: a hostility toward political parties in general, and nationalism. Arturo Uslar Pietri, Miguel Angel Burelli Rivas, and Marcos Pérez Jiménez have all criticized the self-interest of political parties and have charged that Venezuela will not be able to progress until the social unity and stability of the past are re-created. The nostalgia for an idealized, nonpartisan past can gain some votes in the face of contemporary partisan squabbles. Pérez's other strong appeal, his bitter attack on the United States, cut more effectively across ideological lines than his criticism of political parties. Even Cipriano Castro's critic, Pío Gil, reprimanded Juan Vicente Gómez for eliciting U.S. help to punish Castro. Venezuelans have been as jealous of their grudges as of their riches, and many would have flinched at the image of a Venezuelan former president in a Dade County jail. Both the extradition and the opportunity afforded by his defense before the Supreme Court in Venezuela allowed Pérez Jiménez to portray himself as an avid nationalist who had been treated dishonorably by the Yankees. His defiance in the 1960s seemed to some Venezuelans to supplant the quiescence that had characterized Pérez Jiménez in the 1950s.

Indeed, the extradition and trial of Pérez Jiménez assumed a central importance in the whole political competition between Betancourt and Pérez Jiménez. It dramatized their conflicts and the different political systems they represented. One U.S. scholar has recounted the way the AD leaders have attempted to bring Leonardo Ruiz Pineda into the national political mythology as a democratic, nonviolent leader of the resistance against Pérez Jiménez. Charles Ameringer writes: "Because of his style of combat, Ruiz Pineda was the ideal democratic revolutionary. If he had not existed, AD would have had to invent him."[1] The explosive atmosphere of the 1960s called for someone to hate as well as someone to love. AD tried to propose Pérez Jiménez as the antihero. The

[1] Charles Ameringer, "Leonardo Ruiz Pineda: Leader of the Venezuelan Resistance, 1949–1952," *Journal of Interamerican Studies and World Affairs* 21 (May, 1979): 229.

long trial expressed the democratic revulsion toward dictatorship and tried to teach the Venezuelan youth of the evils of the system that they but dimly remembered.

Rather unexpectedly, of course, Pérez Jiménez turned the trial somewhat to his political advantage. He still had gained neither taste nor talent for politics, however, and he refused to challenge the democratic parties for the presidency. No other figure on the Venezuelan horizon was able or willing to assume the task of molding the *perezjimenistas* into a permanent and disciplined party.

The extradition and trial did exact a personal and financial price from Pérez Jiménez, although AD may have wondered whether the precedent was worth the cost. The AD leaders did follow up Pérez's Supreme Court defeat with subsequent judicial actions and political pacts which condemned him, in effect, to perpetual exile. Pérez Jiménez, like Cipriano Castro, became a "man without a country." In the end, Betancourt, who had spent so many years in exile, forced the same fate on his enemy.

Appendix A
Assets in 1948 and Known Sources of Income

Assets

A. *Assets of Lt. Col. Marcos Pérez Jiménez:*
1. Five (5) registered shares in the "SAETA"
   Corporation of this City, of 1,000 bolivares each Bs 5,000.00
2. One (1) share in "Los Cortijos"
   Country Club, with a face value of 5,000.00
3. Furnishings of his residence, valued at 14,000.00
4. A Nash Ambassador automobile, Model 1947,
   Serial No. R-519432 14,000.00
5. Cash 15,000.00

     Subtotal Bs 53,000.00

B. *Assets of Mrs. Flor Chalbaud de Pérez Jiménez:*
1. A house located in the El Conde Development,
   San Augustín Parish, East 12th Street, Block 29,
   in this City, with an estimated value at
   that date of Bs 60,000.00

     Subtotal Bs 60,000.00

     Total Assets Bs 113,000.00

Liabilities

Owed by Col. Marcos Pérez Jiménez:

Balance outstanding on the price of Nash Ambassador
automobile, Model 1947, Serial No. R-519432 Bs 8,000.00

     Total Liabilities 8,000.00

     Net assets Bs 105,000.00

In addition, and in accordance with the respective General Budget Laws of Public Revenue and Expenditures, the said General Marcos Pérez Jiménez (Ret) from November 5, 1948, when he took office as Minister of National Defense, until January 13, 1958, when he was deposed as President of the Republic, should have received the following amounts for salaries and remuneration:

SOURCE: *Pérez Jiménez* v. *Aristeguieta and Maguire* 19,507 (5th cir., 1962), 4:1093–1097.

1. *Fiscal Year 1948–1949*
   a) Salary as Minister of National Defense from
   November 25, 1948, to June 30, 1949 (Official
   Gazette No. 207, special issue of
   July 14, 1948)   Bs   28,800.00
   b) Special end-of-year bonus   2,000.00

                    Subtotal   Bs   30,800.00

2. *Fiscal Year 1949–1950*
   a) Salary as Minister of National Defense, (Official
   Gazette No. 236, special issue of June 30, 1949)   Bs   72,000.00
   b) Expense account as a Member of the
   Government Military Junta   30,000.00
   c) Special end-of-year bonus   3,000.00

                    Subtotal   Bs 105,000.00

3. *Fiscal Year 1950–1951*
   a) Salary as Minister of National Defense, (Official
   Gazette No. 250, special issue of June 30, 1950)   Bs   96,000.00
   b) Expense account as a Member of the
   Government Military Junta   40,000.00
   c) Special end-of-year bonus   4,000.00

                    Subtotal   Bs 140,000.00

4. *Fiscal Year 1951–1952*
   a) Salary as Minister of National Defense, (Official
   Gazette No. 298, special issue of June 30, 1951)   Bs   96,000.00
   b) Expense account as a Member of the
   Government Junta   40,000.00
   c) Special end-of-year bonus   4,000.00

                    Subtotal   Bs 140,000.00

5. *Fiscal Year 1952–1953*
   a) Salary as a Member of the Government Junta,
   from July 1 to December 2, 1952, (Official
   Gazette No. 341, special issue of June 30, 1952)   Bs   58,266.65
   b) Salary as Provisional President of the Republic
   from December 3, 1952, to June 30, 1953,
   as appearing in certificate of office, a duplicate
   of which is attached, marked "B"   87,500.00
   c) Special end-of-year bonus   6,250.00

                    Subtotal   Bs 152,016.65

6. *Fiscal Year 1953–1954*
   a) Salary as President of the Republic, (Official
   Gazette No. 381, special issue of June 30, 1953)   Bs 150,000.00
   b) Special end-of-year bonus   6,250.00

                    Subtotal   Bs 156,250.00

7. *Fiscal Year 1954–1955*
   a) Salary as President of the Republic, (Official
      Gazette No. 417, special issue of June 30, 1954)   Bs 150,000.00
   b) Special end-of-year bonus   6,250.00

                  Subtotal   Bs 156,250.00

8. *Fiscal Year 1955–1956*
   a) Salary as President of the Republic, (Official
      Gazette No. 464, special issue of June 30, 1955)   Bs 150,000.00
   b) Special end-of-year bonus   6,250.00

                  Subtotal   Bs 156,250.00

9. *Fiscal Year 1956–1957*
   a) Salary as President of the Republic, (Official
      Gazette No. 488, special issue of June 30, 1956)   Bs 84,166.50
   b) Special end-of-year bonus   6,250.00

                  Subtotal   Bs 90,416.50

    Total Salary and other remuneration   Bs 1,283,233.15

Appendix B
Pérez Jiménez's Assets by 1958

Date	Description	Bolivares		Dollars
Aug. 27, 1949	Ten Bs 50 par value share certificates in Hotel Tamanaco, 20% paid	Bs 100	$	29.85
Oct. 10, 1950	Purchase by defendant of 239.40 square meters of land in El Paraíso, Caracas	47,880		14,292.54
Feb. 5, 1951	Deposit to account of defendant in National City Bank by Napoleón Dupouy			150,000.00
Oct. 11, 1951	Deposit to account of defendant in National City Bank by Napoleón Dupouy			100,000.00
Dec. 3, 1951	Deposit to account of defendant in National City Bank by Napoleón Dupouy			100,000.00
	Yearly Total		$	350,430.73
Mar. 8, 1952	Purchase by Mrs. Pérez Jiménez of a parcel of land in Santa Monica Real Estate Development	Bs 120,000	$	35,820.89
Apr. 12, 1952	Bill of exchange drawn by Urbanización Caribe C.A. against defendant, paid	840		250.75
May 12, 1952	Bill of exchange drawn by Urbanización Caribe C.A. against defendant, paid	840		250.75
June 12, 1952	Bill of exchange drawn by Urbanización Caribe C.A. against defendant, paid	840		250.75
July 1, 1952	Total C.A. Obras Avenida Bolívar bonds purchased in 1952 per broker's statements in valise	1,001,391		298,922.68

SOURCE: *Pérez Jiménez* v. *Aristeguieta and Maguire* 19,507 (5th cir., 1962), 4:961–969.

Date	Description	Bolivares	Dollars
July 12, 1952	Bill of exchange drawn by Urbanización Caribe C.A. against defendant, paid	840	250.75
July 18, 1952	Purchase by Mrs. Pérez Jiménez of a lot in Caribe Development of 5,117 square meters	143,276	42,768.96
Aug. 12, 1952	Bill of exchange drawn by Urbanización Caribe C.A. against defendant, paid	840	250.75
Sept. 12, 1952	Bill of exchange drawn by Urbanización Caribe C.A. against defendant, paid	840	250.75
Oct. 12, 1952	Bill of exchange drawn by Urbanización Caribe C.A. against defendant, paid	840	250.75
Nov. 4, 1952	Purchase by Mrs. Pérez Jiménez of 20,000 square meters of land in El Peñón	200,000	59,701.49
Nov. 4, 1952	Purchase by Mrs. Pérez Jiménez of 8,190 square meters in El Peñón	81,900	24,447.76
Nov. 12, 1952	Bill of exchange drawn by Urbanización Caribe C.A. against defendant, paid	840	250.75
Dec. 12, 1952	Bill of exchange drawn by Urbanización Caribe C.A. against defendant, paid	840	250.75
	Yearly Total		$ 463,918.53
Jan. 12, 1953	Bill of exchange drawn by Urbanización Caribe C.A. against defendant, paid	Bs 840	$ 240.75
Feb. 12, 1953	Bill of exchange drawn by Urbanización Caribe C.A. against defendant, paid	858	256.12
May 20, 1953	Hotel Tamanaco balance	400	119.40
July 10, 1953	Deposit to account of defendant in National City Bank		1,000,000.00
Aug. 25, 1953	Purchase by Mrs. Pérez Jiménez of house on Sanabria St., El Paraíso, Caracas	100,000	29,850.75

Date	Description	Bolivares	Dollars
Sept. 23, 1953	Purchase by defendant of an estate on second street West of Ejercito Avenue, in El Paraíso	200,000	59,701.49
Nov. 13, 1953	Purchase by Mrs. Pérez Jiménez of 32,000 square meters of land in El Peñón for Bs 320,000 of which Bs 240,000 deferred	80,000	23,880.60
Nov. 13, 1953	Purchase by Mrs. Pérez Jiménez of 25,000 square meters of land in El Peñón for Bs 250,000 of which Bs 187,500 deferred	62,500	18,656.72
	Yearly Total		$ 1,132,715.83
Feb. 10, 1954	Purchase by Mrs. Pérez Bs Jiménez of 6002.75 square meters in El Peñón	60,000	$ 17,910.45
Feb. 15, 1954	Deposit to account of defendant in National City Bank of New York		1,000,000.00
Apr. 30, 1954	Purchase by Mrs. Pérez Jiménez of the "La Constancia" property, of 42,250 square meters in Lagunetica Development.	10,000	2,985.07
May 29, 1954	400 bearer shares, Bs 1,000 par value each, of C.A. El Heraldo registered May 29, 1954. (The record does not disclose when defendant acquired these shares.)	400,000	119,402.98
June 30, 1954	Bonds of C. A. Centro Simón Bolívar. (The date is the issue date of the bonds. The record does not disclose when the defendant acquired these bonds.)	330,000	98,507.46
Aug. 31, 1954	Bonds of Centro Simón Bolívar (The date is issue date of the bonds. The record does not disclose when the defendant acquired these bonds.)	1,500	447.76
Sept. 29, 1954	Purchase by defendant of house and lot on Bolívar Ave. in town of Michelena	30,000	29,850.75

Date	Description	Bolivares	Dollars
Nov. 19, 1954	Purchase by Mrs. Pérez Jiménez of 399.67 square meters on Ejercito Ave., El Paraíso, Caracas	79,934	23,860.90
Dec. 7, 1954	Deposit to account of defendant by Napoleón Dupouy in French American Banking Corporation		1,000,000.00
	Yearly Total		$ 2,301,920.59
Jan. 28, 1955	Purchase by Mrs. Pérez Jiménez of the following real property in El Peñón:		
	1850 square meters Bs	18,500 $	5,522.39
	5000 " "	50,000	14,925.37
	2250 " "	22,500	6,716.42
	900 " "	9,200	2,746.27
	2000 " "	20,000	5,970.15
	900 " "	9,200	2,746.27
	2200 " "	20,000	6,567.16
Jan. 28, 1955	Mortgages on property at El Peñón purchased by Mrs. Pérez Jiménez on Nov. 13, 1953, cancelled	240,000 187,500	71,641.79 55,970.15
Feb. 1, 1955	Purchase by Mrs. Pérez Jiménez of 718.21 square meters in Caribe Development	25,137	7,503.58
Feb. 7, 1955	Purchase by Mrs. Pérez Jiménez of 1,006 square meters of land in Caribe Development	70,420	21,020.90
June 25, 1955	Bonds of Centro Simón Bolívar (The date is issue date of the bonds. The record does not disclose when the defendant acquired these bonds.)	10,000	2,985.07
Oct. 13, 1955	Receipt by Napoleón Dupouy for money to be used in discounting drafts of Instituto Nacional de Obras Sanitarios at 8% per annum to Ingenieros Venezolano, C.A. (IVECA).	2,000,000	597,014.92

Date	Description	Bolivares	Dollars
Oct. 15, 1955	Receipt signed by Antonio Pérez for purchase by defendant of property of C.A. de Inversiones Pecuarias y Agricolas (CADIPIA).	100,000	29,950.75
Dec. 6, 1955	Bill of sale to defendant of Rolls Royce	102,500	30,597.01
	Yearly Total	$	861,778.20
Jan. 19, 1956	Purchase by Mrs. Pérez Jiménez of 20,250 square meters on Suapure St., Colinas de Bello Monte for Bs 708,750 of which Bs 200,000 was paid as a down payment	$	59,701.49
Feb. 9, 1956	Purchase by Mrs. Pérez Jiménez of estate in Vista Alegre Development	Bs 110,000	32,835.82
Feb. 21, 1956	Purchase by Mrs. Pérez Jiménez and Angelina Castro Tejera, equally, on Cristobal Mendoza Avenue, El Paraíso. (Total price Bs 700,000.)	350,000	104,477.61
Feb. 29, 1956	Acknowledgment of defendant's ownership of estate Carbonero	400,000	119,402.98
Mar. 28, 1956	Purchase by Mrs. Pérez Jiménez of the following real properties in Caribe Development:		
	883.30 square meters	24,732.40	7,382.80
	818.15 " "	40,907.50	12,211.19
	758.55 " "	37,927.50	11,321.64
May 4, 1956	Loan to Napoleón Dupouy at 10%	1,000,000	298,507.46
May 16, 1956	Urbanizadora Santa Cruz 6,000 bearer shares. (The date is the registration date. The record does not disclose when the defendant acquired these shares.)	6,000,000	1,791,044.77
May 23, 1956	Down payment on the plantations Chuao and Cepe, owned jointly by Pérez Jiménez and Polinversiones	275,000	82,089.55

Date	Description	Bolivares	Dollars
May 25, 1956	Purchase by Mrs. Pérez Jiménez of 3845 square meters in Colinas de Bello Monte Development	384,500	114,776.12
May 30, 1956	Purchase by Mrs. Pérez Jiménez of 4800 square meters in Colinas de los Chaguaramos Real Estate Development	144,000	42,985.07
Aug. 15, 1956	Purchase of interest in Trans Western de Venezuela	683,375	203,992.54
Aug. 13, 1956	Payment on premium for guarantee on Trans Western de Venezuela	60,000	17,910.45
Dec. 4, 1956	C.A. de Seguros Horizonte 300 shares at Bs 100, purchased at 20% of face value	6,000	1,791.04
	Yearly Total		$ 2,900,430.53
Feb. 25, 1957	Purchase of interest in Edificio Washington through Llovera Páez	Bs 500,000	$ 149,253.73
Mar. 18, 1957	Deposit to account of defendant in National City Bank of New York		300,000.00
Mar. 27, 1957	Deposit to account of defendant in National City Bank of New York		300,000.00
July or Aug., 1957	Purchase of additional interest in Edificio Washington through Llovera Páez	2,500,000	746,268.65
July 29, 1957	Purchase of shares of Banco de Occidente for defendant and his sisters and brother	200,000	59,701.49
Aug. 12, 1957	Trans Western de Venezuela, payment on concessions	250,000	74,626.86
Sept. 23, 1957	100 bearer shares of CADIPA at Bs 5,000. (The record does not disclose when defendant acquired these shares. The date is of amendments to registration.)	500,000	149,253.73
Sept. 27, 1957	Purchase by Mrs. Pérez Jiménez and children of country house "Villa Bertha" in El Paraíso	940,000	280,597.01
Oct. 1, 1957	Deposit by Silvio Gutiérrez to account of defendant in Union Bank of Switzerland		1,000,000.00

Date	Description	Bolivares	Dollars
Nov. 27, 1957	Deposit in Hibernia National Bank in New Orleans to account of defendant by Pedro Gutiérrez Alfaro	1,500,000	447,761.12
Dec. 30, 1957	Deposit for purchase Colonial Trust Company stock through Edificio Washington	3,000,000	895,522.38
	Yearly Total		$ 4,402,989.97

Letter to the Consul-General
of Venezuela in Miami, dated
Oct. 24, 1958, in which defendant stated that he understood
that some valuables in his
valise were not included in the
list of his impounded properties.
He listed those missing as:

Bonds of Centro Simón Bolívar		Bs 3,000,000	$ 895,522.38
Cash (Venezuelan currency)		300,000	89,552.24
Cash (United States currency)			100,000.00
			$ 1,085,074.62
Grand Total			$13,513,576.39

Appendix C
Some Sources of Pérez Jiménez's Wealth

The Venezuelan government was able to establish tentatively that Pérez Jiménez had received the benefit from the following sources. These sums often were qualified by terms such as "at least," "no more than," and the like. The sums were divided into four categories, which are reproduced in the following tables:

I.   Commissions (defense and others); dates are approximate.

		Paid by
July 16, 1951	$ 37,313.43	Empresas Campenon Bernard
Jan. 30, 1952	58,951.50	Aktiebolaget Bofors
Sept. 12, 1951	19,136.25	Venezuelan Government Agency
Sept. 12, 1951	17,885.00	Venezuelan Government Agency
Sept. 12, 1951	145,960.00	Vickers-Armstrong
Oct. 29, 1951	60,000.00	International Standard Electric, New York
March 29, 1953	785,000.00	Ansaldo, S.A.
May 27, 1954	190,272.00	Vickers-Armstrong
May 27, 1954	258,774.00	Government of Venezuela
May 27, 1954	170,175.00	Government of Venezuela
Total	$1,743,467.18	

II. Land Speculations

July 30, 1956	$1,082,794.03	Industrial del Cartón (Issas)
June 7, 1956	991,107.61	Mrs. Rafaela Agreda de Jiménez
Total	$2,073,901.64	

III. Petty Peculation (Improvements on private property at state expense)

1954	$ 4,203.13	Well on "El Peñón"
1955–1958	44,262.39	Gardeners on "El Peñón"
Total	$ 48,465.52	

IV. Profits from Empresa Venezolana de Ingenieria y Construcción, S.A.

1955–Jan. 23, 1958	$ 89,552.24	Profits from EVICSA

Total of I. through IV.

$1,743,467.18
2,073,901.64
48,465.52
89,552.24
$3,955,386.58

SOURCE: *Pérez Jiménez* v. *Aristeguieta and Maguire* 19,507 (5th cir., 1962), 3:860–870.

An estimated $12,000,000 was not tied to specific sources, but the figure was arrived at from indications of his wealth in 1958. See Appendix B.

Appendix D
Articles in the Penal Code with Which Pérez Jiménez Was Charged (Financial Crimes)

Article 195:   Embezzlement or peculation

Every public official who abstracts funds or other personal property, the collection, custody or administration of which has been entrusted to him by virtue of his office, shall be punished by hard labor for three to ten years.

If the loss is not heavy, or if complete reparation is made before the guilty party is brought to trial, he shall suffer imprisonment for three to twenty-one months.

Article 196:   Extortion

Every official who by abusing his office forces a person to give or to promise to him or to any third party any sum of money or other illicit profit or gift shall be punished by imprisonment for eighteen months to five years.

If the amount of thing illicitly given or promised is of little value, the period of imprisonment shall be for three to twenty-one months.

Article 198:   Corruption of Functionaries

Every official who, for the performance of any official duty, receives for his own or another's account, a remuneration, whether in the form of money or any other thing which is not due him, or accepts any offer of such remuneration, shall be punished by imprisonment for one to two months.

Article 199:   Corruption of Functionaries

Every public official who receives, or exacts a promise, money or other benefit, either directly or through another person, for delaying or omitting any official duty, or for doing an act which is contrary to that duty, shall be punished by hard labor for a period of three to five years. The term of hard labor shall be for a period of four to eight years if the offense resulted in:

1. The grant of public office, emoluments, pensions or honors, or the award of contracts in which the agency employing the official has an interest.

2. Tending to cause any loss or injury to any of the parties to a civil action or to a party found guilty in a criminal proceeding.

SOURCE: *Pérez Jiménez* v. *Aristeguieta and Maguire* 19,507 (5th cir., 1962), 3:883–885.

If the act has resulted in a conviction carrying a restriction of personal liberty in excess of six months, the term of hard labor shall be three to ten years.

Article 205:   Profit from public office (lucro de funcionarios)

Every public official who directly, or through an intermediary or by deceit, obtains for himself any personal benefit in any act of public administration in which he performs a function shall be punished with imprisonment for six months to five years.

Bibliography

The most useful primary material was found in the various legal sources and archives. Much of the published material repeated in part some of the court record, books, periodicals, and newspapers used in the court record or the attorneys' guides to the record. Two archives and one set of court records provided the bulk of the material on the extradition and trial of Pérez Jiménez: the papers of Judge William C. Mathes in the Zimmerman Library of the University of New Mexico, the record of the Venezuelan trial of Pérez Jiménez in the archive of the Venezuelan Supreme Court, and the sixteen volumes of the U.S. Fifth Circuit Court of Appeals' record of Pérez Jiménez's petition for a writ of *habeas corpus*. The transcripts of the record of the Fifth Circuit Court of Appeals included copies of the original warrants of arrest, complaints for extradition, court arguments, evidence, and exhibits—in short, the record of the lower court hearings.

Some of the material in the Venezuelan public documents also sums up or repeats documents from the court record. The *Libro amarillo* of the Ministerio de Relaciones Exteriores was especially helpful in tracing Venezuela's attempts to implement the Betancourt Doctrine. The *Informes* of the Comisión Investigadora contra Enriquecimiento Ilícito (CIEI) revealed the problems and procedures of that body.

In addition to secondary studies of recent Venezuelan politics, the most valuable periodicals were some of the Venezuelan publications such as *Política* and *Elite*. Also of great use were newspapers and newsletters, including *El Nacional, El Universal,* the *New York Times,* the *Miami Herald,* and *Latin America.*

Finally, a number of Venezuelan and U.S. books have been quite helpful. The Venezuelan volumes frequently are aggressively partisan, but all have some value for comprehending Venezuelan politics since 1940. Those published by José Agustín Catalá relate most directly to the extradition and the trials of the *perezjimenistas*; many of those volumes published since 1968 might be seen as campaign documents in which the crimes of Pérez Jiménez are publicized in order to limit his political popularity among Venezuelans, especially the young. On the other side, the books by Pérez Jiménez and Rafael Naranjo Ostty and some of the *perezjimenista* groups try to exploit the existing sympathy for the former dictator. A useful series is that edited by José Rivas Rivas which contains reproductions of some of the important news stories from 1936 into the 1960s. Little aside from the court record and newspapers was helpful for the extradition proceedings from the U.S. point of view; Whiteman's *Digest of International Law* did contain several entries from the case and pointed out the legal issues and precedents involved.

Archives

Albuquerque, New Mexico. Zimmerman Library. Coronado Room. William Mathes Papers.

Caracas, Venezuela. Archives of the Corte Suprema de Justicia. Archive 59-95.

Unpublished Works

Baloyra, Enrique A. "Golpes and Democratic Norms in Venezuela." Paper presented at the 8th National Meeting of the Latin American Studies Association, Pittsburgh, Pa., April 7, 1979.

Bigler, Gene E. "The Politicization of Trade and Venezuelan Economic Development." Paper presented at the 8th National Meeting of the Latin American Studies Association, Pittsburgh, Pa., April 7, 1979.

Brossard, Emma B. "Rómulo Betancourt: A Study in the Evolution of a Constitutional Statesman." Ph.D. diss., Claremont Graduate School and University Center, 1971.

Doyle, Joseph. "Venezuela 1958: Transition from Dictatorship to Democracy." Ph.D. diss., George Washington University, 1967.

López Guinazú, Antonio A. "Modernization in Venezuela (1950–1961)." Ph.D. diss., Colorado State University, 1970.

Morales Bello, David, et al. "The Extradition of Pérez Jiménez." Mimeographed. Caracas, Venezuela, n.d.

Stambouli, Andres. "La actuación política de la dictadura y el rechazo del autoritarismo." Paper presented at the 8th National Meeting of the Latin American Studies Association, Pittsburgh, Pa., April 7, 1979.

Thompson, Susan B. "Venezuelan Immigration Policy 1936–1960." Paper presented at the annual meeting of the Committee on Gran Colombian Studies, Washington, D.C., December 29, 1976.

Torres, Arístides. "Formulación e implementación de programas públicos en Venezuela: El caso del Gran Mariscal de Ayacucho." Paper presented at the 8th National Meeting of the Latin American Studies Association, Pittsburgh, Pa., April 7, 1979.

Interviews

Naranjo Ostty, Rafael. Caracas, Venezuela, February 12, 1970.

Velasquez, Ramón. Caracas, Venezuela, June 4, 1970.

Westwood, Howard. Washington, D.C., November 18, 1969.

Government Documents

República de Venezuela, Comisión Investigadora Contra el Enriquecimiento Ilícito de Funcionarios o Empleados Públicos. *Informe que presenta la Comisión Investigadora Contra el Enriquecimiento Ilícito de Funcionarios o Empleados Públicos al Congreso Nacional 1958–1959.*

————, ————. *Informe presentado al Congreso Nacional correspondiente al año 1959–1960.*

————, ————. *Informe presentado al Congreso Nacional correspondiente al periódo 1959–1964.*

————, Fiscalía General de la República. *Informe al Congreso Nacional* for years 1960 through 1964 and 1968. Titles vary.

————, Junta Revolucionaria de Gobierno. *Recopilación de sentencias . . . por el Jurado de Responsibilidad Civil y Administrativa.* Caracas, 1946.

————, Ministerio de Justicia. *Memoria y cuenta presentada al Congreso de la República de Venezuela en sus reuniones ordinarias* for years 1959 and 1960.

————, Ministerio de Relaciones Exteriores. *Libro amarillo de la República de Venezuela* for years 1959 through 1965.

————, Presidencia de la República. *150 años de vida republicana: 1811–1961.* 2 vols. Caracas: Ediciones de la Presidencia de la República, 1963.

————, ————. *Alocución dirigida a los venezolanos por el coronel Marcos Pérez Jiménez, presidente de la república, desde el círculo de las fuerzas armadas.* Caracas, December 2, 1953.

————, ————. *Discurso pronunciada por el coronel Marcos Pérez Jiménez, presidente de la república, desde el destructor Zulia, en el segundo aniversario del 2 de diciembre de 1952.* La Guaira, December 2, 1954.

————, ————. *Discurso pronunciado por el general Marcos Pérez Jiménez, presidente de la república, en al cuarto aniversario del 2 de diciembre de 1952.* Caracas, December 2, 1956.

————, ————. *El Estado Barínas ante la reelección del general Marcos Pérez Jiménez.* 1957.

————, ————. *Mensaje presentado por el coronel Marcos Pérez Jiménez, presidente de la república, al Congreso Nacional en sus sesiones ordinarias de 1954.* Caracas, April 25, 1954.

———, ———. *Mensaje presentado por el coronel Marcos Pérez Jiménez, presidente de la república, al Congreso Nacional en sus sesiones ordinarias de 1955.* Caracas, April 23, 1955.

———, ———. *Mensaje presentado por el general Marcos Pérez Jiménez, presidente de la república, al Congreso Nacional en sus sesiones ordinarias de 1956.* Caracas, April 21, 1956.

———, ———. *Mensaje presentado por el general Marcos Pérez Jiménez, presidente de la república, al Congreso Nacional en sus sesiones ordinarias de 1957.* Caracas, April 25, 1957.

———, Procuraduría de la Nación. *Informe al Congreso Nacional* for years 1957–1958 and 1959.

Periodicals

Ameringer, Charles. "Leonardo Ruiz Pineda: Leader of the Venezuelan Resistance, 1949–1952." *Journal of Interamerican Studies and World Affairs* 21 (May, 1979): 209–232.

Baloyra, Enrique A. "Oil Policies and Budgets in Venezuela, 1938–1968." *Latin American Research Review* 9 (Summer, 1974): 28–72.

———, and John D. Martz. "Culture, Regionalism, and Political Opinion in Venezuela." *Canadian Journal of Political Science* 10 (September, 1977): 527–572.

Bamberger, Michael. "Problems of Political Integration in Latin America: The Barrios of Venezuela." *International Affairs* 44 (October, 1968): 709–719.

Barrios, Gonzalo. "El enriquecimiento ilícito de funcionarios en el plano internacional." *Política* 19 (December, 1961): 42–50.

———. "El enriquecimiento ilícito, problema internacional." *Política* 4 (December, 1959): 88–90.

———. "La recuperación de bienes malversados por los dictadores." *Política* 8 (April, 1960): 119–125.

Berkhouwer, C. "Delitos de los funcionarios públicos." *Politica* 19 (December, 1961): 51–56.

Burggraaff, Winfield J. "Venezuelan Regionalism and the Rise of Táchira." *Americas* 25 (October, 1968): 160–173.

Butler, Robert. "Contemporary Venezuela: Review Essay." *Journal of Interamerican Studies and World Affairs* 17 (May, 1975): 237–244.

Cayuela, José, and David Pachano. "El juicio del siglo." *Elite* 2219 (April 6, 1968): 35–50.

Fontecilla Riquelme, Rafael. "El delito de peculado, ante el derecho internacional." *Política* 10 (June, 1960): 16–38.

Gorkine, M. "Delitos de funcionarios públicos contra la moral y la humanidad." *Política* 19 (December, 1961): 57–63.

Grayson, George W. "Venezuela's Presidential Politics." *Current History* 66 (January, 1974): 23–27+.

Keesing's Contemporary Archives, 1967–1979.

Lairet, Germán. "Corrupción administrativa y corrupción política." *Semana* 352 (February 20–26, 1975): 45.

Latin America, 1967–1979.

Levine, Daniel. "Democracy and the Church in Venezuela." *Journal of Interamerican Studies and World Affairs* 18 (February, 1976): 3–23.

––––––. "Urbanization, Migrants, and Politics in Venezuela." *Journal of Interamerican Studies and World Affairs* 17 (August, 1975): 358–372.

Martz, John. "Venezuela's Generation of '28: The Genesis of Political Democracy." *Journal of Interamerican Studies and World Affairs* 6 (January, 1964): 17–32.

––––––, and Peter B. Harkins. "Urban Electoral Behavior, Caracas 1958–68." *Comparative Politics* 5 (July, 1973): 523–550.

Miami Herald, 1958–1963.

Monjardin, Federico F. "Informe sobre el enriquecimiento ilícito." *Política* 19 (December, 1961): 64–66.

Myers, David J. "Urban Voting, Structural Cleavage, and Party System Evolution: The Case of Venezuela." *Comparative Politics* 8 (October, 1975): 119–151.

Nacional, El (Caracas), 1945–1948, 1958–1959.

New York Times, 1958–1963.

Powell, John D. "Venezuelan Agrarian Problems in Comparative Perspective." *Comparative Studies in Society and History* 13 (July, 1971): 282–300.

Taylor, Philip B., Jr. "Progress in Venezuela." *Current History* 53 (November, 1967): 270–274.

Universal, El. 1958–1959.

Veblen, Eric P., and Gene E. Bigler. "Attitudes Toward the Public Interest and Conflict in Latin American Political Culture." *Latin American Research Review* 11 (Spring, 1976): 173–180.

Von Lazar, A., and V. A. Beadle. "National Integration and Insurgency in Venezuela: An Exercise in Causation." *Western Political Quarterly* 24 (March, 1971): 130–145.

Books

Abreu, José Vicente. *Guasina, donde el río perdió las siete estrellas: Relatos de un campo de concentración de Pérez Jiménez.* Caracas: José Agustín Catalá, 1969.

––––––. *Las cuatro letras.* Caracas: Ediciones Centauro, 1969.

———. *Se llamaba S.N.* 2d ed. Caracas: José Agustín Catalá, 1964.

Acción Democrática. *Rómulo Betancourt: Pensamiento y acción.* Mexico City: Beatriz de Silva, 1951.

Acheson, Dean. *Present at the Creation: My Years in the State Department.* New York: W. W. Norton & Co., 1969.

Alexander, Robert. *The Communist Party of Venezuela.* Stanford, Calif.: Hoover Institution Press, 1969.

———. *Latin American Political Parties.* New York: Praeger Publishers, 1973.

———. *The Venezuelan Democratic Revolution: A Profile of the Regime of Rómulo Betancourt.* New Brunswick, N.J.: Rutgers University Press, 1964.

Ameringer, Charles D. *The Democratic Left in Exile: The Antidictatorial Struggle in the Caribbean, 1945–1959.* Coral Gables: University of Miami Press, 1974.

Arcaya, Pedro Manuel. *The Gómez Regime in Venezuela and Its Background.* Baltimore: The Sun Printing Co., 1936.

———. *La pena de la confiscación general de bienes en Venezuela: Estudio de historia y derecho.* Caracas: Impresores Unidos, 1945.

———. *Tetralogia juridica: Los procesos venezolanos por peculado y enriquecimiento indebido.* Caracas: Impresores Unidos, 1947.

Bannon, John, Robert R. Miller, and Peter M. Dunne. *Latin America.* 4th ed. Encino, Calif.: Glencoe Press, 1977.

Barrios, Gonzalo. *Los días y la política.* Caracas: Editorial Arte, 1963.

Baloyra, Enrique A., and John D. Martz. *Political Attitudes in Venezuela: Societal Cleavages and Political Opinion.* Austin: University of Texas Press, 1979.

Betancourt, Rómulo. *La revolución democrática en Venezuela, 1959–1963: Documentos del gobierno presidido por Rómulo Betancourt.* 4 vols. Caracas: Imprenta Nacional, 1968.

———. *Venezuela: Política y petróleo.* 2d ed. Caracas: Editorial Senderos, 1967.

Blanco Peñalver, Juan. *Historia de un naufragio.* Maracay, Venezuela, 1962.

Blank, David E. *Politics in Venezuela.* Boston, Mass.: Little, Brown & Co., 1973.

Blum, John M., et al. *The National Experience.* 2 vols. New York: Harcourt Brace Jovanovich, Inc., 1977.

Boersner, Demetrio. *Venezuela y el Caribe: Presencia cambiante.* Caracas: Monte Avila, 1978.

Bonilla, Frank. *The Failure of Elites.* Cambridge: MIT Press, 1970.

Briceño-Iragorry, Mario. *Ideario político.* Caracas: Editorial "Las Novedades," 1958.

Brito Figueroa, Federico. *Historia económica y social de Venezuela.* Caracas: Dirección de Cultura, Universidad Central de Venezuela, 1966.

Burggraaff, Winfield. *The Venezuelan Armed Forces in Politics, 1935–1959.* Columbia: University of Missouri Press, 1972.

Capriles, Miguel Angel. *Memorias de la inconformidad.* 2d ed. Caracas, 1973.

Cárdenas, José Rodolfo. *El combate político: Solo para líderes nuevos.* Caracas: Editorial Arte, 1965.

Catalá, José Agustín, ed. *Documentos para la historia de la resistencia, 1948–1952.* Vol. I. Caracas: José Agustín Catalá, 1969.

———. *La denuncia: Crimenes y torturas en la régimen de Pérez Jiménez.* Caracas: José Agustín Catalá, 1969.

———. *Libro negro 1952.* Caracas: Ediciones Centauro, 1974.

———. *Proceso a un ex-dictador: Juicio al general (r) Marcos Pérez Jiménez.* 2 vols. Caracas: José Agustín Catalá, 1969.

Clinton, Daniel Joseph [Thomas Rourke]. *Gómez: Tyrant of the Andes.* New York: William Morrow and Co., 1941.

Colmenares Díaz, Luis. *La espada y el incensario: La iglesia bajo Pérez Jiménez.* Caracas, 1961.

Cova García, D. Luis. *Fundamento jurídico del nuevo ideal nacional.* Caracas: Jaime Villegas, 1955.

Díaz, Julio. *Historia y política.* 2d ed. Caracas: Pensamiento Vivo, 1963.

Equipos Juveniles Perezjimenistas y Desarrollistas. *Marcos Pérez Jiménez: Diez años de desarrollo.* Caracas, 1973.

Estudio de Caracas, vol. VIII, part 1, *Gobierno y político.* Caracas: Ediciones de la Universidad Central de Venezuela, 1967.

Eisenhower, Milton. *The Wine Is Bitter: The United States and Latin America.* Garden City, N.Y.: Doubleday, 1963.

Gabaldón Márguez, Joaquín. *Paginas de evasión y devaneo (1948–1958).* Caracas, 1959.

García Ponce, Guillermo. *Teoria política y realidad nacional.* Caracas: La Muralla, 1967.

Green, Haywood Hackworth. *Digest of International Law.* Washington, D.C.: Government Printing Office, 1941.

Gutiérrez Alfaro, Tito. *La inconstitucionalidad de los tratados internacionales.* Caracas: Academia de Ciencias Políticas y Sociales, n.d.

Institute for the Comparative Study of Political Systems. *The Venezuelan Elections of December 1, 1963.* 3 vols. Washington, D.C.: Operations and Policy Research, Inc., 1964.

International Bank for Reconstruction and Development. *The Economic Development of Venezuela.* Baltimore, Md.: Johns Hopkins Press, 1961.

Kolb, Glen L. *Democracy and Dictatorship in Venezuela, 1945–1958.* New London: Connecticut College, 1974.

Landaeta, Federico. *Mi General: Breve biografía del general Marcos Pérez Jiménez, presidente de la República de Venezuela.* Madrid: La Coruña, 1957.

Lavin, John. *A Halo for Gómez.* New York: Pageant Press, 1954.

Lepervanche Parparcen, René. *Estudio sobre la confiscación.* Caracas: Editorial Bolívar, 1938.

Levine, Daniel H. *Conflict and Political Change in Venezuela.* Princeton: Princeton University Press, 1973.

Lieuwen, Edwin. *Arms and Politics in Latin America.* Rev. ed. New York: Frederick A. Praeger, 1961.

————. *Petroleum in Venezuela: A History.* Berkeley: University of California Press, 1954.

————. *The United States and the Challenge to Security in Latin America.* Columbus: Ohio State University Press, 1966.

————. *Venezuela.* 2d ed. New York: Oxford University Press, 1965.

Liss, Sheldon B. *Diplomacy and Dependency: Venezuela, the United States, and the Americas.* Salisbury, N.C.: Documentary Publications, 1978.

López Borges, Nicanor. *El asesinato de Delgado Chalbaud: Análisis de un sumario.* Caracas: Ediciones Centauro, 1971.

Lugo, Francisco Aniceto. *Pérez Jiménez: Fuerza creadora.* 2d ed. Caracas: Editorial Ragón, 1954.

Luzardo, Rodolfo. *Notas histórico-económicas: 1928–1963.* Caracas: Editorial Sucre, 1963.

————. *Río Grande: Los malos entendimientos en el continente americano.* Caracas: Editorial Sucre, 1965.

Mancera Galletti, Angel. *Civilismo y militarismo.* Caracas, 1960.

Márguez, Pompeyo. *Hacia donde va el 23 de enero?* Caracas: Pensamiento Vivo, 1959.

Martz, John D. *Acción Democrática: Evolution of a Modern Political Party in Venezuela.* Princeton, N.J.: Princeton University Press, 1966.

————. *The Venezuelan Elections of December 1, 1963,* vol. I, *An Analysis.* Washington, D.C.: Operations and Policy Research, Inc., Institute for the Comparative Study of Political Systems, 1964.

————, and Enrique A. Baloyra. *Electoral Mobilization and Public Opinion: The Venezuelan Campaign of 1973.* Chapel Hill: University of North Carolina Press, 1976.

————, and David J. Myers, eds. *Venezuela: The Democratic Experience.* New York: Praeger, 1977.

Maza Zavala, Domingo Felipe. *Paradojas venezolanas: Crónicas de economía y angustia social*. Caracas, 1969.

Moore, John Bassett. *A Digest of International Law*. 8 vols. Washington, D.C.: Government Printing Office, 1906.

Morillo, Gilberto. *El enriquecimiento ilícito en Venezuela*. Caracas: Secretaría Nacional de Fuerza Democrática Popular, 1965.

Morón, Guillermo. *A History of Venezuela*. Ed. and trans. John Street. London: George Allen & Unwin, 1964.

Myers, David J. *Democratic Campaigning in Venezuela: Caldera's Victory*. Caracas: Fundación La Salle, 1973.

Naranjo Ostty, Rafael. *Breve exégesis sobre el caso del general (r) Marcos Pérez Jiménez, ex-presidente de la república de Venezuela*. Caracas: Talleres Tipograficos "Norte," 1964.

————. *Carta a la comision internacional de juristas*. Caracas, 1965.

————. *La verdad de un juicio trascendental*. Caracas: Ediciones Garrido, 1968.

Nixon, Richard. *Six Crises*. Garden City, N.Y.: Doubleday & Co., 1962.

Otero Silva, Miguel. *La muerte de Honorio*. Caracas: Monte Avila, 1968.

Parra Márquez, Hector. *La extradición: Con un estudio sobre la legislación venezolana al respecto*. Mexico: Editorial Guarania, 1960.

Pepper, José Vicente. *Reconstrucción integral de Venezuela*. Valencia, Venezuela: Editorial "Aborigen," 1953.

Pérez, Ana Mercedes. *La verdad inédita: Historia de la revolución de octubre revelada por sus dirigentes militares*. Caracas: Editorial Artes Gráficas, 1947.

————. *Síntesis histórica de un hombre y un pueblo*. Caracas, 1954.

Pérez Jiménez, Marcos. *Frente a la infamia*. Caracas: Cruzada Cívica Nacionalista, 1968.

————. *Pensamiento político del presidente de Venezuela*. Caracas: Imprenta Nacional, 1954.

Pino Iturrieta, Elías. *Positivismo y gomecismo*. Caracas: Ediciones de la Facultad de Humanidades y Educación, Instituto de Estudios Hispanoamericanos, Universidad Central de Venezuela, 1978.

Powell, John Duncan. *The Political Mobilization of the Venezuelan Peasant*. Cambridge, Mass.: Harvard University Press, 1971.

Quevedo, Numa. *El gobierno provisorio*. Caracas: Pensamiento Vivo & Librería Historia, 1963.

Quilarque Quijada, Pedro. *Contribución al estudio del enriquecimiento ilícito de funcionarios y empleados públicos en Venezuela 1813–1959*. Caracas: Ediciones Centauro, 1973.

Ramírez, Alberto. *Esbozo psiquiátrico social del General Juan Vicente*

Gómez. Caracas: Ediciones de la Dirección de Cultura, Universidad de Carabobo, 1974.

Rangel, Domingo Alberto. *Elecciones 1973: El gran negocio.* Caracas: Vadell Hermanos, 1974.

———. *Gómez el amo de poder.* Caracas: Vadell Hermanos, 1975.

Ray, Talton. *The Politics of the Barrios of Venezuela.* Berkeley: University of California Press, 1969.

RIC Universales. *Año Político 1968.* Caracas: RIC Universales, 1969.

Rivas Rivas, José, ed. *El mundo y la época de Pérez Jiménez: Una historia contada en recortes de periódicos.* Caracas: Pensamiento Vivo, 1961.

———, ed. *Las tres divisiones de Acción Democrática.* Caracas: Pensamiento Vivo, 1968.

Rodríguez Iturbe, José. *Iglesia y estado en Venezuela, 1824–1964.* Caracas: Universidad Central de Venezuela, 1968.

Ruggeri Parra, Pablo. *Historia política y constitucional de Venezuela.* Caracas: Editorial Universitaria, Dirección de Cultura Universidad Central, 1949.

Sanz de la Calzada, Carlos, ed. *Diccionario biográfico de Venezuela.* Madrid: Garrido Mezquita, 1953.

Schlesinger, Arthur M., Jr. *A Thousand Days: John F. Kennedy in the White House.* Boston: Houghton Mifflin, 1965.

Servicio Informativo Venezolano. *Venezuela bajo el Nuevo Ideal Nacional: Realizaciones durante el primero año de gobierno del coronel Marcos Pérez Jiménez, 2 de diciembre de 1952–19 de abril de 1954.* Caracas: Servicio Informativo Venezolano, 1954.

Sierralta, Morris. *Vicios de una sentencia.* Caracas: Ediciones "Fabreton," 1968.

Silva Michelena, José A. *The Illusion of Democracy in Dependent Nations.* Cambridge: MIT Press, 1971.

Siso Martínez, José María. *Historia de Venezuela.* 6th ed. Mexico City: Editorial Yocoima, 1962.

Tarnói, Ladislao T. *El Nuevo Ideal Nacional de Venezuela: Vida y obra de Marcos Pérez Jiménez.* Madrid: Ediciones Verdad, 1954.

Taylor, Philip B., Jr., ed. *Venezuela 1969: Analysis of Progress.* Houston: University of Houston, Office of International Affairs, 1971.

———. *The Venezuelan Golpe de Estado of 1958: The Fall of Marcos Pérez Jiménez.* Washington, D.C.: Institute for the Comparative Study of Political Systems, 1968.

Tejera París, Enrique. *Administración pública: Teoría de la estructura administrativa para el desarrollo.* Caracas: Distribuidora America Latina, 1963.

Torres Molina, Bhilla. *Rafael Simón, tremendo guerrillero.* Caracas, 1973.

Tugwell, Franklin. *The Politics of Oil in Venezuela.* Palo Alto, Calif.: Stanford University Press, 1975.

Umaña Bernal, José. *Testimonio de la revolución en Venezuela.* Caracas: Tipografía Vargas, 1958.

Vallenilla Lanz, Laureano, Hijo. *Allá en Caracas.* Caracas: Tipografía Garrido, 1948.

————. *Escrito de memoria.* Caracas: Ediciones Garrido, 1967.

————. *Fuerzas vivas.* Madrid: Editorial Vaher, 1963.

————. *Razones de proscrito.* Caracas: Ediciones Garrido, 1967.

Velásquez, Ramón. *La caída del liberalismo amarillo.* 2d ed. Caracas, 1973.

Venezuela independiente, 1810–1960. Caracas: Fundación Eugenio Mendoza, 1962.

Whiteman, Marjorie M., ed. *Digest of International Law.* 6 vols. Washington, D.C.: Department of State, 1968.

Index

Acción Democrática (AD): and administrative reform, 56; and CCN, 157; clandestine activity of, 38, 77, 80–81; and corrupt firms, 135; desire of, for legal precedent, 145; divisions of, 151–152, 168; efforts of, to disqualify Pérez Jiménez from office, 148–149, 156–158; and elections of 1963, 113–114, 116, 118–119, 153; and elections of 1968, 152–153; and elections of 1973, 162; and elections of 1978, 164–165; and fall of Batista, 57; founding of, 14; in government of 1945–1948, 22–24, 45–46; hostility of, toward Caracas, 118; and Law against Illicit Enrichment, 46, 53; obstructionist role of, in COPEI government, 155; outlawing of, 26–27; Pérez's opinion of, 30, 110–111; publications of, on dictatorship, 163; and revolution of 1945, 18–19, 21; testimony taken by, 75, 82.

Acheson, Dean, 62, 108
AD. *See* Acción Democrática
agrarian reform. *See* agriculture
agriculture, 53–54, 110, 115
Aguilar Mawdsley, Andrés, 47, 74
Allende, Salvador, 160–161
Alliance for Progress, 88–89, 108–109
American Civil Liberties Union (ACLU), 94
Ameringer, Charles, 169
Andean Pact, 152
appeals. *See* extradition proceedings
Araujo Ortega, José, 131–132

Arcaya, Ignacio Luis, 62, 119
Arcaya, Mariano, 43
Ardila Bustamante, Hugo, 120
Arias, Monseñor Rafael, 34
Aristeguieta, Manuel, 64
Arizona Republic, 94
armed forces, Venezuelan: and conspiracy of 1928, 12–13; desire of, for modernization, 11; and golpe of 1948, 25; under Gómez, 9, 17; under Pérez, 29, 31, 39, 140
Ascanio Jiménez, Carlos, 120, 142–143, 148
asylum: diplomatic, 49–50; as part of U.S. tradition, 91, 94; territorial, 58–59, 80

barrios, 40, 154
Barrios, Gonzalo, 21, 57, 151, 158
Barrios, Jonas, 120, 142–143, 148
Bastidas, Arístides, 27
Batista, Fulgencio, 57
Bay of Pigs, 88
Belaúnde Terry, Fernando, 96
Betancourt, Rómulo: and agrarian reform, 54; Betancourt Doctrine of, 23, 52, 95–96, 103, 113, 115–116, 150, 155; and Castro's Cuba, 89–90; distrust of, of Pérez Jiménez, 21, 25; and due process, 53; education and early career of, 3, 11–14; and election of 1968, 151; and election of 1973, 157–158, 163; in exile, 13, 25, 63; and extradition of Pérez, 51, 56, 65, 74, 90, 96–97; hostility of, to Caracas, 117; Pérez's opinion of, 30, 91–92, 136;